ONE Heartbeat Away

Your Journey Into Eternity

Mark Cahill

Author of the bestseller
One Thing You Can't Do in Heaven

One Heartbeat Away: Your Journey Into Eternity
Mark Cahill

Fifteenth Printing, February 2011

ISBN 978-0-9643665-7-2

Published by:
BDM Publishing
2212 Chisholm Trail
Rockwall, Texas 75002
972-771-0568

Bible verses cited are from the King James Version.

Preliminary Editor:
Lynn Copeland, Genesis Publishing Group
www.genesis-group.net

Cover Design, Interior Illustrations, Page Layout & Final Editing:
Russell Barr, BARRgraphics
www.barrgraphics.com

Order additional copies at any bookstore
or at www.markcahill.org.

Printed in the United States of America

Presented to:

From:

Dedication

This book is dedicated to Truth.
If you search for it, you will find it.

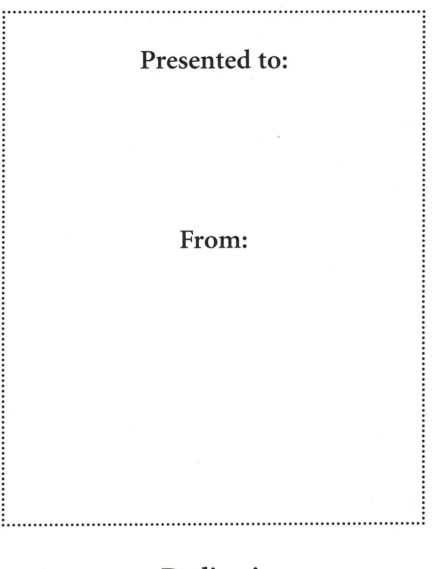

"Keep the Presses Running!"

"I have severe dyslexia, which makes reading a real drag, but when I picked up your book, it was not only understandable, but powerful and fun to consume."
—*Robert Concklin*

"The book you gave me, *One Heartbeat Away*, I have read cover to cover in the last 7 hours, only stopping to eat dinner, check in at the hotel and tell my fiancé about it." —*Todd Jordan*

"This is one of the most remarkable books ever!!" —*Pam Mathews*

"The book that you gave to me has explained to me all of my questions about 'afterlife' and eternity itself. Yes, this book has become my 'journey into eternity.' I find it fascinating to go over its pages..."
—*Vivianna Kotorova*

"Now that my friends and I are closing in on 40 and have children who mean so much to us, we need to be able to answer the most important question there is. 'What happens after this?' If for no other reason than to lead our children the right way. We all are 'One Heartbeat Away!'"
—*Scott Gallagher*

"I just wanted to say that your new book, *One Heartbeat Away*, is done very well and does a fantastic job of explaining who we are and what we're here on earth for. If only all 6 billion people in the world could read this book!"
—*Bart McCurdy*

"I just finished reading your new book, *One Heartbeat Away: Your Journey Into Eternity*—keep the presses running! This book is a 'must have', ready to give a person who is searching for the most important answer. 'Where will you be after you leave this planet?'" —*Rick Brothers*

"This resource can reach a broader range of people than almost any I've come across: young, old, kind or cruel. Solid truth presented in a challenging, readable form. We truly believe that this book will help patients leave our office with their spiritual eyes open."
—*Dr. Steven M. Kirkham, Ophthalmologist*

Contents

Although
we may not realize
it, we all have faith
in something.

Introduction

He who provides for this life but takes no care for eternity
is wise for a moment but a fool forever.
— John Tillotson

It is said that a presidential candidate must be very careful in selecting a running mate, in case they are elected. At any moment, a vice president is just one heartbeat away from becoming the president of the United States of America — the most powerful position in the world.

The truth is that each one of us at any moment can be one heartbeat away from eternity. Your heart beats about 100,000 times in a twenty-four-hour period. One day, one of those beats will be your last.

Does that thought concern you? Most people naturally have a fear of death. Comedian Robin Williams made light of it by joking, "Death is nature's way of saying, 'Your table's ready.'" Actor David Niven stated, "I won't go. I'll kick and scream and make a terrible fuss." And Woody Allen said, "I'm not afraid to die. I just don't want to be there when it happens."

And then, there's the bumper sticker that says, "Death is nature's way of telling you to slow down." Yet, death will eventually happen to each of us, and we will be somewhere for all of eternity. Three hundred million years from now, where will you be?

It is something all of us consider at some point in our lives. Whether it is an illness; a bumpy plane ride; a car crash; the death of a friend or of a famous person like Johnny Carson, Dale Earnhardt or the Pope; or a cataclysmic event like September 11th, the Indian Ocean tsunami, or other natural disasters — some circumstance will turn our thoughts to what happens when we leave this planet.

For that matter, why are we even on this planet? What is the purpose of our existence? Many people think it is just to go to school, party a little, find a job, get married, have kids, attend sporting events, watch their hair turn gray (or turn loose), retire, play golf, and die.

But is that the reason we breathe every day? Isn't there more to this journey of life than living and dying? How can we know whether our time on this planet has been successful?

Some might say they had a good life if they stayed out of jail and didn't hurt anyone. Others define success as having something — or someone — named after them. Maybe to you a good life is if your kids don't get into too much trouble, or if you never have to worry about your finances.

What is the purpose of our existence? Many people think it is just to go to school, party a little, find a job, get married, have kids, attend sporting events, watch their hair turn gray (or turn loose), retire, play golf, and die.

What is most important to you in this lifetime? Is it one of the above-mentioned things? I asked this question of a man at an airport, and he replied that his family was the most important thing to him, which is a typical answer to this question.

I then asked him what would be the most important thing to him on the day he died. When he again answered that it would be his family, I asked what he meant. He explained that he wanted to ensure he left behind enough money to take care of his family after he was gone.

"Wouldn't it be important," I suggested, "to find out where you are going after you die, and for your family to join you there someday?" His eyes widened, and he said he had never thought about that before.

Since we are all part of the ultimate statistic that ten out of ten people die, where we go when we die, and who will be there with us are things we all should think about. You will leave your body behind, but what about your soul? If you believe that there is something more to your existence than simply this life, you're in good company. According to a recent survey by The Barna Group, eight in ten Americans believe in some sort of afterlife. And 79 percent agree that "every person has a soul that will live forever, either in God's presence or absence."[1]

When you die, what do you think will be on the other side? There are many different beliefs. For example:

- Hinduism teaches that an individual is almost endlessly reincarnated, based on the law of karma, which says that the good and bad deeds and thoughts a person sends out in one lifetime are done to them in a later incarnation, over and over and over, until the soul is absorbed into a divine essence.
- The Jewish Bible (called the Old Testament by Christians), as well as the New Testament, teach that there is a heaven and a hell. Jews believe in some form of reward or punishment after death, as do Christians.
- Islam teaches there is a paradise and a hellfire, with martyrdom the only sure ticket to paradise.
- Buddhists believe that, through enlightenment, the soul is continually reincarnated until it reaches an ultimate state of non-existence called nirvana.
- Atheists believe that there is no conscious afterlife. One atheist refers to death as a "celestial dirt nap."
- The New Age movement encompasses many varying beliefs, including the belief that people keep being reborn until reaching oneness with God.

According to The Barna Group, eight in ten Americans believe in some sort of afterlife. And 79 percent agree that "every person has a soul that will live forever, either in God's presence or absence."

There are many possibilities, but which is the one that will happen to you? How can you know what is out there after you draw your last breath? Is it even possible to know?

Although the majority of people believe in the existence of the soul and in life after death, many are unsure of their own destination. One in four adults admits he has "no idea" what will happen after he dies. An amazing two-thirds of atheists and agnostics accept the existence of an afterlife, so it's obvious that many people have not carefully thought through what they believe and why. More importantly, they haven't considered whether there is any evidence to support that belief.[2]

Suppose I were in the northern U.S. in December, and after a few days of below-freezing temperatures, ice begins to form on a nearby lake. I've enjoyed walking on a frozen lake before, so let's say I decide that I'd like to walk on this one. But then I get a better idea: I decide to take a snowmobile out onto the ice. I have seen people do that on TV, and it looks like so much fun.

An amazing two-thirds of atheists and agnostics accept the existence of an afterlife.

Even better, I am going to build a snow ramp so that I can launch the snowmobile into the air, land it on the ice, and slide for a good distance. Now, that sounds like a lot of fun! There is only one problem: No matter how much I believe I can do that, no matter how much faith I have, I would go right through the ice because it would still be very thin. That's reality.

Now suppose it is February at the same lake, and we have had over two straight months of below-freezing temperatures. Although I really want to walk out onto the ice, I'm afraid to do it because a friend fell through the ice a few months earlier. So I'm only willing to take one foot and step ever so lightly onto the ice to make sure it will support my weight. The ice not only holds me up but also would have supported a snowmobile being launched into the air and landing on it. Why? The ice is many inches thick by this time.

What is the difference between these two scenarios? In the first, I had all the faith in the world, but the object of my faith wasn't what I thought it was: The ice was too thin. I would have been taking a blind leap of misplaced faith.

In the second scenario, had I considered the evidence, I could have placed only a small amount of faith into action, and would have been just fine.

Although we may not realize it, we all have faith in something. In fact, you place your faith in many things every day. You have faith each time you drive that other drivers will stop at red lights. You have faith that the chair on which you're sitting will continue to hold you. Every time you fly, you exercise faith that the pilot is not suicidal and planning to crash the plane.

The key is not the amount of faith we have but the object of that faith. That is, are we believing or trusting in something that is actually true? ...it does matter whether the object of our faith is trustworthy and will support our trust.

The key is not the amount of faith we have but the object of that faith. That is, are we believing or trusting in something that is actually true?

So it doesn't really matter what we believe about life after death. But it does matter whether the object of our faith is trustworthy and will support our trust. Are you taking a blind leap onto some "thin ice" for eternity, or is the "ice" you will be landing on many feet thick?

No matter what your answer to that question, your answer is based on faith or belief in something. So ask yourself: What evidence do I have to support that belief?

Oprah Winfrey said that her favorite question to ask show guests is, "What do you know for sure?" Well, one thing we all "know for sure" is that we will die, but the question now is, "Where will we go after that?"

We are all one day closer to eternity than we were yesterday. No matter what or whom you have chosen to place your faith in, you are betting the only life you have — your eternal well-being — on your decision.

Have you examined the evidence to ensure that you're making the right choice? For your own sake, you owe it to yourself to fully explore the options. You don't want to be wrong for all eternity just because you didn't take the time to consider the evidence.

So, before your journey into eternity begins, please take a brief journey with me on a search for evidence of eternal truth. Is there a God? Or isn't there? Is there life after death? Or not? And how trustworthy is the object of your faith?

Sir Winston Churchill said, "Men occasionally stumble over the truth, but most of them pick themselves up and hurry off as if nothing ever happened."[3] I hope that you won't just stumble over the truth and ignore it, but that you will actively seek it — and place your faith in it.

Sir Winston Churchill said, "Men occasionally stumble over the truth, but most of them pick themselves up and hurry off as if nothing ever happened."

Let's take a look at some of the evidence to see "just how thick the ice will be" on the day you die. Let's research the depths of the mystery of eternal truth and see what we find.

Something doesn't just come out of nothing all by itself.

Chapter 1
Nobel Prize

I can see how it might be possible for a man
to look down upon the earth and be an atheist,
but I cannot conceive how he could look up
into the heavens and say there is no God.
— Abraham Lincoln

Many people believe there is no God because they are convinced that science has fully explained how our universe came to be. If there is a natural explanation of our origins, they think, who needs a supernatural one? Perhaps, like many, you see a contest between science and religion, and believe that science has been declared the winner hands down.

But does science alone explain this incredibly beautiful and complex creation in which we live? Doesn't its magnificence make you wonder?

How does the sun provide just the right amount of energy to light and heat our planet? What makes everything in our orderly world work so well together? How is it that we can predict the precise day of a full moon or an eclipse, or determine whether to expect a violent thunderstorm or a fresh snowfall?

Where does lightning come from, or a brilliant rainbow? When we see the startling colors of a sunset, we often wonder how such a spectacular display is created. We marvel at the grandeur of mountains and the beauty of beaches.

As I saw the Grand Canyon for the first time, my jaw dropped. The canyon's vastness was awe-inspiring, and its colors were truly amazing. Where did that canyon come from?

Every time we look at something built by man — a house, for example — we know it had a builder, someone who assembled it. When we see something that has design, like a watch, we know it had a designer who planned it. When we see artwork, like a painting, we know there is an artist who painted it. When we observe order — say twenty Coke cups lined up in a row — we know there was an "orderer" who set them up that way.

When we look around the universe at things not made by man, what do we see? We see creation, design, art, and order. So if everything man-made has a creator, designer, artist, or orderer behind it, why would we not think that there is a Creator, Designer, Artist, and Orderer behind the universe?

Why is it that when we look at Mount Rushmore, we don't say, "Wow, erosion is an amazing thing! Look how it formed the heads of four presidents of the United States"?

Why is it that when we look at Mount Rushmore, we don't say, "Wow, erosion is an amazing thing! Look how it formed the heads of four presidents of the United States"? We realize that would be a foolish statement. Whenever we see creation, design, art, or order, it's obvious that there was some intelligent force behind it to make it happen.

I speak in many venues around the country, so I fly a lot. Once, on the drive from the airport, I saw a beautiful sunset — one of those amazing Technicolor displays that keeps changing like a kaleidoscope. I began to pray that someone would see that beautiful sunset and wonder who painted it in the sky.

The following night was Halloween. I was staying with some friends who had a very large house set back from the road quite a distance. No one had come to the house for candy that night — until there was a ring at the door at around 9:30. As the lady of the house went to answer it, I stuck my head around the corner to take a peek.

At the door were two young ladies, their faces painted like cats. They looked a bit too old to be trick-or-treating, so I asked them their ages. They said they were 20 and 21. I asked them what they were doing trick-or-treating and, of course, they said they wanted some candy!

After chatting a few minutes, I brought up a question about eternity. One girl responded, "You're wasting your time talking to us about God. We're atheists." So I asked them what evidence they had found to prove that there is no God. They didn't have any evidence at all, which I found very interesting.

Like many people, they were probably thinking that reason was on their side. Yet without any evidence to support their belief, what they actually had was blind faith — and they were using that as the basis for their eternal destiny. Some people think it takes blind faith to believe in God. But we use calculated faith for most decisions in life, and we should do the same for our decisions about eternity.

I asked them what would be enough evidence to prove to them that God exists. They didn't have an answer for that either. So I told them I would give them something to think about, and I explained the concept that the universe displays creation, design, art, and order. I asked them, "If everything else has a creator, designer, artist, or orderer behind it, why would you think that there is not a Creator, Designer, Artist, and Orderer behind this universe?"

Suddenly their eyes grew wide. One of the young ladies said, "Yesterday, I walked outside at dusk and saw a gorgeous sunset. And I was wondering to myself, 'Who painted that in the sky?'"

Within twenty-four hours of my prayer, I got to meet someone with whom God had answered that prayer!

Both young ladies were students at a local art college. As artists, they knew that for every beautiful painting, there must be a painter who created that artwork. And logically, the same would have to hold true for all that is in this incredible universe.

Logically, we know that there cannot be an unpainted painting, an unsculpted sculpture, an undesigned design. That just doesn't make sense. And it makes much less sense for us to base our eternal destiny on something that we know is not reasonable.

I was talking with a man one day in downtown Atlanta, and I asked him a question about spiritual matters. He replied that he was an atheist and that there was no way to prove there is a God.

We were standing among tall buildings, so I pointed to one of the skyscrapers and said, "Prove to me that there was a builder for that building." He answered, "That's easy. The building itself is proof that there is a builder."

He was 100 percent correct. We know that you don't just gather some concrete, pipes, windows, paint, wires, etc., then turn around and look back to suddenly find a building. A building requires a builder.

I said, "Exactly. The building is proof that there is a builder." I then added, "The sun, the moon, the stars, the oceans, the sand, each unique snowflake, the three billion pieces of your DNA that are different from mine, are absolute proof that there had to be a Creator of this universe."

The fact that you can't see, touch, taste, smell, or hear the builder of a skyscraper doesn't mean that such a person doesn't exist.

He looked at me. I could see the light bulb flash on behind his eyes, and then he glanced away. As he thought about that statement, he realized he had provided his own proof.

The fact that you can't see, touch, taste, smell, or hear the builder of a skyscraper doesn't mean that such a person doesn't exist. You don't need any amazing faith to believe there was a builder of a building you can see; you just need to look at the evidence and make an informed decision. And the best piece of evidence you could have is the work that builder left behind.

The same holds true for the God of this universe. The evidence left for us to look at is all the evidence we will ever need in order to know that our universe has a Creator.

Something from Nothing

Imagine this scenario:

> Billions of years ago a dark substance began to evolve from nothing. It came out of nowhere. Then there was a big bang. We don't know what caused the bang or why, but it happened.

> As many millions of years passed, this substance developed a fizz to it and became sweet. Millions of years later some aluminum molecules formed from nothing, gathered together, and wrapped themselves around this liquid in the perfect shape of a cylinder. The aluminum then formed a pop top on the cylinder.
>
> Forty or fifty years ago, some red and white paint molecules fell onto the can, forming the words "Coca-Cola," an expiration date, and a complete ingredient list. Wow — that is amazing!

This example, given by a friend of mine, describes an absurd way of thinking. It would be an insult to your intellect if I insisted that the above scenario were true. This universe is infinitely more complex than a can of Coke, yet for some reason people are content to believe that it just came out of nowhere — that something came from nothing. But if a Coke can and its contents couldn't happen by random chance processes, how could something as orderly and as intricately designed as our universe have been assembled merely by chance? Logically, we know that's impossible.

One night I noticed a youth football practice going on across the street from where I was speaking, so I went over and began a conversation with a man who was there to watch his son play. As we chatted, he told me that he was Jewish. We talked a little about the Jewish faith, but he mentioned that not only was he not practicing his faith, he was actually an atheist. I found a Jewish atheist to be a very interesting combination.

It was a beautiful night — nice and chilly, with a bright moon and a canopy of stars. I asked him, "When you see this beautiful creation on a night like tonight, doesn't it make you think of the Creator who made this place?" He admitted, "That's what I am struggling with." He was struggling because he knew, when he looked at the sky, that this awesome creation had to come from somewhere. Someone created it, but the question is, "Who?"

Many people don't believe that a God created the universe because they can't imagine a Being that is eternal. Surely God must have had a beginning, they think. Where did He come from? Who made Him? If they don't have satisfactory answers, then they refuse to believe.

I find it interesting that, before coming up with the "big bang" theory, scientists believed that the universe was eternal. They couldn't explain how it came into being by itself, so they claimed that it simply always was — it had no beginning.

Scientists now proclaim that the universe began with a big bang. But that provides more questions than it does answers. There had to be something to go "bang." Where did the matter come from? What energy source caused the bang? What was the catalyst that set the matter into motion to form the universe? How could order have come from disorder?

Think about that. If you believe matter existed for all eternity, and it had the ability to spontaneously start up the universe, and it was powerful and intelligent enough to put our immense universe together with order and precision and beauty — haven't you just defined God? He's not as difficult to believe in as you may have thought. You might not understand Him, but that's no reason to believe that He doesn't exist.

As I came home late one evening, I turned on the TV and saw the David Letterman show was on. His guest was an 80-year-old scientist from England who had just won the Nobel Prize. I love the British accent, so I was drawn to listen to the conversation.

The scientist made the statement, "David, we have reached the point in science where we know for a fact that there was a beginning to this universe." Letterman suddenly straightened up in his chair and looked with surprise at his guest. He said, "Wait a minute. Wait just a minute. If we know that there is a beginning to this universe, doesn't that imply…"

How would you have finished that sentence if you were speaking? Some people might say, "...doesn't that imply that there is an end to the universe?" But Letterman continued, "...doesn't that imply that there must be a Beginner to this universe?" As you can see, our mind logically leads us to conclude that if there was a beginning, there must be a Beginner to this universe — someone to set it all in motion. The scientist's response was amazing. He stared at the floor for a moment, then looked at Letterman and replied, "That is a place that we don't like to go to in science." What an incredible admission! He was stating that, because he was a scientist, he didn't want to even think about it. We can choose to turn off our logic in our search for truth as we journey through life, but I don't believe that is a very wise thing to do. Like Letterman, we know intuitively that beginnings require Beginners.

Cause and Effect

There is something in science called the Law of Cause and Effect. This is an indisputable, universal law that says that for every material effect, there had to be a cause. There is nothing in the universe that doesn't have a cause behind its existence. Your parents caused you, your grandparents caused your parents, etc.

There is something in science called the Law of Cause and Effect. This is an indisputable, universal law that says that for every material effect, there had to be a cause.

But if you continue going further and further back, there will not be an infinite regression. You must eventually reach a First Cause (or an Uncaused Cause), which created that first effect. Something doesn't just come out of nothing all by itself. In other words, there had to be some causal agent that began the process and set our whole universe in motion.

Robert Jastrow, founder of the Goddard Institute for Space Studies at NASA, acknowledges this requirement:

> The universe, and everything that has happened in it since the beginning of time, are a grand effect without a known cause. An effect without a cause? That is not the world of science; it is a world of witchcraft, of wild events and the whims of demons, a medieval world that science has tried to banish.[4]

Even Charles Darwin admitted:

> The impossibility of conceiving that this grand and wondrous universe, with our conscious selves, arose through chance, seems to me the chief

> argument for the existence of God ... I am aware that if we admit a first cause, the mind still craves to know whence it came, and how it arose.[5]

Some scientists may not like to admit what that causal agent might be, yet according to this law, it is irrefutable that everything that has a beginning has a cause, including the universe. The universe (an effect) cannot simply bring itself into being. It requires a cause that is outside itself.

Scholar C. S. Lewis wrote, in *God in the Dock*:

> An egg which came from no bird is no more "natural" than a bird which had existed from all eternity. And since the egg-bird-egg sequence leads us to no plausible beginning, is it not reasonable to look for the real origin somewhere outside the sequence altogether? You have to go outside the sequence of engines, into the world of men, to find the real originator of the rocket. Is it not equally reasonable to look outside Nature for the real Originator of the natural order?[6]

You will never hear of a tornado whipping through a junkyard and leaving a fully formed 747 jet, a Mercedes, and a skyscraper in its wake. Why? Blind chance cannot do that.

What do *you* think?

Louis Pasteur, the famous scientist, said of our world: "The more I study nature, the more I stand amazed at the work of the Creator."[7] His logic convinced him that our complex, orderly creation requires a Creator.

Sir Isaac Newton stated, "This most beautiful system of the sun, planets, and comets could only proceed from the counsel and dominion of an intelligent and powerful Being."[8] You may find it hard to believe that God could make everything out of nothing, but the alternative is that nothing turned itself into everything. Which takes more faith to believe?

Evidence of Design

As we've seen with the Coke can example, blind, random chance does not give rise to design. You will never hear of a tornado whipping through a junkyard and leaving a fully formed 747 jet, a Mercedes, and a skyscraper in its wake. Why? Blind chance cannot do that.

If you placed all the pieces of a watch into a shoebox and shook it for ten minutes, do you believe it would shake into a functioning watch? Of course not. What if you shook it for a year? Would a functioning watch *then* come out of the box? Say you were able to shake it for five billion years; would you then have a functioning watch? There is no possible way for that to happen.

And if it couldn't happen by chance to something relatively simple like a watch, it most certainly couldn't happen by chance to our magnificently complex universe.

Consider some of the amazing aspects of design that are evident in our solar system:

1. The earth is positioned at just the right distance from the sun so that we receive exactly the proper amount of heat to support life. The other planets of our solar system are either too close to the sun (too hot) or else too far (too cold) to sustain life.
2. Any appreciable change in the rate of rotation of the earth would make life impossible. For example, if the earth were to rotate at 1/10th its present rate, all plant life would either be burned to a crisp during the day or frozen at night.
3. Temperature variations are kept within reasonable limits due to the nearly circular orbit of the earth around the sun.
4. The moon revolves around the earth at a distance of about 240,000 miles, causing harmless tides on the earth. If the moon were located 1/5th of this distance away, the continents would be completely submerged twice a day!
5. The thickness of the earth's crust and the depth of the oceans appear to be carefully designed. Increases in thickness or depth of only a few feet would so drastically alter the absorption of free oxygen and carbon dioxide that plant and animal life could not exist.
6. The earth's axis is tilted 23 degrees from the perpendicular to the plane of its orbit. This tilting, combined with the earth's revolution around the sun, causes our seasons, which are absolutely essential for the raising of food supplies.

7. The earth's atmosphere (especially the ozone layer) serves as a protective shield from lethal solar ultraviolet radiation, which would otherwise destroy all life.
8. The earth's atmosphere also serves to protect the earth by burning up approximately twenty million meteors each day that enter it at speeds of about 30 miles per second! Without this crucial protection, the danger to life would be immense.
9. The two primary constituents of the earth's atmosphere are nitrogen (78 percent) and oxygen (20 percent). This delicate and critical ratio is essential to all life forms.
10. The earth's magnetic field provides important protection from harmful cosmic radiation.[9]

All of this happened just by chance? I think someone would have to commit intellectual suicide to believe that. What does your logic say as you consider the evidence?

Even well-known astrophysicist Stephen Hawking concluded:

> The universe and the laws of physics seem to have been specifically designed for us. If any one of about 40 physical qualities had more than slightly different values, life as we know it could not exist: Either atoms would not be stable, or they wouldn't combine into molecules, or the stars wouldn't form the heavier elements, or the universe would collapse before life could develop, and so on.[10]

"The universe and the laws of physics seem to have been specifically designed for us."
— Stephen Hawking

Unlike the gentleman on David Letterman's show, many scientists have been willing to honestly, logically weigh the evidence and have determined that blind chance cannot be given credit for creating our highly ordered universe. Though he remains an evolutionist, Hawking admitted, "It would be very difficult to explain why the universe should have begun in just this way, except as the act of a God who intended to create beings like us."[11]

Consider the conclusions other scientists have reached about the universe's design:

Sir Fred Hoyle (British astrophysicist):

A common sense interpretation of the facts suggests that a super intellect has monkeyed with physics, as well as with chemistry and biology, and that there are no blind forces worth speaking about in nature. The numbers one calculates from the facts seem to me so overwhelming as to put this conclusion almost beyond question.[12]

Paul Davies (Australian astrophysicist):

There is for me powerful evidence that there is something going on behind it all.... It seems as though somebody has fine-tuned nature's numbers to make the universe.... The impression of design is overwhelming.[13]

Alan Sandage (the greatest living cosmologist and winner of the Crawford prize in astronomy):

The world is too complicated in all its parts and interconnections to be due to chance alone. I am convinced that the existence of life with all its order ... is simply too well put together.[14]

John O'Keefe (NASA astronomer):

We are, by astronomical standards, a pampered, cosseted, cherished group of creatures ... If the universe had not been made with the most exacting precision we could never have come into existence. It is my view that these circumstances indicate the universe was created for man to live in.[15]

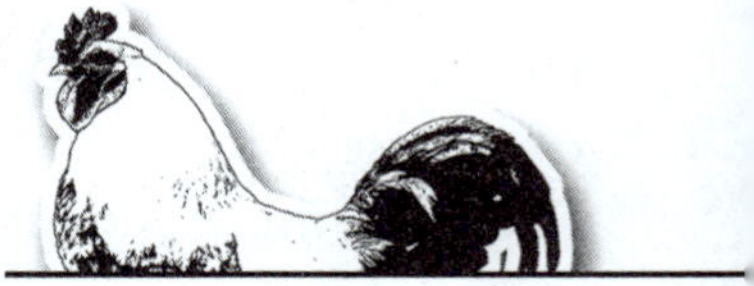

"As we survey all the evidence, the thought insistently arises that some supernatural agency — or, rather, Agency — must be involved."

— George Greenstein

Arno Penzias (Nobel Prize winner in physics):

Astronomy leads us to a unique event, a universe which was created out of nothing, one with the very delicate balance needed to provide exactly the conditions required to permit life, and one which has an underlying (one might say "supernatural") plan.[16]

George Greenstein (astronomer):

As we survey all the evidence, the thought insistently arises that some supernatural agency — or, rather, Agency — must be involved. Is it possible that suddenly, without intending to, we have stumbled upon scientific proof of the existence of a Supreme Being? Was it God who stepped in and so providentially crafted the cosmos for our benefit?[17]

Albert Einstein, one of the greatest scientists of all time, said, "I want to know how God created this world."[18] Maybe his desire is something all of us should ponder as we survey the evidence.

Moral Law

Another argument for God's existence is the reality of moral law. Man is a moral being, but evolution cannot explain where our sense of morality comes from. How can we know intuitively that something is wrong unless there is a right? Why do right and wrong exist?

Our moral nature can also be seen in our desire for justice. Although we don't always do what is right ourselves, we certainly don't have any trouble knowing when we've been wronged. And when that happens, we demand that justice be done! This moral law that humans live by had to come from somewhere. But where? Mindless, random chance processes cannot explain the existence of a moral code.

The moral code is also related to the Law of Cause and Effect, which we looked at earlier. This law dictates that an effect never precedes its cause, and is never greater than or superior to its cause. Therefore, there must be something that existed before the universe was brought into being, and that cause must be superior to our awesome universe in every way. As with a building, the universe exhibits design, so it must have a Designer. Since it exhibits intelligence, its Designer must be intelligent; since it has life, its Designer must have life; and since it exhibits morality, its Designer must be moral.

When you really get down to it, it takes more faith to believe that there is no God than to believe that there is a God. How could matter come into being by itself from nothing? How could an effect come from no cause? How could life come from non-life? How could intelligence come from non-intelligence? How could meaning come from meaninglessness? These are all things that an atheist must believe in order to be consistent — and they all contradict the irrefutable Law of Cause and Effect.

How does that sit with your logic? Always base your decisions on evidence, facts, and truth. Don't just go with feelings when making decisions; feelings may be important in some aspects of life, but they do not determine what is true.

Well, the ice beneath you is beginning to thicken. When considering the evidence from creation, design, art, order, science, and moral law, it is obvious that our search for eternal truth is beginning to narrow.

In the next chapter, we will look more closely at the design process for our universe; then in Chapter 3, we will consider who this Designer might be.

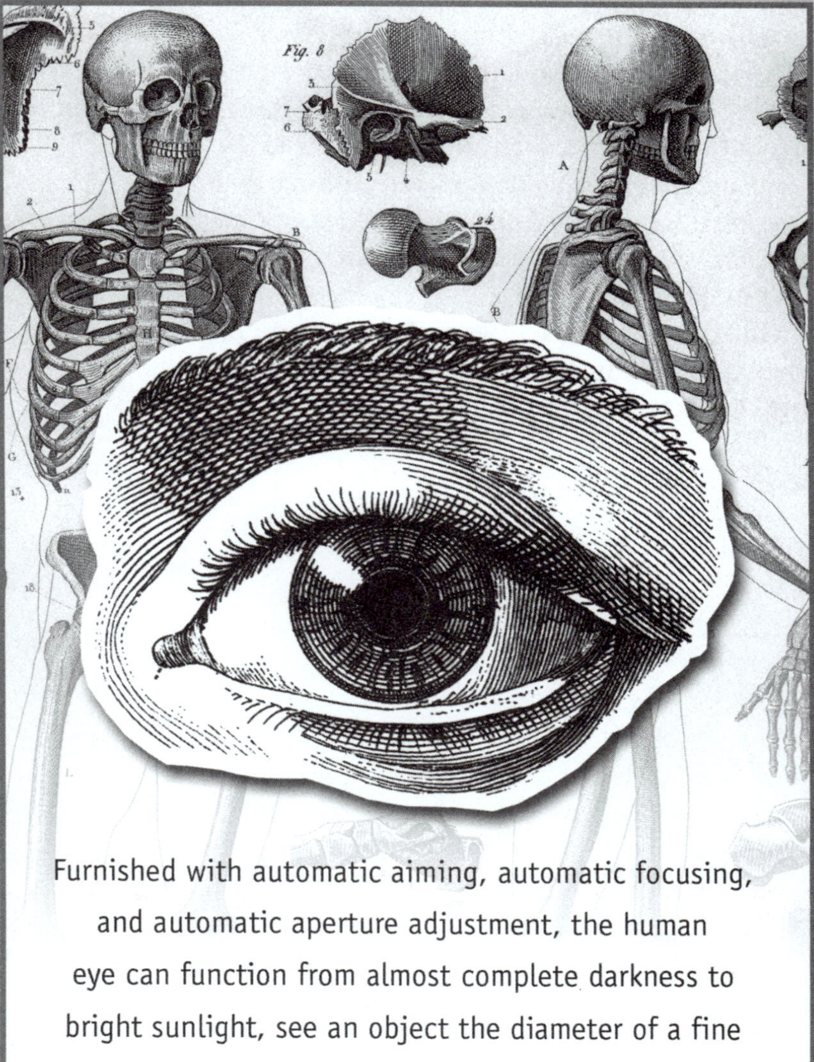

Furnished with automatic aiming, automatic focusing, and automatic aperture adjustment, the human eye can function from almost complete darkness to bright sunlight, see an object the diameter of a fine hair, and make about 100,000 separate motions in an average day...and then while we sleep, it carries on its own maintenance work.

Dr. Scott Huse

Chapter 2
I Can See Clearly Now

To suppose that the eye with all its inimitable contrivances for adjusting the focus to different distances, for admitting different amounts of light, and for the correction of spherical and chromatic aberration, could have been formed by natural selection, seems, I freely confess, absurd in the highest degree.
— Charles Darwin

As we've seen in the previous chapter, the evidence is pretty solid that our universe is designed. Yet, despite the logical evidence pointing to the existence of a Creator, many people still reject the idea of God because they believe evolution is a fact.

We were all told in kindergarten that when a frog becomes a prince, that is a fairy tale. But when I was in high school and college, they told us that when a frog becomes a prince, that is science!

So people tend to think that if some scientists say they have conclusive proof that the entire universe came into being by itself, then no fairy-tale "Creator" need apply.

Because I grew up in a public-school environment and attended a public university, I was one of the many children taught evolution from the time I started school. So as an adult, I thought, "Couldn't evolution be how all of creation came into being?" Then I decided to do some searching — and I was surprised by what I found.

Since this issue is so important in determining not only whether God exists but what kind of God He is, let's take a few minutes to honestly examine the evidence and see where it leads.

What Is Evolution?

First, let's look at what is meant by "evolution." Evolution has two main branches. One is microevolution, which involves minor variations within a species. We see evidence of this all the time, such as when bacteria become resistant to antibiotics. This is also called adaptation or natural selection. Microevolution is scientific because it is observable and measurable.

The other branch is macroevolution, which is the concept that successive small changes can, over time, gradually change one species to another. It involves not only minor variations but also the addition of completely new features and body types.

Microevolution is limited by the genetic code. No features that are not already present in a creature's DNA can ever be produced by natural selection.

Dr. J. P. Moreland summarizes it in this way:

> Macroevolution is the general theory that all life arose from nonlife in some prebiotic soup (where chemical reactions plus some form of energy gave rise to the first life), and all life evolved from the first life up to Homo Sapiens.[19]

Macroevolution — the belief that the variations we can see taking place in microevolution (within a species) are supposedly continuous and limitless, so that one species will continue to change and eventually become a new species — is the heart of evolutionary theory.

Macroevolution, however, has never been observed; therefore, it is not scientific.

As I was searching for the truth about evolution, one of the most compelling facts I learned was that microevolution is limited by the genetic code. No features that are not already present in a creature's DNA can ever be produced by natural selection.

So, while there is variation within species, it is always within these limits. For example, there are many different types of dogs — from the Chihuahua to the Irish wolfhound, from the Mexican hairless to the Yorkshire terrier — yet they are all still dogs.

In *The Answers Book*, Ken Ham describes this limitation of microevolution:

> Adaptation and natural selection are biological facts; amoeba-to-man evolution is not. Natural selection can only work on the genetic information

> present in a population of organisms — it cannot create new information. For example, since no known reptiles have genes for feathers, no amount of selection will produce a feathered reptile. Mutations in genes can only modify or eliminate existing structures, not create new ones.[20]

Thus, there are always natural limits to biological change. Natural selection is just that — selection. It cannot create anything new; it can only select from the information contained in the organism's genetic blueprint.

Yet evolutionists ignore this key fact and claim that one species can gain new information and evolve into another species. Unfortunately for their theory, evolutionists don't have any evidence for this. It has never been proven or observed in nature and, indeed, never can be.

Let's take a closer look at the two conditions of macroevolution, both of which are necessary for the theory of evolution to be true.

The first assertion of macroevolution is that living matter came from non-living matter. There is only one problem with that: It has been shown to be impossible.

The Origin of Life

The first assertion of macroevolution is that living matter came from non-living matter. There is only one problem with that: It has been shown to be impossible. The scientific method requires repeatable observation to prove something, yet despite scientists' earnest attempts, and even baseless claims, they have never been able to create life from non-life. In fact, the opposite is the case.

Evolutionist Martin Moe admitted that "a century of sensational discoveries in the biological sciences has taught us that life arises only from life."[21] Therefore, it is unscientific and inaccurate for evolutionists to claim that spontaneous generation occurred — that is, that nonliving chemicals produced living organisms sometime in the distant past.

Louis Pasteur and others have shown the impossibility of spontaneous generation and have proved the Law of Biogenesis: Life can arise *only* from pre-existing life and will perpetuate *only* its own kind.

Eminent evolutionist George Gaylord Simpson and his colleagues noted:

> There is no serious doubt that biogenesis is the rule, that life comes only from other life, that a cell, the unit of life, is always and exclusively the product or offspring of another cell.[22]

Since the Law of Biogenesis dictates that life comes only from life,… Where did the first life in the universe come from?

Since the Law of Biogenesis dictates that life comes *only* from life, this should raise a question in our minds: Where did the first life in the universe come from? If life always comes from life, the only logical conclusion is that life has always existed. Remember, there cannot be an effect without a cause, and the effect cannot be greater than its cause. Therefore, the only possibility is that we came from an eternal, living Creator.

Nobel Prize winner Francis Crick stated:

> The great majority of sequences [required for life] can never be synthesized at all, at any time.… An honest man, armed with all the knowledge available to us now, could only state that in some sense the origin of life appears to be almost a miracle, so many are the conditions which would have had to be satisfied to get it going.[23]

In addition to life arising *only* from life, the Law of Biogenesis also states that life only perpetuates its own kind. Each creature's genes are uniquely programmed to reproduce only within that same species. This explains why whales produce only whales, cows produce cows, ants produce ants, and humans produce humans — which leads us to the next problem with evolution.

Transitional Forms

The other claim of macroevolution is that one species gradually changes over time to form another species.

To prove macroevolution, scientists line up various creatures, point to the similarities, and tell us that they're obviously descended from a common evolutionary ancestor. I'm sure you've seen these charts in school textbooks showing a progression from fish to reptiles to mammals.

But let's say I lined up cars of various styles from a certain manufacturer according to their size, from sub-compact to luxury car, and pointed out their similarities. Would you believe that they obviously descended from a common evolutionary ancestor — or would you just use your common sense and think they simply had a common maker?

At best, the fossils used to create these charts demonstrate microevolution, such as the variety within horses, but is there any proof of one species changing to another? No. In fact, there's proof that they didn't, for if macroevolution were true, all species would have spent more time in transition than in completion. Thus the fossil record would reveal millions upon millions of transitional forms — creatures in the intermediate stages of evolution. No such fossils exist.

Charles Darwin, who championed the theory of evolution in *On the Origin of Species by Means of Natural Selection or The Preservation of Favored Races in the Struggle for Life*, acknowledged this lack of transitional forms as one of his theory's fatal flaws. He stated:

> As by this theory, innumerable transitional forms must have existed, why do we not find them embedded in the crust of the earth? Why is all nature not in confusion instead of being as we see them, well-defined species? Geological research does not yield the infinitely many fine gradations between past and present species required by the theory; and this is the most obvious of the many objections which may be argued against it. The explanation lies, however, in the extreme imperfection of the geologic record.[24]

Darwin knew exactly what was required to prove his theory true, and he was honest enough to say so. He also recognized that there were numerous valid objections against the theory, one of which was the lack of transitional forms. There should be millions upon millions of fossils in intermediate stages if evolution were true. The problem, Darwin proposed, was that we just have not seen enough of the fossil record yet. Well, that has now been remedied with modern geology.

Almost 150 years after Darwin, what do we find in the fossil record? We find fossils of fully formed woolly mammoths, whole fish, whole reptiles, and so on. Everything in the fossil record appears fully formed and true to its own kind. There are no creatures with partially formed skeletons, or partial fins or beaks. Among the billions of fossils found, we don't see one single example of the transitional forms Darwin said must exist if his theory of evolution were true.

Everything in the fossil record appears fully formed and true to its own kind. There are no creatures with partially formed skeletons, or partial fins or beaks. Among the billions of fossils found, we don't see one single example of the transitional forms Darwin said must exist if his theory of evolution were true.

What does that tell us? That there is something very wrong with his theory.

The fossil record should show gradual transition from lesser forms to the more complex forms for this theory to be true. Take a look at what the experts say.

George Gaylord Simpson admitted:

> The regular absence of transitional forms is not confined to mammals, but is an almost universal phenomenon, as has long been noted by paleontologists.[25]

A. J. Marshall stated:

> The origin of birds is largely a matter of deduction. There is no fossil of the stages through which the remarkable change from reptile to bird was achieved.[26]

H. W. Smith of NYU, speaking of the lack of fossils that should exist for the vertebrates, wrote:

> The gap remains unbridged and the best place to start the evolution of the vertebrates is in the imagination.[27]

After spending forty years searching for evidence of evolution, and failing to find any, Nils Heribert-Nilsson wrote:

> The fossil material is now so complete that it has been possible to construct new classes, and the lack of transitional series cannot be explained as being due to the scarcity of material. The deficiencies are real; they will never be filled.[28]

It is conclusive: There is no evidence in the fossil record for macroevolution — that is, for one species changing to another. Evolutionists try to defend the lack of transitional forms by claiming that species evolved so rapidly that they left no fossil record. But they also tell us that no one can see evolution taking place today because it occurs too slowly.

So, in reality — whether it is supposedly too fast or too slow to notice — there is no fossil evidence of macroevolution. So no one can actually *see* any evidence of evolution anywhere!

Can we call it the "fact" of evolution with no evidence to back it up? That doesn't even make for a good theory!

In the journal *Evolution*, David Kitts reminded his fellow evolutionists:

> Despite the bright promise that paleontology provides a means of 'seeing' evolution, it has presented some nasty difficulties for evolutionists, the most notorious of which is the presence of 'gaps' in the fossil record. Evolution requires intermediate forms between species, and paleontology does not provide them.[29]

What the fossil record shows instead is not gradual change but sudden appearance and stability: most fossil species appear all at once, fully formed.

According to paleontologist Robert Carroll:

> The most striking features of large-scale evolution are the extremely rapid divergence of lineages near the time of their origin, followed by long periods in which basic body plans and ways of life are retained. What is missing are the many intermediate forms hypothesized by Darwin....[30]

In the period that paleontologists call "the Cambrian explosion," virtually every major animal group appears suddenly from nowhere, with no transitional forms preceding them. So, instead of animals diverging from a common parent, what the fossil record shows is that all the major groups arose abruptly *at one time.* Think about that. Does this evidence support the theory that life evolved gradually by accident — or does it point to a Creator?

Evolutionists usually argue that the necessary transitional fossils are there but they haven't been found yet, or that they've been destroyed. When you believe something without having any proof, does that fall within the realm of science — or is it faith?

Why would someone choose to believe by faith in evolution, which has no evidential proof — and which, in fact, the evidence disproves — but not believe by faith in a Creator for whom we *do* have evidence?

According to Dr. Kent Hovind, the test of any theory is whether or not it provides answers to basic questions. How would you answer these?

1. When, where, why, and how did life come from non-living matter?
2. When, where, why, and how did life learn to reproduce itself?
3. With what did the first cell capable of sexual reproduction reproduce?
4. Why would any plant or animal want to reproduce more of its kind since this would only make more mouths to feed and decrease the chances of survival? (Does the individual have a drive to survive, or the species? How do you explain this?)
5. How can mutations (recombining of the genetic code) create any new, improved varieties? (Recombining English letters will never produce Chinese books.)
6. Natural selection works only with the genetic information available, and tends only to keep a species stable. How would you explain the increasing complexity in the genetic code that must have occurred if evolution were true?
7. When, where, why, and how did:
    a) Single-celled plants become multi-celled? (Where are the two- and three-celled intermediates?)
    b) Fish change to amphibians?
    c) Amphibians change to reptiles?
    d) Reptiles change to birds? (Their lungs, bones, eyes, reproductive organs, heart, method of locomotion, body covering, etc., are all very different!) How did the intermediate forms live?

8. When, where, why, how, and from what did:
   - a) Whales evolve?
   - b) Sea horses evolve?
   - c) Bats evolve?
   - d) Hair, skin, feathers, scales, nails, claws, etc., evolve?
9. Which of the following evolved first (how, and how long, did it work without the others)?
   - a) The digestive system, the food to be digested, the appetite, the ability to find and eat the food, the digestive juices, or the body's resistance to its own digestive juice (stomach, intestines, etc.)?
   - b) The drive to reproduce or the ability to reproduce?
   - c) The lungs, the mucus lining to protect them, the throat, or the perfect mixture of gases to be breathed into the lungs?
   - d) The plants, or the insects that live on and pollinate the plants?
   - e) The bones, ligaments, tendons, blood supply, or muscles to move the bones?
   - f) The immune system or the need for it?[31]

Now take a minute to thoughtfully consider your answers. Are you sure they're reasonable and scientifically provable, or do you just hope and believe that it may have happened that way? Do you really think evolution makes sense?

Scientists want to convince us that new body plans and complex organs — with all their interrelated functions — simply appeared in order to meet a creature's new need.

But when you stop to consider it logically, it just isn't possible. Natural selection is fine for explaining certain small-scale changes in organisms, like the beaks of birds adapting to small environmental changes. It can take existing structures and refine them. But it can't explain how you get complex structures in the first place.

We also need to follow the idea of transitional forms to its logical conclusion: Can a fish survive with a partial gill? No, it would die. Can a bird survive with half a wing? No, it would be lunch for some other animal! Could we digest food with an incomplete digestive system? Or see with an undeveloped eyeball? Could a cheetah run without fully formed legs? Common sense tells us the answer.

The Missing Link

And that leads us to the pinnacle of transitional forms — the missing link between ape and man. If humans evolved from apes, the fossil record should reveal a multitude of transitional forms. And because humans are said to have evolved relatively recently, the fossils would have had less time to decay and should therefore be plentiful.

So what have scientists found? Nebraska Man, Piltdown Man, Java Man, Peking Man, Neanderthal Man, and Lucy are all supposed to be "missing links." But did you know that *every single one of these* has been disproved scientifically? Yet they were included in my school books, and — though scientifically disproved — many can still be seen in textbooks today!

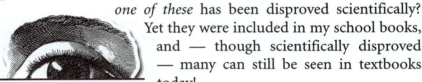

Because humans are said to have evolved relatively recently, the fossils would have had less time to decay and should therefore be plentiful.

Let's take a look at the evidence:

Nebraska Man was created from a single tooth discovered in Nebraska. Based on only one tooth (and a lot of imagination), Nebraska Man was sketched complete with a skull, skeleton, tools, and even a family. The only problem is that the tooth was later found to have come from an extinct pig!

Piltdown Man has been revealed to be a deliberate hoax. The skull fragment actually came from a modern human, and the jawbone portion and two teeth were from an orangutan. The teeth had been filed down to make them look human, and the bones and teeth had been stained to give them the appearance of being ancient. The entire "discovery" was forged from the outset to fool people who would not search for the truth.

Java Man was constructed from widely-scattered bones — a skullcap and femur found far apart in a gravel deposit. They were actually unrelated parts of a human being and a giant gibbon.

Peking Man was based only on monkey-like skulls that were bashed in at the back. Because they were found with various animal bones and tools, it was assumed that these "tool-using apes" were man's ancestors. Instead, it was discovered that these animals were man's meal, and the tools were used *on* them rather than *by* them.

Neanderthal Man was determined to be completely human — just plain, modern people with a well-developed culture, art, and religion, but who suffered from dietary deficiencies.

Lucy could not be a "missing link" because it has been determined that man walked upright before the time of Lucy.

"The missing link" is still missing — and will forever remain missing because the rule holds for humans as for all other life forms: There are no transitional forms. Everything appears in the fossil record suddenly, and perfectly formed.

Again, while there is plenty of evidence for microevolution (adaptation within a species), macroevolution — the supposed development of one species into another — has no evidence to support it. None. Scientists have found no transitional fossils and no missing links.

Dr. Colin Patterson, director of the British Museum of Natural History, and a highly respected evolutionist, wrote a book about evolution. When asked why his book didn't include any illustrations of transitional fossils, Dr. Patterson, who has seven million fossils in his museum, replied:

> I fully agree with your comments on the lack of direct illustration of evolutionary transitions in my book. If I knew of any, fossils or living, I certainly would have included it.... I will lay it on the line. There is not one such fossil for which one might make a watertight argument.[32]

Niles Eldridge, a leading expert in vertebrate fossils, decided to honestly weigh the evidence. Here is his conclusion:

> No wonder paleontologists shied away from evolution for so long. It never seems to happen. Assiduous collecting up cliff faces yield zigzags, minor oscillations, and the very occasional slight accumulation of change — over millions of years, at a rate too slow to account for all the prodigious change

> that has occurred in evolutionary history. When we do see the introduction of evolutionary novelty, it usually shows up with a bang, and often with no firm evidence that the fossils did not evolve elsewhere! Evolution cannot forever be going on somewhere else. Yet that's how the fossil record has struck many a forlorn paleontologist looking to learn something about evolution.[33]

Wow! What a couple of statements: They just said *there is no evidence* to back up the theory of evolution.

So, after doing a bit of research to discover the truth, I did "learn something about evolution." I learned that the evidence just isn't there to put my faith in. How about you?

Evolution cannot forever be going on somewhere else. Yet that's how the fossil record has struck many a forlorn paleontologist looking to learn something about evolution.
— Niles Eldridge

Probability

As we've already seen, the Law of Biogenesis proves that evolution is not possible. And the complete lack of fossil evidence supports that conclusion.

Another fact that led me to reject evolution was the Law of Probability, which also shows the impossibility of life arising from non-life.

According to Distinguished British astronomer Sir Frederick Hoyle, the number of trial assemblies of amino acids needed to give rise to the enzymes required for life, and their discovery by random shuffling, turns out to be less than 1 in 1 x $10^{40,000}$.[34] Just to give you an idea of how astronomical this number is, one trillion is only 10^{12}. And it is estimated that there are only 10^{80} electrons in the entire universe! So $10^{40,000}$ of anything is almost impossible even to imagine. Mathematicians say that any event in which the chances are beyond one in 10^{50} is impossible — it is an event that we can state with certainty will never happen, no matter how much time is allotted and no matter how many conceivable opportunities could exist for the event to take place.

Recall that Hoyle said the probability of an enzyme arising spontaneously was less than one in $10^{40,000}$ — which is an incredibly lesser probability than the 1 in 10^{50} that makes an event impossible.

Dr. Harold Morowitz, former professor of biophysics at Yale University, estimated that the probability for the chance formation of the smallest, simplest form of a living organism known is one chance in $10^{340,000,000}$.

And the famous astronomer and evolutionist Carl Sagan estimated that the chance of life evolving on any single planet, including Earth, is one chance in $10^{2,000,000,000}$.

Do you realize how huge that number is? It would take 6,000 books with 300 pages each just to write this number out. So if ever anything were impossible, spontaneous generation would have to be it.

According to the Law of Probability, then, the odds of life arising from non-life are far beyond the realm of possibility. And that's just for a single molecule to come to life. How would you explain the complexity of life forms, or the formation of the extremely detailed DNA code?

Human DNA, for example, contains three billion pieces of information — literally tens of thousands of pages worth. Did that information develop and evolve one page at a time?

How could undirected, random chance have created complex information such as this? It boggles the mind to think about it. It certainly does not indicate chance, but rather design.

A man once posed this question to me: If you lined up a computer, a robot, a 747 jet, and a lowly worm, which one would a scientist say is the most intricately designed of those four?

I thought it would be the worm. He told me that I was right, and that is also what scientists say. When you examine the function of a digestive system, or any least physical system, you begin to appreciate the highly ordered inner workings of that system.

We know for a fact that the computer had a creator and designer; we know the robot had a creator and designer; we know the 747 had a creator and designer; but somehow we think the worm happened by luck and by chance over time? That just doesn't make sense. If the inanimate objects needed a creator and a designer, not only would the complex, living, self-replicating worm have to have had a creator and designer, but it would have to have had a much *greater* Creator and Designer than those three inanimate objects. And if this is true even of the "simple" worm, imagine what it would take for something as amazingly complex as the human brain to form.

Even Carl Sagan admits:

> The information content of the human brain expressed in bits is probably comparable to the total number of connections among neurons — about a hundred trillion, 10^{14} bits. If written out in English, that information would fill some twenty million volumes — as many as in the world's largest libraries. The equivalent of twenty million books is inside the head of every one of us. The brain is a very big place in a very small space.... The neurochemistry of the brain is astonishingly busy, the circuitry of a machine more wonderful than any devised by humans.[35]

If humans cannot devise something as astonishing as the brain, who can — and who did?

World-renowned crusader for Darwinism, Professor Richard Dawkins, states:

> We have seen that living things are too improbable and too beautifully "designed" to have come into existence by chance.[36]

Irreducible Complexity

Biochemist Dr. Michael Behe, who argues that evolution could never have given rise to the intricate structures of life, has identified something he calls "irreducible complexity."

This refers to an organism which is so complex that it could not have come together piece by piece and still function; all the parts must have come about at once in order to have any function at all. Behe explains:

> By "irreducibly complex" I mean a single system composed of several well-matched, interacting parts that contribute to the basic function, wherein the removal of any one of the parts causes the system to effectively cease functioning.

> An irreducibly complex system cannot be produced directly (that is, by continuously improving the initial function, which continues to work by the same mechanism) by slight, successive modifications of a precursor system, because any precursor to an irreducibly complex system that is missing a part is by definition nonfunctional…
>
> Since natural selection can only choose systems that are already working, then if a biological system cannot be produced gradually it would have to arise as an integrated unit, in one fell swoop, for natural selection to have anything to act on.[37]

He cites the simple mousetrap as an example. All the pieces must be present at one time in order for it to function. A piece of wood won't catch a mouse. A piece of wood and a spring won't catch a mouse. A piece of wood, a spring, and a hinge won't catch a mouse. All the parts must be present, and arranged correctly, in order for the mousetrap to function. The same would be true for any irreducibly complex system.

A piece of wood won't catch a mouse. A piece of wood and a spring won't catch a mouse. A piece of wood, a spring, and a hinge won't catch a mouse. All the parts must be present, and arranged correctly, in order for the mousetrap to function.

For instance, the knee joint consists of at least 16 essential characteristics, each requiring thousands of pieces of information to exist simultaneously in the genetic code. Therefore, the knee could not have evolved gradually but must have been created all at once as a whole, fully functioning joint.

Amazingly, Charles Darwin himself admitted that an idea such as "irreducible complexity," if proven true, would demolish his theory. In *The Origin of Species* he wrote:

> If it could be demonstrated that any complex organ existed which could not possibly have been formed by numerous, successive, slight modifications, my theory would absolutely break down.[38]

Darwin, as quoted at the beginning of this chapter, said he had a most difficult time with the human eye. He admitted that it would be "absurd in the highest degree" to claim that the eye, with its amazing complexity, could have evolved.

Dr. Scott Huse points out what the human eye can do:

> Furnished with automatic aiming, automatic focusing, and automatic aperture adjustment, the human eye can function from almost complete darkness to bright sunlight, see an object the diameter of a fine hair, and make about 100,000 separate motions in an average day, faithfully affording us a continuous series of color stereoscopic pictures. All of this is performed usually without complaint, and then while we sleep, it carries on its own maintenance work.[39]

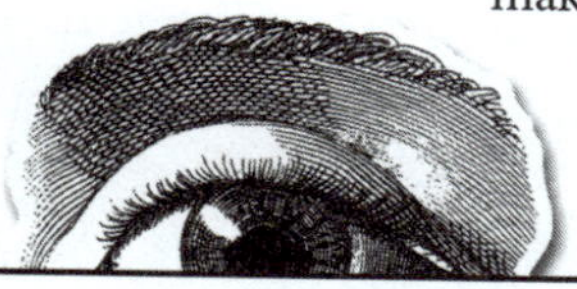

The flagellum is a little motor-driven propeller that sits on the backs of certain bacteria and drives them through their watery environment. It spins at 100,000 rpm and can change direction in a quarter turn. The intricate machinery in this molecular motor — including a rotor, a stator, O-rings, bushings, and a drive shaft — requires the coordinated interaction of approximately forty complex protein parts.

Then look at the flagellum of some bacteria — a marvel of engineering. Harvard biologist Howard Berg refers to in his public lectures as "the most efficient machine in the universe."

The flagellum is a little motor-driven propeller that sits on the backs of certain bacteria and drives them through their watery environment. It spins at 100,000 rpm and can change direction in a quarter turn. The intricate machinery in this molecular motor — including a rotor, a stator, O-rings, bushings, and a drive shaft — requires the coordinated interaction of approximately forty complex protein parts.

If any part is missing or not available in the right proportions, no functional flagellum will form. So, how could it have evolved?

According to Michael Behe, we know of only one sufficient cause that can produce functionally integrated, irreducibly complex systems: an Intelligent Designer.

Molecular biology has shown that even a single cell is incredibly complex. Bruce Alberts, a leading cell biologist and president of the National Academy of Sciences, writes:

> We have always underestimated cells.... The entire cell can be viewed as a factory that contains an elaborate network of interlocking assembly lines, each of which is composed of a set of large protein machines. Why do they call them machines? Precisely because, like machines invented by humans to deal efficiently with the macroscopic world, these protein assemblies contain highly coordinated moving parts.[40]

And all the parts must be in place simultaneously or the cell can't function.

Since life is built of these "machines," the idea that natural processes could have made a living system is absurd.

Behe acknowledges that:

> Systems of horrendous, irreducible complexity inhabit the cell. The resulting realization that life was designed by an intelligence is a shock to us in the twentieth century who have gotten used to thinking of life as the result of simple natural laws.[41]

Although the highly intricate machines in cells often resemble those designed by humans, in many cases they are *much more advanced* than what man has been able to create!

Evolutionist Richard Dawkins said of the DNA in cells, "The machine code of the genes is uncannily computer-like."[42]

Microsoft's cofounder Bill Gates stated, "DNA is like a computer program, but far, far more advanced than any software we've ever created."[43]

Since Gates hires programmers to design his software, doesn't it make sense that the "software" in a cell — which is far more advanced than any man-made software — had a designer also?

In fact, researchers believe DNA could be the basis of a staggeringly powerful new generation of computers. After computer scientist Leonard Adleman realized that human cells and computers process and store information in much the same way, researchers around the world began creating tiny biology-based computers, using test tubes of DNA-laden water to crunch algorithms and spit out data.

Researchers are also hoping that genetic material can self-replicate and grow into processors so powerful that they can handle problems too complex for silicon-based computers to solve.

The journal *Nature Biotechnology* tells of two scientists who built a biologically based computer that can't lose a game of tick-tack-toe to a human, and doesn't need any prompting from outside sources to compete.

Question: If the basic building block of life is smarter than man, don't you think it required something smarter than man to design it?

According to molecular biologist James Shapiro:

> There are no detailed Darwinian accounts for the evolution of any fundamental biochemical or cellular system, only a variety of wishful speculations. It is remarkable that Darwinism is accepted as a satisfactory explanation for such a vast subject — evolution — with so little rigorous examination of how well its basic theses work in illuminating specific instances of biological adaptation or diversity.[44]

Even Shapiro, a staunch evolutionist, suggests examining the evidence — which he has already admitted is not there.

Evolution-Defying Creatures

If any creature can be found that defies the rules of evolution in such a way that it could not possibly have evolved, then it must have been created.

And if there is even one animal that required God as its Creator, why not believe in God as the Creator of everything else as well? When you honestly examine the evidence, it just doesn't make sense that design could have come about without a designer. Here are some examples of wonderfully designed creatures that defy evolution.

The Tick: The first "wonderfully designed" creature we're going to look at is the detestable common tick.

Dr. Jose Ribeiro, of the National Institutes of Health, gives the tick a lot of credit: "Ticks know everything we know and don't know [chemically], about pharmacology."[45]

The tiny tick has dozens of elaborate chemical weapons in its saliva, which it injects into the wound. To help it camp out on its host for a few days and avoid detection, the tick's saliva contains an anesthetic so the host won't feel it and interrupt the meal.

To keep the host's blood flowing, the tick's saliva contains compounds to disable the clotting mechanism. It also tricks the host's immune system into keeping white cells away so the tick enjoys a feast of the red cells it needs.

Entomologist Stephen Wikel, who has studied 10,000 ticks, stated, "We probably have a lifetime of work ahead of us,"[46] in order to discover how this complex process works.

Dr. Ribeiro said these tiny creatures "have a very ancient wisdom."[47] Do you think random natural processes could have come up with this incredible chemical cocktail — or could this come only from an intelligent Creator?

The Gecko Lizard: Next, consider the amazing gecko lizard, which can walk across the ceiling upside down without falling off. On its toe pads are an estimated 500 million tiny fibers tipped with little suction cups. In addition, the tips of the lizard's toes bend upward so that it can peel off the suction cups gradually at each step and not get stuck to the surface.

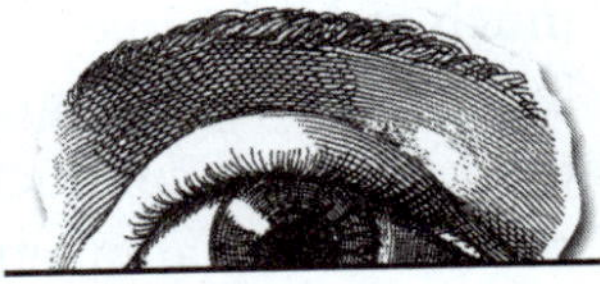

Why would the process of random mutations and blind chance put suction cups on the gecko's feet?

Dr. Robert Kofahl explains:

> The extraordinary microscopic structure of the gecko lizard's toe pads clearly indicates intelligent purposeful design. No remotely plausible scheme for the origin of the gecko's suction cups by random mutations and natural selection has yet been proposed by evolutionary theorists. And should some scientist with a clever imagination succeed in devising such a scheme, he would still be without a scrap of fossil evidence to demonstrate that the hypothetical process of evolution actually took place in the past.[48]

Why would the process of random mutations and blind chance put suction cups on the gecko's feet? Only half a suction cup would make the gecko lunch for some other creature! Too much suction and the gecko isn't going anywhere!

How did mindless evolution know to also create toes that curl upward to control the suction? Only the hand of God could have created the purposeful design of the gecko lizard.

The Ocean Sponge: Another creature that boggles the mind is the seemingly simple ocean sponge, which scientists have discovered actually produces fiber optics better than our most sophisticated manufacturing methods.

The sponge's thin glass fibers are capable of transmitting light better than industrial fiber optic cables used for telecommunication. Commercial manufacturing methods require high temperatures and produce relatively brittle cable that can crack if bent too far. The sponge's fibers, grown at cold temperatures, are much more flexible, and can even be tied in a knot without breaking. By adding traces of sodium to the fibers, the sponge increases their ability to conduct light — something that cannot be done in commercial manufacturing. Scientists at Bell Laboratories hope to eventually learn how to duplicate the manufacturing process of this lowly sponge.

Joanna Aizenburg at Bell Labs admitted, "Modern technology cannot yet compete with some of the sophisticated optical systems possessed by biological organisms."[49] Most of us would think that an ocean sponge is a pretty rudimentary life form on the evolutionary chart, yet top scientists are trying to copy its "sophisticated optical system"!

Do they see evidence of intelligent design and give credit where credit is due? Surprisingly, no. Chemist Geri Richmond said of the sponge:

> …It's such a wonderful example of how exquisite nature is as a designer and builder of complex systems. We can draw it on paper and think about engineering it, but we're in the stone age compared to *nature* [*emphasis added*].[50]

According to the journal *Nature*, there is an emerging field called biomimetics, in which scientists try to understand how biological systems are engineered and apply the principles to developing technology.

Doesn't it strike you that something that's "engineered," and that's more advanced than what scientists can create, couldn't have just happened by mindless, random chance processes? That's what the statistical analyses we looked at before tell us, too.

Most of us would think that an ocean sponge is a pretty rudimentary life form on the evolutionary chart, yet top scientists are trying to copy its "sophisticated optical system"!

Other recent discoveries include: a glowing protein in jellyfish that allows surgeons to illuminate cancerous tissue while they operate to remove it; and a starfish called the brittlestar, coated with tiny lenses that act as a collective "eye," which engineers are using as a model for creating sensors and guidance systems.

Randy Kochevar, a marine biologist, described the brittlestar as incredible:

> We're looking at these things that are not known to be visual animals yet we're finding these fascinating optical properties that are built into their bodies.[51]

In his book *Superforce: The Search for a Grand Unified Theory of Nature*, Australian astrophysicist Paul Davies asks us to consider these insightful questions:

> If nature is so "clever" as to exploit mechanisms that amaze us with their ingenuity, is that not persuasive evidence for the existence of intelligent design behind the universe? If the world's finest minds can unravel only with difficulty the deeper workings of nature, how could it be supposed that those workings are merely a mindless accident, a product of blind chance?[52]

The Giraffe: Being a rather tall person myself (6'6"), there are not many beings I look up to — except at the zoo, where I was surprised to find myself looking up — way up! — to a bunch of giraffes! Despite their height — up to 18 feet — they could run very gracefully (unlike me!). I wanted to find out more about this unusual animal.

One thing I learned is that the giraffe needs a powerful heart to pump blood up its long neck to the brain.

If we want to believe in evolution, let's imagine that the very first giraffe manages to evolve the two-foot-long heart it needs to get blood up a neck that long. Its heart is now so powerful that, as the giraffe bends its head down, the increased blood pressure is more than enough to burst the blood vessels in its brain.

So this first giraffe must be intelligent enough to realize that an improvement is needed and then set out to somehow grow an incredibly complex organic structure to fix the problem.

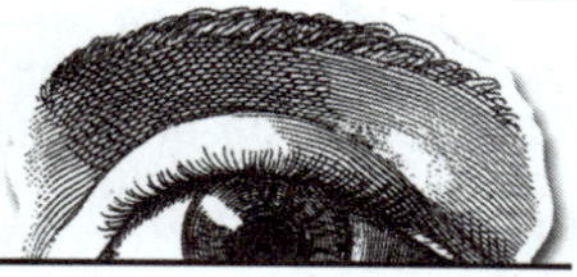

Through evolution, which is imagined to consist of mindless, processes over long periods of time, the creature manages to quickly devise a protective mechanism to prevent it from blowing its brains out when it gets its first drink of water.

And it must do so within a matter of days — before it dies of thirst or brain damage — or else this new species will shortly be extinct. (Of course, how would it know an improvement was needed unless it had first had a brain hemorrhage? And then it wouldn't know anything; it would be dead.)

Through evolution, which is imagined to consist of mindless, totally random accidental chance processes occurring over long periods of time, the creature manages to quickly devise a protective mechanism to prevent it from blowing its brains out when it gets its first drink of water.

Dr. Jobe Martin describes this amazingly detailed solution:

> As the bull bends its head down…, valves in the arteries in its neck begin to close. Blood beyond the last valve continues moving toward the brain. But instead of passing at high speed and pressing into the brain and damaging or destroying it, that last pump is shunted under the brain into a group of vessels similar to a sponge…. The brain is preserved as the powerful surge of oxygenated blood gently expands this "sponge" beneath it.

> However, from this mechanism another problem arises. A lion creeps up and prepares to kill its spotted prey. The giraffe quickly raises its head and, without something to compensate for the reduced blood flow, passes out. It got up too fast, generating low blood pressure and diminished oxygen content in the brain. The lion eats a hearty meal, and the giraffe, were it alive, would realize that it had better evolve some mechanism to re-oxygenate its oxygen-deprived brain! We all know that animals that have been eaten by a lion don't evolve anything, even though evolutionists would have us believe that creatures evolve the necessary-for-life improvements as they are needed for survival.
>
> But the giraffe survives! … as he begins to raise his head, the arterial valves open. The "sponge" squeezes its oxygenated blood into the brain; the veins going down the neck contain some valves, which close to help level out the blood pressure, and the giraffe can quickly be erect and running without passing out and becoming lion lunch.[53]

And it does all of this automatically. The giraffe is another amazing creature that defies the theory of evolution. Do you really think there's any way the giraffe could have gradually evolved and developed its special features randomly over time, as evolution demands?

Remember, if there is even one creature that could not have evolved, then there must be a Creator.

Follow the Evidence

After examining this evidence — which is only a small part of the total body of such evidence — we've seen that scientists do not have any proof for the theory of evolution.

And we've seen that macroevolution does not explain how life could have come into being, or how life could have evolved from simple to complex forms.

Let's look at just a few more quotes from those who have considered the evidence — or lack thereof.

On the origin of life, noted evolutionist, Nobel Prize winner and Harvard professor George Wald said:

> One has only to contemplate the magnitude of this task to concede that the spontaneous generation of a living organism is impossible. Yet here we are as a result, I believe, of spontaneous generation.[54]

This eminent scientist *acknowledges* that spontaneous generation is scientifically impossible, yet he chooses to believe that this is how life began! Here's someone intelligent enough to win a Nobel Prize, yet stubborn enough to deny the obvious facts.

Sir Ernest Chain, co-holder of the Nobel Prize for developing penicillin, addresses the other main aspect of evolution:

> To postulate that the development and survival of the fittest is entirely a consequence of chance mutations seems to me a hypothesis *based on no evidence and irreconcilable with the facts.* These classical evolutionary theories are a gross over-simplification of an immensely complex and intricate mass of facts, and it amazes me that they are swallowed so uncritically and readily, and for such a long time, by so many scientists without a murmur of protest. [*emphasis added*][55]

If you want to find the truth, always follow the evidence, no matter where it leads.

Evolution from one species to another is one of the biggest lies ever perpetrated on mankind. As Adolf Hitler said, "The bigger the lie, the more people will believe in it." I bought into the lie of evolution for years. However, the evidence just isn't there; the facts don't support it. So I'm not swallowing the lie anymore, and I hope you won't either.

But why is it that people just believe the theory without taking a hard look at the evidence to see where it leads? Why would scientists accept it so uncritically?

For an amazing statement that gets to the heart of the matter, consider this honest admission by evolutionist Richard Lewontin, Harvard genetics professor:

> Our willingness to accept scientific claims that are against common sense is the key to an understanding of the real struggle between science and the supernatural. We take the side of science *in spite* of the patent absurdity of some of its constructs...in spite of the tolerance of the scientific community for unsubstantiated just-so stories, because we have a prior commitment, a commitment to materialism....
>
> Moreover, that materialism is absolute, for we cannot allow a Divine Foot in the door. To appeal to an omnipotent deity is to allow that at any moment the regularities of nature may be ruptured, that miracles may happen. [*emphasis in the original*][56]

And there you have it. A moment of truth. Dr. Lewontin actually admits that no matter where the evidence leads, he is not going to consider it. If the evidence clearly points to "a Divine Foot in the door," he will not accept it.

Why? The reason is the same for all: Once we know there is a God, we know we must answer to that God. And some people, despite the evidence, just don't want to go there. Which way are you going to let the evidence take you?

Robert Jastrow, director of NASA's Goddard Institute for Space Studies, clearly points out the options:

> Perhaps the appearance of life on earth is a miracle. Scientists are reluctant to accept that view, but their choices are limited; either life was created on the earth by the will of a being outside the grasp of scientific understanding, or it evolved on our planet spontaneously, through chemical reactions occurring in non-living matter lying on the surface of the planet.[57]

There are only two options: Our immensely complex universe came into being by chance, or it was created by the hand of God. Which one will you choose? Be sure your choice is based on the facts, not blind faith. Your future depends on it.

Here's another truth to consider. If you choose not to believe in a God who created you, but instead think you're nothing but an accidental result of random chance processes, then you believe the following:

- There is no qualitative difference between humans and animals.
- There ultimately is no meaning in life.
- There is no life after death.
- There is no purpose to human history.

"The bigger the lie, the more people will believe in it."
— Adolph Hitler

Do these thoughts fit well with your reasoning? Or do you intuitively know that humans have special value and that there is a purpose behind your life?

Like some people, you may not want to acknowledge that there is a God to whom you are accountable. We all will die one day. Eventually we all will have to face that fact, even if we deny it with every breath in our body. Remember the "ultimate statistic": Ten out of ten people die. And when we take our last breath, God will still be there. Then what?

When taking a look at the amazing evidence in this chapter, you can see that it is true that if a frog turns into a prince, it is only a fairy tale, and it will never be a scientific fact.

The evidence tells us that we were made by a Creator. We are not here by accident; we were created for a reason.

The mystery of life is getting clearer as our search for eternal truth narrows. Let's see where the evidence leads us now.

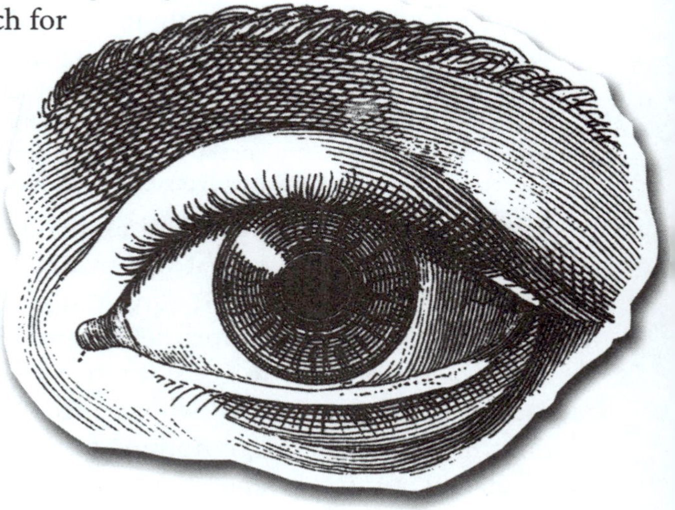

Take the state of Texas,
fill it two feet deep in silver dollars,
paint one of them red...

Chapter 3
The Red Silver Dollar

Within a century, the Bible will be extinct.
— Voltaire (1694–1778)

Now that we know that the evidence for a Creator is solid *and* that not a shred of evidence for evolution exists, we need to ask: Who is this Creator? Surely He wants His created beings to be able to know Him.

Why would He create us and then leave us floundering around in the dark on our own? It's only logical that a God would give humans a way to find Him — a written record telling us about Himself, His character, and His plan for mankind.

There are many possible answers to who this God might be. Buddhists don't believe so much in a God as in continual reincarnation leading to one's eventual re-absorption into the universe. The Muslim god, Allah, is distant and unknowable by man. To New Agers, everyone and everything is a god — you and I are gods. Many Hindus view God as Brahman, a universal spirit that everyone is a part of. But while many Hindus don't acknowledge a Supreme Being, they do worship 330 million lesser gods.

To Jews, God is the Creator — a personal, all-powerful Spirit who revealed Himself to Abraham and to the prophets, promising someday to manifest as the Messiah.

To Christians, God is that same Creator. They believe He manifested as Jesus, the Messiah, in order to destroy the sin barrier between man and God by the sacrifice of Himself, and that He will come again to judge everyone.

There are many other beliefs about who or what God is.

Some people think it's intolerant or arrogant for anyone to claim that only one belief system is true so all the others are false.

But as you can see, each religion offers a concept of God that is contradictory to that of other religions. Therefore, they can't *all* be true. It's possible that they're all wrong, but they certainly can't all be right.

How do we decide which one — if any — is right?

In order to determine the validity of each option, first we would have to examine the religious texts of the various belief systems. Then we would have to apply some sort of test to see which one is true.

Some of the texts include the *Egyptian Book of the Dead*, the *Book of Mormon*, the *Pearl of Great Price*, the *Koran*, the *Hadith*, the *Bible*, the *Bhagavad Gita*, the *Vedas*, the *Holy Dhammapada*, and so on.

What basic tests can we apply to a text to determine whether it is true?

Be careful that you search for what is true, not just for something that you already believe. Make sure you have evidence to prove you're taking a calculated leap of faith.

When selecting a test of validity, remember: It doesn't matter what we believe; it matters what is true. I might believe the earth is flat, but that is not true. I might believe the sky is green, but that is not true. I might believe I'm a millionaire, but that is not true. Truth is what reality says it is.

So be careful that you search for what is true, not just for something that you already believe. Make sure you have evidence to prove that you're taking a *calculated* leap of faith into eternity, not a *blind* leap.

Once you have found a true religious text, you have your answer about which belief is true. So let's talk about tests.

Let's say you were taking a multiple-choice test and had the following question:

2 + 2 = a) 4; b) 5; c) 3; d) 6

Once you know that the answer is a, how much time do you need to study options b, c, and d? None at all.

Why not study the other options? Because all truth, by definition, is narrow. There is *only one* answer to 2 + 2 =. One right answer and *millions* of wrong answers.

For example, there is only one person who is currently president of the United States of America: One right answer and six billion wrong ones.

You can't have a wrong answer unless there is a what?

The same holds for any type of truth, even eternal truth. Eternal truth will also be narrow, and you certainly want to be sure you find the right answer.

On one of my many flights, a man seated next to me was taking notes on an article titled "Spirituality in the Neighborhood." I noticed pictures of Buddha statues throughout the article and was curious what it was about.

He told me that he was a Unitarian Universalist minister, and that in his congregation were Jews, Christians, Buddhists, atheists, etc. He had a little bit of everything in his church.

When I asked him, "When you die, what do you think is on the other side?" He replied, "I really don't know." He said he was hoping in reincarnation, but that people could believe anything they wanted to. His church was into social justice by doing good things for others, so they thought that whatever happens on the other side, they will be OK.

I challenged him with this question: "Is it possible that a person could believe something is going to be on the other side after death, but when he dies he finds that what he thought was going to be there was not actually there?"

He answered, "Of course."

"You are right," I said. "If someone believes there is nothing when he dies and there is something, then he is 100 percent wrong. But you can't have a wrong answer unless there is a what?"

He looked at me and gulped. He replied, "A right answer."

"Exactly. There has to be a right answer for eternity, and you just said so. That means there is eternal truth. That being the case, then some people in your congregation have wrong answers for eternity. What are you going to do about it?"

His logic forced him to admit that there were right and wrong answers, yet he didn't believe in right or wrong. But either there *is* something when we die or there is *nothing*. We can't all be right when it comes to our opinions on eternity.

And if there can be a wrong answer for eternity, then there has to be a right one. Do you know what that right answer is?

I've always wondered: Who or what is able to keep track of each deed of each person who has ever lived in order to make the karmic circle work?

Since reincarnation is one of the popular beliefs (in Hinduism, Buddhism, Transcendental Meditation, and various occult and New Age circles, among others), I'd like to take a minute to think through how it might work.

The mechanism of reincarnation is based on the supposed "law of karma," in which good deeds and bad deeds are tallied and used as the basis for determining a person's fate in the next life.

One's good karma may earn them a better status or some good fortune in the next life, while one's bad karma will bring suffering into that life that matches the wrong done in the past.

Reincarnation typically ends only when one has advanced enough to have *neither* good karma nor bad karma, but to be totally neutral. Then one will be absorbed into an impersonal "universal consciousness," or "cosmic consciousness," in which the individual self ceases to exist. That is, the end result is the complete annihilation of the finite self. The individual becomes "one with the universe."

I've always wondered: Who or what is able to keep track of each deed of each person who has ever lived in order to make the karmic circle work? Such an entity would have to be:

- *everywhere* (omnipresent) — to be able to see all people at all times and know their thoughts and motivations;
- *all-knowing* (omniscient) — in order to keep a running tally of all those billions of individuals and their actions, and to determine whether someone deserves a cosmic thumbs-up or thumbs-down for the next life;
- *all-powerful* (omnipotent) — able to enforce its decisions;
- *good* — having a pure sense of morality that knows exactly what is "good" and what is "bad" in every particular situation. It also must be righteous enough to make a just judgment in assigning how the person will be spending that future life.

It would be the height of cruelty for an individual to have worked hard for a lifetime to accumulate 7,258,206,418 good deeds — and then find out (in the next lifetime, as a cockroach) that he was just one good deed short of the amount needed for advancement!

Now we've defined what "the universe" would have to be like in order to implement reincarnation. But it seems that rather than some impersonal "cosmic force," these requirements describe a separate, personal, all-knowing, ever-present, all-powerful, moral, just, intelligent, righteous Being.

In addition, if individuals will have their actions justly judged as right or wrong, they would have to know in advance what the definitions of right and wrong are.

They would also need to be able to see where they are on the karmic scale. After all, wouldn't a fair God let people know where they stand? It would be the height of cruelty for an individual to have worked hard for a lifetime to accumulate 7,258,206,418 good deeds — and *then* find out (in the next lifetime, as a cockroach) that he was just one good deed short of the amount needed for advancement!

That would be a shame. And wouldn't be a fair God at all. Surely a fair, righteous, just God would tell us very clearly who He is, how we can know Him, and what we can expect in eternity. He would also give us clear guidelines as to what is right and wrong, and let us know how we're doing.

Surely a fair, righteous, just God would tell us very clearly who He is, how we can know Him, and what we can expect in eternity. He would also give us clear guidelines as to what is right and wrong, and let us know how we're doing.

Unlike other religious writings, the Bible actually does that.

What is the Bible? It is a compilation of 66 books written by more than 40 writers over a period of 1600 years that reads like one book by one author. The unity, harmony, and accuracy of the Bible cannot be compared with that of any other book. The Bible is, by its very existence, evidence of a Divine Hand writing through devoted men.

If you have a favorite holy book other than the Bible, you may want to argue that. Let me explain to you why the Bible is unique.

One Bible scholar stated it this way:

> Consider for a moment the sheer miracle of the Bible. It was written by over 40 writers during the span of more than 60 generations (around 1,600 years)! These writers were from a variety of backgrounds: kings, herdsmen, soldiers, fishermen, poets, statesmen, scholars, priests, and prophets.
>
> The writers wrote on the continents of Asia, Africa and Europe in the languages of Hebrew, Greek, and Aramaic. Yet [the Bible] manages to [present] one unfolding drama of redemption. How is it possible that the Bible could have been written in the most complex and counterproductive way imaginable, and yet manage to fit together so accurately?[58]

The Bible is the best-selling book of all time. Many books have sold thousands, some have sold millions, some have even passed the ten million mark. By comparison, Bible sales are about 150 million per year, with approximately four billion Bibles in print, in over 2,000 languages.[59] No other book even comes close. There is something about it that draws people all over the world to want to read it.

Now, the fact that there are billions of copies around doesn't mean that the Bible is true, but because it is the best-selling book in history, shouldn't you take a look at it? You don't want to be one of those people who feel free to critique or claim to "know" the Bible without actually having read it.

The Bible claims to be written by God. All other religious texts were written by men who claimed to be speaking for God. Men wrote the Bhagavad Gita; men who knew Mohammed, or knew of him, wrote the Koran long after his death; a man wrote the Book of Mormon, claiming that an angel gave him the translation of ancient golden plates; Mary Baker Eddy wrote the central book of Christian Science, *Science and Health with Key to the Scriptures*, first published by Eddy in 1879.

Only the Bible claims to have been written by God speaking to men. Over 3,000 times the Bible says, "Thus saith the Lord." What other book ever written has ever said something like that so many times? In no way, shape, or form is that book claiming human authorship.

When I discovered this fact, my question was, "Is there any evidence to prove the supernatural origin of the Bible?" I found out that there is a wealth of information — from history, archaeology, science, and prophecy — that shows the Bible is indeed the Word of God.

Don't agree with me until you read the following evidence. Then decide for yourself, one way or the other.

Historical evidence supports the Bible. To prove something historically, you have to look at several things. One thing to consider is the original or early manuscripts of that document. Then we must ask: How close to the original is what we have today? In the case of the Bible, today we have over 24,000 ancient copies of portions of the New Testament. The next closest in all of antiquity is Homer's *Iliad*, of which we have 643 ancient copies.

John Warwick Montgomery said:

> To be skeptical of the resultant text of the New Testament books is to allow all of classical antiquity to slip into obscurity, for no documents of the ancient period are as well attested bibliographically as the New Testament.[60]

Also, among ancient writings, there is no other text that has manuscripts that come as close in time to the original writing as the Bible does. We would never dismiss any old texts of the *Iliad* or the *Odyssey*, and we shouldn't dismiss the Bible when it has much better documentation to back it up.

In addition, the book must also be free of any known contradictions. If a book contradicts itself, then it isn't reliable. Dr. Gleason Archer said:

> As I have dealt with one apparent discrepancy after another and have studied the alleged contradictions between the biblical record and the evidence of linguistics, archaeology, or science, my confidence in the trustworthiness of Scripture has been repeatedly verified and strengthened.[61]

Many people claim that there are contradictions in the Bible, but when asked to identify one, they can't. Some say they have read it cover to cover — but they only did it once, years ago.

This tells us some people are basing their eternal destiny on what they read when they were twelve. Be sure you don't just believe what other people say without checking out the facts for yourself.

The *external* evidence for the Bible is also amazing. Tacitus, a Roman historian, and Josephus, a Jewish historian, both support the historical accuracy of the Bible. For example, there were seventeen secular historians who wrote about the death of Jesus by crucifixion. This could not have been concocted by a group of men: External historical records attest to the truth of the Bible.

The Bible accurately describes history down to the smallest of details, and history attests to the accuracy of Scripture. For example, the rise and fall of great empires like Greece and Rome (*Daniel 2:39–40*) and the destruction of major cities (for instance, Tyre, Sidon; *Isaiah 23*) are described in the Bible.

Tyre's demise is also recorded by other ancient historians. They tell how — after King Nebuchadnezzar of Babylon failed in a thirteen-year attempt to capture the seacoast city — Alexander the Great laid siege to it for seven months and completely destroyed it and its inhabitants.

Intensive and prolonged study have shown that the historical accuracy of the Bible is far superior to the written records of Egypt, Assyria, and other early nations.

Archaeological evidence supports the Bible. There have been over 25,000 archaeological finds that provide support regarding people, their titles, and their locations mentioned in the Bible. Interestingly, not one of those finds has contradicted the Bible. As a matter of fact, these discoveries reveal the Bible as being true. Nelson Glueck, the renowned Jewish archaeologist, wrote:

> It may be stated categorically that no archaeological discovery has ever controverted a biblical reference.[62]

That is amazing: The text is historically trustworthy.

Millar Burrows states:

> The Bible is supported by archaeological evidence again and again. On the whole, there can be no question that the results of excavation have increased the respect of scholars for the Bible as a collection of historical documents.[63]

There have been over 25,000 archaeological finds that provide support regarding people, their titles, and their locations mentioned in the Bible. Interestingly, not one of those finds has contradicted the Bible.

Scientific evidence supports the Bible. One of the most convincing pieces of evidence supporting the truth of the Bible is the scientific nature of that book. I was always led to believe that science and the Bible did not and could not mesh together — that the two were in fact opposed to each other.

Now read how wrong I was:

About 2,500 years ago, science said that there were around 1,100 stars in the sky. But at about the same time, the prophet Jeremiah said (*33:22*), "...the host of heaven cannot be numbered, neither the sand of the sea measured..." Jeremiah said they were uncountable. And now, after looking at the awe-inspiring pictures sent back to earth by the Hubble Deep Space Telescope, we know that the stars of the sky *are* uncountable to man.

"It's just turtles all the way down."

(Of course, they are not uncountable to God, who "...telleth the number of the stars; he calleth them all by *their* names." *Psalm 147:4*)

Science used to teach that the world sat on the back of a large animal. The reason scientists taught this is because they couldn't believe that the flat earth wasn't supported by something.

I recently read that a small boy, confronted with the awesome fact that the earth simply hangs in space, decided to believe instead that it rested on the back of a turtle. When asked what the turtle was standing on, he said, "Another turtle." When asked what *that* turtle was standing on, he said, "It's just turtles all the way down."

Job 26:7 says of God, "He stretcheth out the north over the empty place, and hangeth the earth upon nothing." That statement was written 3,500 years ago. The Bible has always said that the earth is hanging in space. And, of course, with our science and our space exploration today, we know that to be a fact.

In the book of Hebrews, one can read this statement:

> Through faith we understand that the worlds were framed by the word of God, so that things which are seen were not made of things which do appear. (*Hebrews 11:3*)

That statement was written almost 2,000 years ago. From this, we see that the Bible has always stated that things that we see are made of invisible things. This never made sense to most people — until, of course, it was discovered that there really are invisible elements called "atoms."

In the book of Job, written 3,500 years ago, we read, "Canst thou send lightnings, that they may go, and say unto thee, 'Here we are?'" (*Job 38:35*)

> The Bible here is making a scientifically ludicrous statement — that light can be sent, and then manifest itself in speech. But did you know that radio waves move at the speed of light? This is why you can have instantaneous wireless communication with someone on the other side of the earth. Science didn't discover this until 1864 when the British scientist James Clerk Maxwell suggested that electricity and light waves were two forms of the same thing.[64]

Once again, the Bible is scientifically accurate. 2,800 years ago, Isaiah also made an interesting observation. He said:

> *It is* he that sitteth upon the circle of the earth, and the inhabitants thereof *are* as grasshoppers; that stretcheth out the heavens as a curtain, and spreadeth them out as a tent to dwell in. (*Isaiah 40:22*)

Ray Comfort, in *Scientific Facts in the Bible,* said:

> The Bible informs us here (*Isaiah 40:22*) that the earth is round. At a time when science believed that the earth was flat, it was the Scriptures that inspired Christopher Columbus to sail around the world. He wrote:
>
> > "It was the Lord who put it into my mind. I could feel His hand upon me … there is no question the inspiration was from the Holy Spirit because He comforted me with rays of marvelous illumination from the Holy Scriptures."[65]

At a time when science believed that the earth was flat, it was the Scriptures that inspired Christopher Columbus to sail around the world.
— RAY COMFORT

The Creator of the universe, of course, knows how His creation operates, and He has given us evidence of that fact throughout the Bible.

One day as I walked into a magazine shop in an airport, I noticed Vanilla Ice, a popular rap artist from a few years ago. I started a conversation with him, and at one point I said, "I heard that you had gotten into Christianity." He replied, "I used to be into that." That's an interesting statement.

As we continued to talk, he said that according to the Bible, someone who commits suicide will go to hell. He was trying to quote the Bible, but he didn't know what it said. I told him there are six suicides mentioned in the Bible, and not one time is it said it's the right thing to do. But it also doesn't say it is an automatic ticket to hell.

What do you think is the only book in the world that contains hundreds of very detailed prophecies and records of the fulfillment of those prophecies? The answer is the Bible.

He also mentioned that he was really into science, so I shared some of the scientific evidence that the Bible contains. He was very interested in the evidence, and he even gave me his address so that I could send him a book with more information!

Our logic and our conscience tell us that we really do want to know the evidence that will lead us to the right answer for this life — *and* the next.

Are your logic and conscience telling you that?

Fulfilled prophecy supports the Bible. The scientific evidence for the Bible is absolutely stunning, but it doesn't even begin to compare with the fact that showed me beyond a shadow of a doubt that the Bible is the Word of God.

What fact was that? What was it that would prove there is no way that the Bible could be from man, but must be from the hand of Almighty God? One hundred percent accuracy in foretelling the future. If we could find that in a religious text, we would have the answer we are seeking.

Next question: What do you think is the only book in the world that contains hundreds of very detailed prophecies and records of the fulfillment of those prophecies? The answer is the Bible. The Book of Mormon for Latter Day Saints doesn't; the Koran for Muslims doesn't; the Bhagavad Gita for Hindus doesn't.

In all the writings of Buddha, Confucius, and Lao-Tse, you will not find a single example of prophecy being fulfilled. In the Koran, the only instance of a specific prophecy is when Mohammed predicted that he himself would return to Mecca — a prophecy very easy for him to fulfill himself.

The Bible, on the other hand, contains more than 2,000 detailed prophecies in the Old Testament alone. In fact, twenty-five percent of the Bible is predictive in nature. And except for the prophecies that tell about the End Time return of Jesus, every single prophecy — including those about political, religious, intellectual, and geographic events leading up to the return of Jesus Christ to earth — has been fulfilled down to the smallest detail.

One of the interesting things about the Bible is that it says that anyone who does not predict with 100 percent accuracy is a false prophet. The fact that people "predict" something in the *National Enquirer*, it doesn't make them true prophets.

In Old Testament times, if someone claimed to be speaking for God and the prophecy did not come true, the penalty was death by stoning. (God takes misrepresenting Him very seriously.) So when prophets spoke, they made sure they were properly representing God's words, and not their own! Prophecy is so important because it demonstrates who God is and that He can be trusted.

> Remember the former things of old: for I *am* God, and *there is* none else; *I am* God, and *there is* none like me.
>
> Declaring the end from the beginning, and from ancient times *the things* that are not *yet* done, saying, My counsel shall stand, and I will do all my pleasure:
>
> … yea, I have spoken *it*, I will also bring it to pass; I have purposed *it*, I will also do it. (*Isaiah 46:9–11*)

God says that He will declare the end from the beginning. If He says through His prophets that He will do something, He will do it. Let's see if that is true.

The Old Testament was finished more than 400 years before the New Testament was written. To see how good God's predictive ability was, let's take a look at a small portion of those Old

Testament prophecies that predict who the Messiah, the expected Savior, would be.

1. In the Old Testament, Isaiah 7:14 reads, "Therefore the Lord Himself shall give you a sign; Behold, a virgin shall conceive, and bear a son, and shall call his name Immanuel."

This prophecy was fulfilled by Yeshua (the Hebrew name of Jesus), as we read in the New Testament:

> Now the birth of Jesus Christ was on this wise: When as his mother Mary was espoused to Joseph, before they came together, she was found with child of the Holy Ghost.
>
> Then Joseph her husband, being a just *man*, and not willing to make her a publick example, was minded to put her away privily.
>
> But while he thought on these things, behold, the angel of the Lord appeared unto him in a dream, saying, Joseph, thou son of David, fear not to take unto thee Mary thy wife: for that which is conceived in her is of the Holy Ghost.
>
> And she shall bring forth a son, and thou shalt call his name JESUS: for he shall save his people from their sins.
>
> Now all this was done, that it might be fulfilled which was spoken of the Lord by the prophet, saying,
>
> Behold, a virgin shall be with child, and shall bring forth a son, and they shall call his name Emmanuel, which being interpreted is, God with us.
>
> Then Joseph being raised from sleep did as the angel of the Lord had bidden him, and took unto him his wife:
>
> And knew her not till she had brought forth her firstborn son: and he called his name JESUS. (*Matthew 1:18–25*)

God said that He would bring forth a Son from a virgin, and He did.

2. The Old Testament prophesies that this Messiah, this Son who would be "Immanuel, God with us," would truly be the incarnation of Almighty God:

> For unto us a child is born, unto us a son is given: and the government shall be upon his shoulder: and his name shall be called Wonderful, Counsellor, The mighty God, The everlasting Father, The Prince of Peace. (*Isaiah 9:6*)

And the New Testament says:

> [Jesus said] But ye shall receive power, after that the Holy Ghost is come upon you: and ye shall be witnesses unto me both in Jerusalem, and in all Judaea, and in Samaria, and unto the uttermost part of the earth.
>
> And when he had spoken these things, while they beheld, he was taken up; and a cloud received him out of their sight.
>
> And while they looked stedfastly toward heaven as he went up, behold, two men stood by them in white apparel;
>
> Which also said, Ye men of Galilee, why stand ye gazing up into heaven? this same Jesus, which is taken up from you into heaven, shall so come in like manner as ye have seen him go into heaven. (*Acts 1:8–11*)
>
> Jesus said unto them, Verily, verily, I say unto you, Before Abraham was, I am. (*John 8:58*)

God said that Messiah would be "The Mighty God, The everlasting Father," in human form — and He was.

3. The Old Testament also prophesies that, even while occupying a human body in this world, the Savior Messiah would be the Son of God.

> I will declare the decree: the LORD hath said unto me, Thou *art* my Son; this day have I begotten thee. (*Psalm 2:7*)

This prophecy was fulfilled in Matthew 3:17, which says:

> And lo a voice from heaven, saying, This is my beloved Son, in whom I am well pleased.

It was again confirmed in Matthew 17:5:

> While he yet spake, behold, a bright cloud overshadowed them: and behold a voice out of the cloud, which said, This is my beloved Son, in whom I am well pleased; hear ye him.

Luke 22:66–71 says:

> And as soon as it was day, the elders of the people and the chief priests and the scribes came together, and led him into their council, saying,
>
> Art thou the Christ? tell us. And he said unto them, If I tell you, ye will not believe:

And if I also ask *you*, ye will not answer me, nor let *me* go.

Hereafter shall the Son of man sit on the right hand of the power of God.

Then said they all, Art thou then the Son of God? And he said unto them, "Ye say that I am.

And they said, "What need we any further witness? for we ourselves have heard of his own mouth.

We see that God said He would have a Son, and He did.

4. Furthermore, the Old Testament prophesies that, whoever this Messiah would be, He would be born in Bethlehem. At the time of Jesus' birth, Bethlehem had only about 1,000 inhabitants:

But thou, Beth-lehem Ephratah, *though* thou be little among the thousands of Judah, *yet* out of thee shall he come forth unto me *that is* to be ruler in Israel; whose goings forth *have been* from of old, from everlasting. (*Micah 5:2*)

Matthew 2:1 shows the fulfillment:

Now when Jesus was born in Bethlehem of Judaea in the days of Herod the king, behold, there came wise men from the east to Jerusalem.

God said His Son would be born in Bethlehem, and He was.

5. Micah also mentions (above) the pre-existence of Messiah: "whose goings forth *have been* from of old, from everlasting."

When He was in Judea, Jesus Himself said He fulfilled this prophecy when He told some people who opposed Him:

Your father Abraham rejoiced to see my day: and he saw *it*, and was glad.

Then said the Jews unto him, Thou art not yet fifty years old, and hast thou seen Abraham?

Jesus said unto them, Verily, verily, I say unto you, Before Abraham was, I am. (*John 8:56–58*)

This prophecy is also fulfilled in Colossians 1:17, which says:

And he is before all things, and by him all things consist.

God said His Son pre-existed all things, and He did.

6. Deuteronomy 18:18 says that Messiah would be a prophet:

I will raise them up a Prophet from among their brethren, like unto thee, and will put my words in his mouth; and he shall speak unto them all that I shall command him.

This prophecy was fulfilled in Matthew 21:11, when:

... the multitude said, This is Jesus, the prophet of Nazareth of Galilee.

God said His Son would be a prophet, and He was.

7. The Messiah would have an unusual manifestation of the Holy Spirit. Isaiah 11:2 says of this:

And the spirit of the LORD shall rest upon him, the spirit of wisdom and understanding, the spirit of counsel and might, the spirit of knowledge and the fear of the LORD.

Matthew tells us of events that confirmed the fulfillment of this prophecy, including Matthew 3:16–17, which states:

And Jesus, when he was baptized, went up straightway out of the water: and, lo, the heavens were opened unto him, and he saw the Spirit of God descending like a dove, and lighting upon him:

And lo a voice from heaven, saying, This is my beloved Son, in whom I am well pleased.

God said His Son would have an unusual manifestation of the Holy Spirit, and He did.

8. The Messiah would also have a ministry of miracles, as foretold in Isaiah 35:6:

Then shall the lame *man* leap as an hart, and the tongue of the dumb sing: for in the wilderness shall waters break out, and streams in the desert.

This prophecy was fulfilled continually in the ministry of Jesus. For instance, Matthew 9:35 says:

And Jesus went about all the cities and villages, teaching in their synagogues, and preaching the gospel of the kingdom, and healing every sickness and every disease among the people.

And Matthew 15:29–31 tells us that:

And Jesus departed from thence, and came nigh unto the sea of Galilee; and went up into a mountain, and sat down there.

And great multitudes came unto him, having with them *those that were* lame, blind, dumb, maimed, and many others, and cast them down at Jesus' feet; and he healed them:

Insomuch that the multitude wondered, when they saw the dumb to speak, the maimed to be whole, the lame to walk, and the blind to see: and they glorified the God of Israel.

God said that His Son would perform miracles, and He did.

9. The Old Testament prophesies that the Messiah would rise from the dead. Psalm 16:10 says:

> For thou wilt not leave my soul in hell; neither wilt thou suffer thine Holy One to see corruption.

We are told by an apostle, in Acts 2:31, that this prophecy was fulfilled by Jesus' resurrection, and he referred to the above verse:

> He seeing this before spake of the resurrection of Christ, that his soul was not left in hell, neither his flesh did see corruption.

What an amazing prophecy! Hundreds of years before the Son of God walked on Planet Earth, it was predicted that He would rise from the dead, and He did!

10. Scripture tells us that Messiah would be betrayed by a friend. Among other references to this event, Psalm 41:9 says:

> Yea, mine own familiar friend, in whom I trusted, which did eat of my bread, hath lifted up *his* heel against me.

Matthew 10:4 clearly speaks of "Judas Iscariot, who also betrayed him."

And John 13:21–22, 25–26 tells more specifically how it was fulfilled:

> ... he was troubled in spirit, and testified, and said, Verily, verily, I say unto you, that one of you shall betray me.
>
> Then the disciples looked one on another, doubting of whom he spake.
>
> ... He then lying on Jesus' breast saith unto him, Lord, who is it?
>
> Jesus answered, He it is, to whom I shall give a sop, when I have dipped *it*. And when he had dipped the sop, he gave *it* to Judas Iscariot, *the son* of Simon.

Thus Judas, knowing he'd planned to betray his best friend, took the bread and ate it.

God said His Son would be betrayed by a friend who ate with Him, and He was.

11. The prophets said that Messiah would be betrayed for thirty pieces of silver. Zechariah 11:12 says of the betrayer:

And I said unto them, If ye think good, give *me* my price; and if not, forbear. So they weighed for my price thirty *pieces* of silver.

Matthew 26:15 shows the fulfillment:

And said *unto them*, What will ye give me, and I will deliver him unto you? And they covenanted with him for thirty pieces of silver.

Jesus was betrayed by a friend for the exact price that had been predicted hundreds of years before. ***God had said that the price of His Son's betrayer would be thirty pieces of silver, and it was.***

12. The Old Testament prophesies that Messiah would be mocked.

But I *am* a worm, and no man; a reproach of men, and despised of the people.

All they that see me laugh me to scorn: they shoot out the lip, they shake the head, *saying*,

He trusted on the Lord *that* he would deliver him: let him deliver him, seeing he delighted in him. (*Psalm 22:6–8*)

In Matthew 27:29, its fulfillment is described:

And when they had platted a crown of thorns, they put *it* upon his head, and a reed in his right hand: and they bowed the knee before him, and mocked him, saying, Hail, King of the Jews!

Matthew 26:67 says:

Then did they spit in his face, and buffeted him; and others smote *him* with the palms of their hands,

God said His Son would be mocked, and He was.

13. The book of Psalms describes how the Messiah would die. Psalm 22:14–20 describes His death in detail:

I am poured out like water, and all my bones are out of joint: my heart is like wax; it is melted in the midst of my bowels.

My strength is dried up like a potsherd; and my tongue cleaveth to my jaws; and thou hast brought me into the dust of death.

For dogs have compassed me: the assembly of the wicked have enclosed me: they pierced my hands and my feet.

I may tell all my bones: they look *and* stare upon me.

They part my garments among them, and cast lots upon my vesture.

> But be not thou far from me, O Lord: O my strength, haste thee to help me.
>
> Deliver my soul from the sword; my darling from the power of the dog.

When He reached Psalm 22, which so fully and completely described the scene around him, He said the first words loudly enough that bystanders — who all knew the Psalm… — would begin to recite along with him.

This amazing description of the physical effects of execution by crucifixion was written hundreds of years before it was used by the Romans.

Crucifixion was first practiced about 200 B.C., and first practiced in a Jewish province in 63 B.C. Yet it was predicted in detail in Psalm 22, written by King David, who was born more than a 1,000 years before Jesus. Yes, it was predicted that Messiah would die that way, and He did. The fact that His hands and feet would be pierced and that His garments would be gambled for are also striking prophetic details in Psalm 22.

Notice how it was fulfilled. Luke 23:33–34 describes the scene of the crucifixion:

> And when they were come to the place, which is called Calvary, there they crucified him, and the malefactors, one on the right hand, and the other on the left.
>
> Then said Jesus, Father, forgive them; for they know not what they do. And they parted his raiment, and cast lots.

In Matthew 27:35, we read:

> And they crucified him, and parted his garments, casting lots: that it might be fulfilled which was spoken by the prophet, They parted my garments among them, and upon my vesture did they cast lots.

God said His Son would die in a certain manner, and He did.

14. The Old Testament prophesies that there would be a cry from this Messiah at His death. Psalm 22:1 describes it:

> My God, my God, why hast thou forsaken me?…

Matthew 27:46 describes the fulfillment of this prophecy:

> And about the ninth hour Jesus cried with a loud voice, saying, Eli, Eli, lama sabachthani? that is to say, "My God, my God, why hast thou forsaken me?

Religious Jews, both men and women, have always, and still do, memorize and recite the Psalms continuously — especially when facing difficult situations, and even more so when surrounded by unbelievers. I believe that when Jesus shouted the beginning of Psalm 22, it signified that He had been reciting the Psalms to Himself right along, as the Jewish custom was and still is.

And when He reached Psalm 22, which so fully and completely described the scene around him, He said the first words loudly enough that bystanders — who all knew the Psalm, and who also knew that it was a messianic prophecy — would begin to recite along with him.

Then suddenly, as they recited it, they would realize that it was being fulfilled before their eyes in ways Jesus could not have arranged: His body was being wracked in a particular way. His garments were being gambled for. Soldiers pierced His hands and feet with huge nails. People were shouting insults at Him that were predicted in this Psalm and elsewhere (Isaiah 53).

The people would go on to remember what all this meant, in the messianic prophecy of Isaiah:

> Surely he hath borne **our** griefs, and carried **our** sorrows: yet we did esteem him stricken, smitten of God, and afflicted.
>
> But he *was* wounded for **our** transgressions, *he was* bruised for **our** iniquities: the chastisement of **our** peace *was* upon him; and with his stripes **we** are healed.
>
> All **we** like sheep have gone astray; **we** have turned every one to his own way; and the LORD hath laid on **him** the iniquity of us all.
>
> He was oppressed, and he was afflicted, yet he opened not his mouth: he is brought as a lamb to the slaughter, and as a sheep before her shearers is dumb, so he openeth not his mouth.
>
> He was taken from prison and from judgment: And who shall declare his generation? for he was cut off out of the land of the living; for the transgression of my people was he stricken.
>
> And he made his grave with the wicked, and with the rich in his death; because he had done no violence, neither *was any* deceit in his mouth.

> Yet it pleased the Lord to bruise him; he hath put *him* to grief: **when thou shalt make his soul an offering for sin, he shall see *his* seed**, he shall prolong *his* days, and the pleasure of the Lord shall prosper in his hand.
>
> He shall see of the travail of his soul, *and* shall be satisfied: by his knowledge shall my righteous servant justify many; for he shall bear **their** iniquities. (*Isaiah 53:4–11*) [*emphasis added*]

God said His Son would cry out at His death, and He did.

15. The Old Testament prophesies that the Messiah would be pierced. We have already read prophecies of His hands and feet being pierced, and how they were fulfilled. For example:

> And I will pour upon the house of David, and upon the inhabitants of Jerusalem, the spirit of grace and of supplications: and they shall look upon me whom they have pierced, and they shall mourn for him, as one mourneth for *his* only *son*, and shall be in bitterness for him, as one that is in bitterness for *his* firstborn. (*Zechariah 12:10*)

But there was more piercing that took place. John describes how Jesus' side was pierced, and why — showing that it was because prophecy was being fulfilled:

> But when they came to Jesus, and saw that he was dead already, they brake not his legs:
>
> But one of the soldiers with a spear pierced his side, and forthwith came there out blood and water.
>
> And he that saw *it* bare record, and his record is true: and he knoweth that he saith true, that ye might believe.
>
> For these things were done, that the scripture should be fulfilled, A bone of him shall not be broken.
>
> And again another scripture saith, They shall look on him whom they pierced. (*John 19:33–37*)

God said His Son would be pierced, and He was.

16. Darkness would prevail over the land. Amos says:

> And it shall come to pass in that day, saith the Lord God, that I will cause the sun to go down at noon, and I will darken the earth in the clear day: (*Amos 8:9*)

The fulfillment is described by Matthew:

Now from the sixth hour there was darkness over all the land unto the ninth hour. (*Matthew 27:45*)

What time is "the sixth hour"? The Jewish clock began at 6:00 a.m. So the sixth hour was actually noon.

God said that He would make the earth dark at noon , and He did — for a three-hour period!

Consider: These are just a very few of many hundreds of prophecies that have been fulfilled with amazing accuracy.

The reason all these prophecies are so *important* is something called compound probability. When we consider having a *great many* requirements fulfilled by the same person, the likelihood of finding such a person decreases with every requirement. And the more unusual the requirement, the less likely we are to find such a person.

Now consider this: Jesus Christ fulfilled more than 300 prophecies in his life. Here's something that can help you appreciate the odds of this happening: If *only eight* of those 300 prophecies came true in any one person, it would be comparable to this:

- Build a small fence around the state of Texas,
- fill it two feet deep in silver dollars,
- paint one of them red,
- mix them all up,
- then — starting at the Louisiana border — walk blindfolded as far into Texas as you want to go,
- then lean over, still blindfolded,
- and pick up the red silver dollar.

What do you think the chances are that you would pick up the *red* one? Would you bet your retirement on picking up that red silver dollar? Would you bet your eternal life on odds like that? All of us do, because those are only the odds for *eight* prophecies coming true in one person. But Jesus had more than 300 prophecies about Him come true.

Rabbis used to wonder if there would be two Messiahs because He was spoken of as both a Suffering Servant, coming to remove the barrier of sin from between people and God, and as a Conquering King, coming to deliver His people from worldly oppression. But they were reading about two visits of the same Messiah. One down, and one to go!

The rabbis also used to wonder if there were going to be three Messiahs, because it is written that He would be born in Bethlehem, that God would call Him out of Egypt, and that He would be called a Nazarene.

They couldn't imagine one man fulfilling all three requirements. But Jesus was born in Bethlehem, was taken by his parents into Egypt to escape being murdered by Herod, and lived there until God told Joseph it was OK to return to Israel. Then they went to live in Nazareth, where Jesus grew up and learned and worked until he was thirty.

If it was difficult to imagine one man fulfilling only those three requirements of Messiah, imagine contemplating the odds for the 300 prophecies that have come true in Jesus!

First, you would have to go down to the neutron, proton, electron level of an atom to get a sample size big enough. There just aren't enough other items in the universe to describe the unlikelihood of this happening. We know it is absolutely impossible for man to predict the future with 100 percent accuracy. Certainly not to this magnitude. Only God could do that, and He did!

Matthew says:

> But he answered and said, It is written, Man shall not live by bread alone, but by every word that proceedeth out of the mouth of God.
> (*Matthew 4:4*)

We have those words that proceed out of His mouth here in the Bible. What is it going to tell us about eternity?

John records that:

> Pilate saith unto him, What is truth? And when he had said this, he went out again unto the Jews, and saith unto them, I find in him no fault *at all*.
> (*John 18:38*)

Like Pilate, we are all searching for truth that we can depend on — not a blind faith, but faith based on good, solid evidence.

John says:

Sanctify them through thy truth: thy word is truth. (*John 17:17*)

Putting It All Together: God's Word about Messiah, recorded in the Bible, has been shown to be true.

Investigating the actual findings of science, history, archaeology, and prophecy has shown us that — based on the evidence — saying there is no God makes no sense, because everything in the universe points to intelligent design and because no one but God could give so many complete, detailed prophecies — sometimes thousands of years in advance — and then simply and elegantly fulfill them in one Man's life.

So far, we have seen that science cries out for a Creator who made us and everything else. Then we found that the Bible is a reliable, true document. How does this all fit together? Does the Bible support those same positions of science? Let's take a look.

The Bible, Nature, Science, and Truth

As you search out eternal truth, remember that the Lord says to use your reason. Use your logic. It is not intellectual suicide to believe *truth*. Logic exists to help us find truth. Be reasonable, and watch as the truth continues to unfold.

Come now, and let us reason together, saith the LORD.... (*Isaiah 1:18*)

Saying that the Bible was written by error-prone men doesn't invalidate the statement that the Bible's words are from God. The amazing fulfillment of prophecy is major evidence of that.

Furthermore, human beings don't *always* err. Not all of the time. We can write without error. In fact, we *must* do it quite often — in school, at work, and in our checkbooks and other financial affairs.

Ninety-two times the Bible says, "It is written...," meaning that God used a man to write something that must now be regarded as God speaking.

When you see a beautiful painting, do you think the painter painted it? Or do you think the brush painted it? Of course, we know that the painter painted it, but we also know that the painter used the brush. In the same way, you can see that God is claiming authorship of the Bible, but He used mankind to put it down on parchment and to preserve it through time.

Someone once said, "God can draw a straight line with a crooked stick." That is, He can use an imperfect person to do something perfectly.

We know that God can't err. And now that we know that the Bible is the Word of God, we know that the Bible can't err either. Surely God would preserve His Word and keep it free from mistakes. We just need to look at the evidence to see that this is true:

• The Bible says that what has been made speaks very clearly of the One who made it:

> The heavens declare the glory of God; and the firmament sheweth his handywork.
>
> Day unto day uttereth speech, and night unto night sheweth knowledge.
>
> *There is* no speech nor language, *where* their voice is not heard.
>
> Their line is gone out through all the earth, and their words to the end of the world. In them hath he set a tabernacle for the sun,
>
> Which *is* as a bridegroom coming out of his chamber, *and* rejoiceth as a strong man to run a race.
>
> His going forth *is* from the end of the heaven, and his circuit unto the ends of it: and there is nothing hid from the heat thereof. (*Psalm 19:1–6*)
>
> In the beginning God created the heaven and the earth. (*Genesis 1:1*)

• When we looked at the evidence in Chapter 1, we concluded someone would have to be unreasonable not to believe the universe had a Creator. Long before us, God came to the same conclusion and commented on those who would deny His existence:

> Because that which may be known of God is manifest in them; for God hath shewed *it* unto them.
>
> For the invisible things of him from the creation of the world are clearly seen, being understood by the things that are made, *even* his eternal power and Godhead; so that they are without excuse: (*Romans 1:19–20*)
>
> THE fool hath said in his heart, *There is* no God. They are corrupt, they have done abominable works, *there is* none that doeth good. (*Psalm 14:1*)

• God also declared the beginning of things when He said that He made this universe:

> He hath made the earth by his power, he hath established the world by his wisdom, and hath stretched out the heavens by his discretion.
>
> When he uttereth His voice, *there is* a multitude of waters in the heavens, and he causeth the vapours to ascend from the ends of the earth; he maketh lightnings with rain, and bringeth forth the wind out of his treasures.
>
> Every man is brutish in *his* knowledge: every founder is confounded by the graven image: for his molten image *is* falsehood, and *there is* no breath in them. *(Jeremiah 10:12–14)*
>
> My help *cometh* from the LORD, which made heaven and earth. (*Psalm 121:2*)
>
> Happy *is he* that *hath* the God of Jacob for his help, whose hope *is* in the LORD his God:
>
> Which made heaven, and earth, the sea, and all that therein *is*: which keepeth truth for ever: (*Psalm 146:5–6*)
>
> Thou, *even* thou, *art* LORD alone; thou hast made heaven, the heaven of heavens, with all their host, the earth, and all *things* that *are* therein, the seas, and all that *is* therein, and thou preservest them all; and the host of heaven worshippeth thee. (*Nehemiah 9:6*)

"God can draw a straight line with a crooked stick."

• God said that He created animal life:

> But ask now the beasts, and they shall teach thee; and the fowls of the air, and they shall tell thee:
>
> Or speak to the earth, and it shall teach thee: and the fishes of the sea shall declare unto thee.
>
> Who knoweth not in all these that the hand of the LORD hath wrought this?
>
> In whose hand *is* the soul of every living thing, and the breath of all mankind. (*Job 12:7–10*)

• God holds the breath of every living being in His hands and His hands alone!

> LORD, thou hast been our dwelling place in all generations.
>
> Before the mountains were brought forth, or ever thou hadst formed the earth and the world, even from everlasting to everlasting, thou *art* God. (*Psalm 90:1–2*)
>
> Know ye that the LORD he *is* God: *it is* he *that* hath made us, and not we ourselves; *we are* his people, and the sheep of his pasture. (*Psalm 100:3*)

> Thus saith God the Lord, he that created the heavens, and stretched them out; he that spread forth the earth, and that which cometh out of it; he that giveth breath unto the people upon it, and spirit to them that walk therein: (*Isaiah 42:5*)

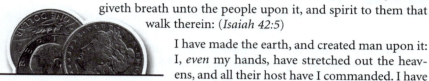

> I have made the earth, and created man upon it: I, *even* my hands, have stretched out the heavens, and all their host have I commanded. I have raised him up in righteousness, and I will direct all his ways: he shall build my city, and he shall let go my captives, not for price nor reward, saith the Lord of hosts....
>
> Verily thou *art* a God that hidest thyself, O God of Israel, the Saviour.
>
> They shall be ashamed, and also confounded, all of them: they shall go to confusion together *that are* makers of idols.
>
> *But* Israel shall be saved in the Lord with an everlasting salvation: ye shall not be ashamed nor confounded world without end.
>
> For thus saith the Lord that created the heavens; God himself that formed the earth and made it; he hath established it, he created it not in vain, he formed it to be inhabited: I *am* the Lord; and *there is* none else. (*Isaiah 45:12–13, 15–18*)

For thus saith the Lord that created the heavens; God Himself that formed the earth and made it; He hath established it, He created it not in vain, He formed it to be inhabited: I am the Lord; and there is none else.
— Isaiah 45:18

• God made both animals and man each after its own kind. That is, a kind produces the same kind, and not another kind:

> And God created great whales, and every living creature that moveth, which the waters brought forth abundantly, after their kind, and every winged fowl after his kind: and God saw that *it was* good.
>
> And God blessed them, saying, Be fruitful, and multiply, and fill the waters in the seas, and let fowl multiply in the earth.
>
> And the evening and the morning were the fifth day.
>
> And God said, Let the earth bring forth the living creature after his kind, cattle, and creeping thing, and beast of the earth after his kind: and it was so."
>
> And God made the beast of the earth after his kind, and cattle after their kind, and every thing that creepeth upon the earth after his kind: and God saw that *it was* good.

> And God said, Let us make man in our image, after our likeness: and let them have dominion over the fish of the sea, and over the fowl of the air, and over the cattle, and over all the earth, and over every creeping thing that creepeth upon the earth. (*Genesis 1:21–26*)

• The Bible gets even more specific, insisting that macroevolution never happened:

> All flesh *is* not the same flesh: but *there is* one *kind of* flesh of men, another flesh of beasts, another of fishes, *and* another of birds. (*1 Corinthians 15:39*)

Just as the scientific evidence showed us, each kind of flesh is different, and each kind of flesh can produce only its own kind of flesh. The Bible says the exact same thing!

Bottom Line: Truth has been found. The Bible tells us all we need to know in order to choose where we will spend eternity. In fact, we might say BIBLE is a great acronym for "Basic Information Before Leaving Earth."

It doesn't matter who you are — Michael Jordan, the president, you, or me — we will all be leaving earth one day. If you have the right information about eternity and do the right thing with it, you will end up at the right destination.

But if you have the *wrong* information, or do the wrong thing with the *right* information, you will end up at the wrong destination.

The ice is getting much thicker beneath us now. Since we know the Bible to be true, eternal truth continues to grow clearer and clearer.

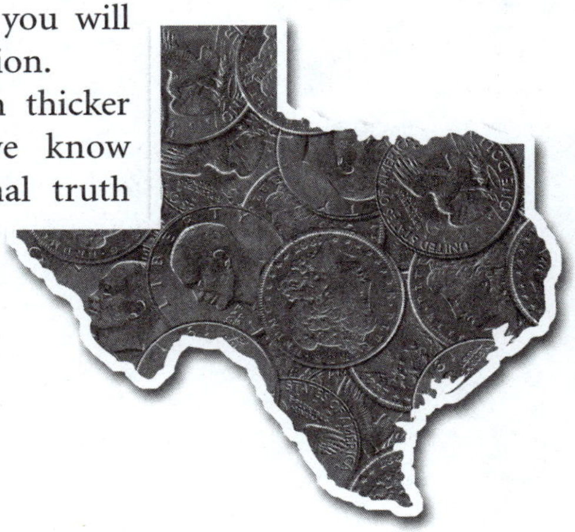

We don’t put “Death” on our day planner,
but one day it just shows up.

Chapter 4
"The Flames! The Flames!"

Between us and heaven or hell there is only life,
which is the frailest thing in the world.
— Blaise Pascal

Now that the mystery of whether the Bible is true has been solved, the way is open toward the next step of our journey: finding what the Bible says about our eternal destination.

Do you recognize these words?

To every thing there is a season,
And a time to every purpose under the heaven:
A time to be born, and a time to die;
A time to plant, and a time to pluck up that which is planted;
A time to kill, and a time to heal;
A time to break down, and a time to build up;
A time to weep, and a time to laugh;
A time to mourn, and a time to dance....

Some people think these words were written decades ago for a song by The Byrds, but actually these timeless words were inspired thousands of years before that by God (*Ecclesiastes 3:1–4*).

These words hit us deeply because they're true: There *is* a time to live, and a time to die, for each one of us. The question is, what will happen to us once our time to die comes? What happens to us after that last heartbeat? Are you ready if today happens to be that day for you?

God has placed an awareness of eternity in the heart of every man and woman. Deep down in our hearts, we all know intuitively that there is more than just this life, that there is something beyond the grave. The Bible says that we each have a body, soul, and spirit (*1 Thessalonians 5:23*). You will leave your body behind at death, but what will happen to your soul and spirit? Where will *you* spend eternity?

When you look at the words etched on a tombstone, you see the deceased person's name, date of birth, and date of death. If there are seventy or eighty years between the person's birth and death dates, most of us would consider that the person had a nice full life.

Yet eternity is infinitely longer than eighty years. I can guarantee that you will be alive somewhere after your physical death a whole lot longer than you will be alive here on earth.

We never see a U-Haul behind a hearse because we take nothing with us when we die. The only thing that will be important on the day you die will be whether or not you know the God who created you.

Since that's true, it makes sense to learn what we can about what is on the other side instead of simply focusing on things that are temporary. One hundred and fifty years from now, will it matter whether or not you made a million dollars, drove a convertible Mercedes, owned an incredible house, or played in the Final Four? No. We never see a U-Haul behind a hearse, because we take nothing with us when we die.

The only thing that will be important on the day you die will be whether or not you know the God who created you. If you *do*, you will be with Him forever … and ever and ever. And if you *don't*, you will be without Him forever … and ever and ever, because you will have rejected His loving presence and accepted the consequences that go with that rejection.

It is only the eternal things — not the temporary things — that will matter. Ask yourself this question: Are you more concerned about your relationships and possessions in this brief life than you are about where and how you will spend eternity?

The Bible tells of a wealthy man who was quite satisfied with all the possessions he'd acquired during his lifetime. He said to himself:

> ...This will I do: I will pull down my barns, and build greater; and there will I bestow all my fruits and my goods.
>
> And I will say to my soul, Soul, thou hast much goods laid up for many years; take thine ease, eat, drink, *and* be merry.
>
> But God said unto him, *Thou* fool, this night thy soul shall be required of thee: then whose shall those things be, which thou hast provided?
>
> So *is* he that layeth up treasure for himself, and is not rich toward God. (*Luke 12:18–21*)

Death is sudden. Death is uninvited. Death is certain. We don't put "Death" on our day planners, but one day it just shows up.

It is a journey from which there is no return. Now, none of us ever wants to be called a fool, neither in this lifetime nor in the next. So, how can we make sure that we don't find out we've been foolish one minute *after* we die?

Life offers numerous choices, no matter what we're considering: what kind of car we will buy, what we will eat tonight, where we will go to school, who we will marry, what college we will attend, how we will spend our time, and so on. Eternity, though, offers only two choices. The Bible tells us that each of us will wind up in one of two final destinations after we die:

We don't put "Death" on our day planners, but one day it just shows up.

> ... them that sleep in the dust of the earth shall awake, some to everlasting life, and some to shame *and* everlasting contempt. (*Daniel 12:2*)

We will all be fully awake and aware, either happily in heaven, or in disgrace and everlasting contempt in hell.

Mark Twain made a joke of it, suggesting we should "go to heaven for the climate, hell for the company." However, it will not be a joke for you or anyone else if you end up in hell.

"Imagine There's No Heaven"

In his song *Imagine*, John Lennon didn't take what God's Word says about eternity seriously. (*Full lyrics can be found on the internet.*) The world as Lennon imagined it had "no heaven," "no hell," "no countries," "nothing to kill or die for," "no religion," and "no possessions."

Lennon's imaginings about what would make this world happy were dead wrong. People want happiness, but getting rid of possessions, countries, and God has proven not to be the way to achieve that happiness.

Is it really a good idea to throw out God and all the things the Bible says He wants for us — possessions, countries, and so on? Not if God is real. And all the evidence we've examined so far says He is.

Lennon's imaginings about what would make this world happy were dead wrong. People want happiness, but getting rid of possessions, countries, and God has proven not to be the way to achieve that happiness.

As far as what is out there after we die, let's find out if those destinations that Lennon denied actually do exist. Since God has a much better view of eternity than we do — and He wants us to know the truth so that we can spend eternity with Him — let's see what the Bible has to say about what awaits us on the other side. You may be surprised at what you find.

According to a Barna Group survey, a majority of Americans (76 percent) believe heaven exists. Forty-six percent of those describe it as "a state of eternal existence in God's presence," while 30 percent view it as "an actual place of rest and reward where souls go after death." Another 14 percent think heaven is just "symbolic."[66]

What do you think heaven is like?

Many people picture heaven as the ultimate playground, where they can be reunited with all their old friends and family and enjoy endless fun and pleasure. They believe that the whole purpose of heaven will be personal enjoyment and that they'll have every whim catered to. But if everyone is selfishly thinking of himself,

doesn't that sound a bit like life on earth, where people are striving to get what they want, even at the expense of others? In fact, according to C. S. Lewis, "a ruthless, sleepless, unsmiling concentration upon self…is the mark of hell," not of heaven.

"A ruthless, sleepless, unsmiling concentration upon self… is the mark of hell," not of heaven.
— C. S. Lewis

That's not how God's Word describes the kingdom of heaven. The Bible describes heaven as:

> … a better *country*, that is, an heavenly: Wherefore God is not ashamed to be called their God: for he hath prepared for them a city. (*Hebrews 11:16*)

Jesus said that heaven contains many dwelling places, and that He would go there to prepare a place for us (*John 14:2*).

In heaven, there will be no material decay or corruption; it will be a place where we can safely trust everything to be good:

> But lay up for yourselves treasures in heaven, where neither moth nor rust doth corrupt, and where thieves do not break through nor steal: (*Matthew 6:20*)

We will have new "spiritual" bodies that have a physical substance. They will be whole and healthy and free from all the physical flaws from which we suffer on earth (*1 Corinthians 15:44*). There will be no more hunger or thirst, no more tears or pain, for all of eternity (*Revelation 7:16–17*). In heaven, the Bible explains, we will receive rewards and be able to rest from our labors. Heaven is a place of peace and comfort for the weary, and it is a better country than you live in now. It is where God and His angels will be. We have to ask ourselves if it is where *we* will be.

One of my friends died recently — a Christian. He was hooked up to a dialysis machine when his heart stopped. The doctors rushed over with defibrillator paddles and shocked his heart back to life.

He looked at his father sitting next to him and said, "Dad, you would not believe what I just saw!" The amazing thing about that statement was that *he had not seen in twenty years*; he had lost his eyesight decades earlier from the diabetes that was slowly killing him.

I heard a story of a young boy who looked up at the summer sky and said, "If heaven is that beautiful on the outside, I wonder how beautiful it must be on the inside!"

He explained that his soul had lifted out of his body, and he could see the flat line on the heart monitor next to his bed. He then began to take off on a journey. He said there was a white, consuming light with a glorious presence of love that came over him, and he saw flowers that had the most vibrant, beautiful colors he had ever seen! He told his father, "Dad, if that is what death is, death is OK!" Five days later he died.

Heaven is a very real destination where you may go one day.

At the funeral for her Christian husband, a woman was heard to say, "He's the lucky one; I wish I were going to heaven today. Why couldn't it have been me?" When we know where our loved ones are going, and where we're going, death is something we can look forward to without fear.

I heard a story of a young boy who looked up at the summer sky and said, "If heaven is that beautiful on the outside, I wonder how beautiful it must be on the inside!" None of us has any real clue about the glorious nature of what God has prepared for those who follow Him. The Bible says that in heaven there will be streets of gold and walls made of pearls, emeralds, and precious stones.

I thought it was interesting that what we highly value here on earth is something that we'll walk on in heaven — a plain, ordinary paving material! What does that say about heaven's spectacular beauty?

Words cannot describe how amazing it will be. No pain, no suffering, no disease, no crying, no death. The best thing about heaven, though — the only thing we'll care about when we finally get there — is that heaven is where we will be able to talk face to face with our awesome Creator.

Will that be your destination for all of eternity?

"No Hell Below"

The other choice is a place called hell. John Lennon's song asks us to imagine there's "no hell below." Hell is out of fashion today, but it is not out of business! Just because we don't like the idea of hell doesn't mean that it does not exist. Many people say they don't believe in hell, so hell can't exist. But remember: It doesn't matter what we believe; it matters what is true. Unbelief doesn't change reality. We may believe that poison won't kill us, but it will. We may believe that the earth is flat, but it is not. Be sure you search for truth, and not just for something you'd like to believe in.

Many people have told me that they wouldn't mind going to hell because all their friends would be there. But hell is not a place of rehab or enjoyment. It is a place of punishment. Only one-third of adults think that hell is an actual place of torment, according to Barna Group research, while four in ten view it simply as eternal separation from God's presence.[67] Regardless of what we think, though, how does God's Word describe it?

According to the Bible, hell is a very real place. We know of thirty-three times that Jesus spoke of it, describing its horrors in graphic detail. It is a place of eternal, conscious torment, where there is terrible suffering and "unquenchable fire." (*Matthew 3:12*) The Bible says that those who do not obey God will "be punished with everlasting destruction" (*2 Thessalonians 1:9*), and will be cast "into the furnace of fire; in that place there shall be weeping and gnashing of teeth" (*Matthew 13:41–42*). It is called "hell fire" (*Matthew 5:22*), where its inhabitants will face "everlasting punishment" (*Matthew 25:46*), and "indignation and wrath, tribulation and anguish, upon every soul of man that doeth evil" (*Romans 2:8–9*).

Jesus warns us to avoid hell at all costs:

> And if thy hand offend thee, cut it off: it is better for thee to enter into life maimed, than having two hands to go into hell, into the fire that never shall be quenched: Where their worm dieth not, and the fire is not quenched.
>
> And if thy foot offend thee, cut it off: it is better for thee to enter halt into life, than having two feet to be cast into hell, into the fire that never shall be quenched: Where their worm dieth not, and the fire is not quenched.
>
> And if thine eye offend thee, pluck it out: it is better for thee to enter into the kingdom of God with one eye, than having two eyes to be cast into hell fire: Where their worm dieth not, and the fire is not quenched. (*Mark 9:43–48*)

We are told that when angels in heaven rebelled against Him, God "cast them down to hell, and delivered them into chains of darkness, to be reserved unto judgment" (*2 Peter 2:4*). Try to imagine how dark such a place will be. Have you ever been on a tour of a cave? Usually the tour guide will shut off all the lights to give people a sense of the total blackness. With the complete absence of light, it is so utterly black that you could stick your finger in your eye and not see it coming. The darkness is so oppressive that people sometimes start to panic after only a minute. Imagine how many minutes there are in an unending eternity. The darkness alone would be torment enough.

The Bible refers to hell as the "kingdom of darkness" and declares that "the children of the kingdom shall be cast out into outer darkness: there shall be weeping and gnashing of teeth" (*Matthew 8:12*). It says that people who reject God do so because they love the deeds of darkness rather than the light. Since darkness is what these people want, it is what they get for all of eternity. And there is no escape from this place because there is only an entrance — no exit.

Why Hell?

Some people choose not to believe in the God of the Bible because they don't like the thought of an angry God who would punish people eternally in hell. I used to think the same thing. Before I became a Christian, I didn't know that there were many attributes of God. Most people are familiar with the Bible verse

"God is love." And He is. But He is also just. He is holy. He is righteous. And because of these other attributes, He also has a tough side — and rightfully so.

God hates sin. Period. None of us on earth can fully realize just how much God hates even the smallest sin. I had not pictured a God who had this stern side. One day, however, I realized that I couldn't just create the God that I wanted. God is not an exercise in imagination, or visualization, or mind projection. He exists independent of my thoughts about Him. But that's what I was trying to do as I ignored what the Bible had to say about God. The *real* God is the one I will certainly stand before when I die, not my imaginary "God."

The Bible refers to hell as the "kingdom of darkness" and declares that "the children of the kingdom shall be cast out into outer darkness: there shall be weeping and gnashing of teeth" (Matthew 8:12).

Since we know the Bible to be true, we also know that the God we will face will be the God of the Bible. So we need to discover, and really understand, why He has this wrathful side. And we need to know what we can do to make sure we *don't* see that side of Him when we die. The Bible, God's Word, tells us why we incur His wrath and how we can avoid it:

> Mortify therefore your members which are upon the earth; fornication, uncleanness, inordinate affection, evil concupiscence, and covetousness, which is idolatry:
>
> For which things' sake the wrath of God cometh on the children of disobedience: (*Colossians 3:5–6*)

We also read in the Bible that:

> … the wrath of God is revealed from heaven against all ungodliness and unrighteousness of men, who hold the truth in unrighteousness. (*Romans 1:18*)
>
> But after thy hardness and impenitent heart treasurest up unto thyself wrath against the day of wrath and revelation of the righteous judgment of God:

> Who will render to every man according to his deeds:
>
> To them who by patient continuance in well doing seek for glory and honour and immortality, eternal life:
>
> But unto them that are contentious, and do not obey the truth, but obey unrighteousness, indignation and wrath, (*Romans 2:5–8*)

So if people face God's wrath and go to hell, it will be because they choose to. The God who created this universe has given us proof of His existence, yet many refuse to acknowledge it.

The Bible explains that the "lake of fire" was originally prepared "for the devil and his angels," but people who obey these evil beings will go into the lake of fire with them.

> Then shall he say also unto them on the left hand, Depart from me, ye cursed, into everlasting fire, prepared for the devil and his angels: (*Matthew 25:41*)
>
> Know ye not, that to whom ye yield yourselves servants to obey, his servants ye are to whom ye obey; whether of sin unto death, or of obedience unto righteousness? (*Romans 6:16*)

It isn't God's desire that people go to hell, but He gives us the free will to choose.

As we read in Psalm 139:8, "If I ascend up into heaven, thou art there: if I make my bed in hell, behold, thou art there."

There is a saying, "You made your bed; now lie in it!" So "making our bed" is a preparation for lying in it. That is, our actions determine our future — like it or not.

While we spend our time *preparing* to go to hell, God is with us. We can turn to Him at any moment and say, "God, I'm sorry I've offended you. Please get me out of this mess and put me on the right track," and He will help us. But once we're dead and in hell, it's too late to ask for help.

In the Matthew passage above we learned that hell wasn't originally created with people in mind. Heaven was:

> Then shall the King say unto them on his right hand, Come, ye blessed of my Father, inherit the kingdom prepared for you from the foundation of the world: (*Matthew 25:34*)

The Bible is very explicit about the fact that God takes no pleasure in the death of the wicked. He says:

> ...*As* I live, saith the Lord God, I have no pleasure in the death of the wicked; but that the wicked turn from his way and live ... (*Ezekiel 33:11a*)

> The Lord is not slack concerning his promise, as some men count slackness; but is longsuffering to us-ward, not willing that any should perish, but that all should come to repentance. (*2 Peter 3:9*)

It is not a happy day for Him when someone dies and goes to hell. Will it be a bad day for God when you die?

Many people believe it is unfair for God to send individuals to hell for eternity. God is being entirely fair, based on their rejection of Him.

If people don't want anything to do with Him here on earth, why would we think they would want anything to do with Him on the other side? If they hate the thought of God in this life, they will hate being with Him in the next.

There are two kinds of people: those who say to God, "Thy will be done," and those to whom God says, "All right, then, have it your way."
— C. S. Lewis

Author Frank Harber stated:

> For God to force people to go to heaven against their wishes wouldn't be heaven — it would be hell. Atheist author Jean-Paul Sarte noted that the gates of hell are locked from the inside by the free choice of men and women.[68]

C. S. Lewis wrote:

> There are two kinds of people: those who say to God, "Thy will be done," and those to whom God says, "All right, then, have it your way."[69]

We are given the freedom to choose between evil and good, between God's will and our own. God is simply honoring our choices — and allowing us to face the consequences.

One of the things I was told years ago is that hell is simply being separated from the presence of God for all of eternity. But according to Revelation 14:10–11, that is not a true statement in the way most people understand it.

None of us can fully comprehend what the absence of God in our lives would mean. Regardless of whether we credit His existence or not, "in him we live and move and have our being" (*Acts 17:28*), and "by him all things consist" (*Colossians 1:17*). Existence without His sustaining presence is horrifying. But we don't have to imagine anything; the Bible presents us with that reality:

> And the smoke of their torment ascendeth up for ever and ever: and they have no rest day nor night, who worship the beast and his image, and whosoever receiveth the mark of his name. (*Revelation 14:11*)

God is experienced by those in hell in two very terrible ways: First, He is present as a witness, along with the holy angels:

> And the third angel followed them, saying with a loud voice, If any man worship the beast and his image, and receive *his* mark in his forehead, or in his hand,
>
> The same shall drink of the wine of the wrath of God, which is poured out without mixture into the cup of his indignation; and he shall be tormented with fire and brimstone **in the presence of the holy angels, and in the presence of the Lamb.** (*Revelation 14:9–10*) *[emphasis added]*

Second, He is there in the memory of the damned. One of the greatest torments for them will be to remember how God spoke to them continually, in the depths of their hearts, telling them "This is the way; walk ye in it" (*Isaiah 30:21*). And they will remember that they refused to listen to Him. In hell, people aren't able to "get away" from God. They rejected and denied His all-loving presence for every second of every minute of their lives on earth, and must exist, riddled with regret, for every second of eternity.

But over and over, God has clearly said we are choosing. For example:

> He that believeth on him is not condemned: but he that believeth not is condemned already, because he hath not believed in the name of the only begotten Son of God. (*John 3:18*)
>
> For if we would judge ourselves, we should not be judged. (*1 Corinthians 11:31*)

God is the glory of heaven and the terror of hell. It is the wrath of God that makes hell hell. If you wind up in hell, you end up being away from the glory of the Lord — His goodness — but you will never get away from His wrath.

Some people think Satan is in charge of hell, but Satan is a defeated foe and isn't in charge of anything. God is always in charge! He is the sovereign ruler over all of heaven and earth — and hell. Hell is not a kingdom for Satan to rule, or a place for people to party. It is a place of eternal punishment.

The worst part of hell is not the torment, but that the torment will never end. If you are one of those rejecting the truth of God, it will be a fearful thing for you to stand before God one day. Picture the scene as portrayed by the prophet and apostle, John:

> And I saw a great white throne, and him that sat on it, from whose face the earth and the heaven fled away; and there was found no place for them.
>
> And I saw the dead, small and great, stand before God; and the books were opened: and another book was opened, which is *the book* of life: and the dead were judged out of those things which were written in the books, according to their works.
>
> And the sea gave up the dead which were in it; and death and hell delivered up the dead which were in them: and they were judged every man according to their works.
>
> And death and hell were cast into the lake of fire. This is the second death.
>
> And whosoever was not found written in the book of life was cast into the lake of fire. (*Revelation 20:11–15*)

Some people think Satan is in charge of hell, but Satan is a defeated foe and isn't in charge of anything.

The first death is when our soul separates from our body. At that moment, if we are believing in and loving God, our soul also will go to be with God. Paul wrote when pondering the inevitability of his own death:

> We are confident, I say, and willing rather to be absent from the body, and to be present with the Lord. (*2 Corinthians 5:8*)

The second death happens at the last judgment, when a soul who didn't go to be with God, and who has been in hell until then, is formally sentenced along with the rest of condemned mankind to separation from the all-loving presence of God and goes into the lake of fire for eternity.

We will all experience the first death, but how can you and I make sure that we don't experience the second death? We will see very shortly what determines the difference between eternal life in heaven and eternal suffering in hell. You will want to be sure you never go anywhere near there for even ten seconds, let alone for ten-million-plus years.

"It's Not Safe to Die"

I talked with a young man one day who mentioned that he had been injured and wound up on an emergency-room operating table. He said his heart had stopped beating and, as his soul rose up out of his body, immediately the sense of an evil presence began to come over him and he could hear an evil hissing laughter. He told me he was so glad to get back into his body and be alive! He now knows how real evil is.

A respiratory nurse who works in an emergency room told me about a patient who had gone "code red" — he flat-lined. She and some other medical personnel rushed over with the defibrillator to try to bring him back to life. They applied the paddles and revived him. She said that he started screaming and shouting, "The heat, the heat!" Then his heart stopped again. They brought him back a second time. He shouted, "The flames, the flames!" They lost him again. Four times the man flat-lined and was brought back, each time shouting about the heat or the flames. After the last time, he died and they couldn't bring him back. She said all the doctors and nurses just stood there for a few minutes and stared at the body. They all knew that man went to hell. He was screaming it to them before he even got out of here.

I have met several people (*all in a non-drug and non-alcohol-induced state*) who experienced a burning hell rather than being with Jesus, or the typical "tunnel and white light" scenario. So don't believe that sweetness-and-light near-death stories are the only kind people report.

Dr. Maurice Rawlings, a cardiologist, has witnessed numerous patients during and after their near-death experiences and reported his findings in *Beyond Death's Door*. After interviewing 300 patients immediately after resuscitation, Dr. Rawlings says that nearly half of them reported seeing a lake of fire, devil-like figures, and other sights reflecting the reality of hell. "There is a life after death," Rawlings said, "and if I don't know where I'm going, it's not safe to die."

He also discovered that when patients who had described their experiences in hell vividly were asked about those experiences a few days later, they couldn't recall them. This may explain why many researchers find only "good cases." He believes some patients change their story because they're embarrassed to admit where they've been, even to their families, while those who had heavenly visions remember and report the details.[70]

So don't get a false sense of security that what follows death is always a pleasant thing. Hell is a very real place — one that you really *don't* want to go to when you die.

Voltaire, the famous French author, philosopher, and atheist, was once asked if he would say something to comfort a friend who was dying. Voltaire responded, "I don't think I can do that. The thought that there might really be a hell plagues me continually."

There is a hell, and one of the clearest pictures of it in the Bible is the well-known story of the rich man and Lazarus:

> There was a certain rich man, which was clothed in purple and fine linen, and fared sumptuously every day:
>
> And there was a certain beggar named Lazarus, which was laid at his gate, full of sores,
>
> And desiring to be fed with the crumbs which fell from the rich man's table: moreover the dogs came and licked his sores.
>
> And it came to pass, that the beggar died, and was carried by the angels into Abraham's bosom: the rich man also died, and was buried;
>
> And in hell he lift up his eyes, being in torments, and seeth Abraham afar off, and Lazarus in his bosom.

> And he cried and said, Father Abraham, have mercy on me, and send Lazarus, that he may dip the tip of his finger in water, and cool my tongue; for I am tormented in this flame.
>
> But Abraham said, Son, remember that thou in thy lifetime receivedst thy good things, and likewise Lazarus evil things: but now he is comforted, and thou art tormented.
>
> And beside all this, between us and you there is a great gulf fixed: so that they which would pass from hence to you cannot; neither can they pass to us, that *would come* from thence.
>
> Then he said, I pray thee therefore, father, that thou wouldest send him to my father's house:
>
> For I have five brethren; that he may testify unto them, lest they also come into this place of torment.
>
> Abraham saith unto him, They have Moses and the prophets; let them hear them. And he said, Nay, father Abraham: but if one went unto them from the dead, they will repent.
>
> And he said unto him, If they hear not Moses and the prophets, neither will they be persuaded, though one rose from the dead. (*Luke 16:19–31*)

Notice that when the rich man was in hell, all five of his senses worked just fine. He was in such torment that he begged for even a drop of water. One thing that hits me hard as I read this is that there is no crossing over. Judgment is set once you take your last breath. The rich man could not have someone bring him water, and Lazarus could not run over to help, even if he wanted to.

After you die, you cannot change your eternal destination. You have a one-way ticket to eternity. You must know *before* your last heartbeat which side of the chasm you will be on forever … and ever and ever. The rich man wanted his brothers warned so that they wouldn't end up in hell with him for all of eternity. I hope you will consider this book your warning. God doesn't want you to go to hell, and neither do I.

If the people taking a recent Barna survey were accurate in their opinion, which I don't believe they were, hell would be a pretty sparsely populated place. Only one-half of one percent of Americans said they expect to go to hell when they die, while nearly two-thirds (64 percent) think they are headed for heaven.[71]

But what did Jesus say?

> Enter ye in at the strait gate: for wide *is* the gate, and broad *is* the way, that leadeth to destruction, and many there be which go in thereat. (*Matthew 7:13*)
>
> Therefore be ye also ready: for in such an hour as ye think not, the Son of man cometh. (*Matthew 24:44*)

What is it that determines your final destination? What criteria will decide where you are going? That crucial question is the topic of our next chapter, as our search for eternal truth continues to narrow.

Bosses, coaches, teachers, and others judge us on the work that we do or don't do. Society, as a whole, doesn't know any other way.

Chapter 5
It's the Law!

I wanted a perfect ending. Now I've learned, the hard way, that some poems don't rhyme, and some stories don't have a clear beginning, middle, and end. Life is about not knowing, having to change, taking the moment and making the best of it, without knowing what's going to happen next. Delicious ambiguity.
— Gilda Radner

Gilda Radner, the famous comedienne, didn't know what was going to happen next — but you do. You know that there are only two destinations when you leave this world, and you head for one or the other just after your last heartbeat.

That leaves us with another question — one that most people are keenly aware of.

On a flight to Cincinnati one day, I was sitting next to a man who worked for Proctor and Gamble. I asked him what he thought was out there after he died.

He said, "I believe there is a heaven or hell after we die. What I can't figure out is what is the criterion for who gets which place?"

And, of course, that is the question: What is the separating factor that will put us in one or the other place for all of eternity?

> For by grace are ye saved through faith; and that not of yourselves: *it is* the gift of God:
>
> Not of works, lest any man should boast. (*Ephesians 2:8–9*)
>
> Not by works of righteousness which we have done, but according to his mercy he saved us, by the washing of regeneration, and renewing of the Holy Ghost; (*Titus 3:5*)

The first point that amazed me is that we can't take credit for enough good works, hoping to gain entrance into heaven. This totally goes against almost all of our thinking. Bosses, coaches, teachers, and others judge us on the work that we do or don't do. Won't God do the same?

I remember sitting in church one time as a teenager, and a major moment of my life happened to me: I began to think about how God would judge me. I pictured that God had this big scorecard in heaven and that I got a check mark for every time I was nice to my brothers and sister, a check mark for each time I threw a quarter into the collection plate, a check mark each time I turned in my homework, a check mark for going to church, etc.

But I was left with one big question: How many check marks did I need to get into heaven? Was it 500 or 501? What was the answer? What gets us into heaven?

And what gets us into hell? People get pretty upset even thinking about that! Here's an example from the *Seattle Post-Intelligencer*, Wednesday, February 4, 2004:

> GIRL SAYS "HELL" IN SCHOOL, SUSPENDED
> Dan Nephin, Associated Press writer
>
> Pittsburgh, AP — … Brandy McKenith, 7, was suspended for swearing …saying the word "hell," but her family says she was referring to the biblical location of fire and brimstone.
>
> She served the suspension Tuesday.
>
> The Pittsburgh Public Schools' student code of conduct prohibits profanity, but doesn't provide a definition, spokeswoman Pat Crawford said. The school would not comment further.
>
> …"The school's policy says 'no profanity' and that's not further defined," Walczak said. "How should this little girl know that 'hell' is not allowed? It's questionable whether 'hell' is even a profanity, and it certainly isn't in the way that she used it."
>
> McKenith, a suburban Pittsburgh police detective, said family members aren't "religious fanatics," but there's a healthy respect for the Lord, so he accepts his daughter's explanation.
>
> "She's under the assumption that good people go to heaven and …bad people go to hell," he said Wednesday.

I pictured that God had this big scorecard in heaven and that I got a check mark for every time I was nice to my brothers and sister, a check mark each time I turned my in homework …

Why would that second-grader think good people go to heaven and bad people go to hell? And why do almost all of us think the same way?

On the day that Terri Schindler Schiavo died, I was listening to Bill O'Reilly's radio show. He said, "I hope she is in Paradise. What is wrong in believing in that? Don't you hope that bad people are punished and that good people are rewarded?"

The word "sin" means "miss the mark," referring to the bull's-eye on a target. God's Word is saying that if you miss that bull's-eye and your arrow lands off to the side, you have "sinned" — you have "missed the mark."

I don't know how so many people get the idea that good people go to heaven, and bad people go to hell, but it seems ingrained in all of us.

As my search continued, I began to realize that no matter what the world was telling me about being "good enough" to get to heaven, God had a different standard. And I realized that I needed to know what that standard is so that I could make correct decisions about eternity. Our eternal destinations will be determined by that standard.

So what does God's trustworthy Word say about that standard? And what determines whether a person has or has not lived up to that standard, making them "good" or "bad"?

Romans 3:23 tells us that:

> For all have sinned, and come short of the glory of God;

What does it mean when it says that we have all "sinned"? The word "sin" means "miss the mark," referring to the bull's-eye on a target. We want to hit it right in the middle, but here God's Word is saying that if you miss that bull's-eye and your arrow lands off to the side, you have "sinned" — you have "missed the mark."

The Apostle Paul tells us that:

> For the wages of sin *is* death; but the gift of God *is* eternal life through Jesus Christ our Lord. (*Romans 6:23*)

So my next question was very simple: What is the mark all of us must hit in order to avoid death and receive eternal life?

Romans 3:19–20 says:

> Now we know that what things soever the Law saith, it saith to them who are under the Law: that every mouth may be stopped, and all the world may become guilty before God.
>
> Therefore by the deeds of the Law there shall no flesh be justified in His sight: for by the Law *is* the knowledge of sin.

It is now obvious that this Law will give me the knowledge of sin. What is this Law? Psalm 19:7 tells us:

> The Law of the Lord *is* perfect, converting the soul: the testimony of the Lord *is* sure, making wise the simple.

This Law can turn me back to God? What is this Law?
1 John 3:4 clearly states:

> Whosoever committeth sin transgresseth also the Law: for sin is the transgression of the Law.

If you break this Law, it is sin? What is this Law?
Romans 7:7 asks:

> What shall we say then? *Is* the Law sin? God forbid. Nay, I had not known sin, but by the Law: for I had not known lust, except the Law had said, Thou shalt not covet.

And here we have the huge clue we were looking for! We can recognize that a Law is being quoted here — "Thou shalt not covet." That is the tenth of the Ten Commandments!

In the first five books of the Bible, written by Moses, God gives us the Ten Commandments twice (*Exodus 20:1–17; Deuteronomy 5:6–21*). All I know is that when I was a kid and my mom said something twice, her son better not forget it! Since God repeated these commandments within a short space of time, it must be important for us to know what these commandments are and how to follow them.

Ted Koppel, host of ABC's *Nightline*, said in a commencement address at Duke University:

> We have actually convinced ourselves that slogans will save us. "Shoot up if you must, but use a clean needle." "Enjoy sex whenever with whoever you wish; but wear a condom." No! The answer is no. Not no because it isn't cool or smart or because you might wind up in jail or dying in an AIDS

> ward — but no because it's wrong. What Moses brought down from Mt. Sinai were not the Ten Suggestions, they are Commandments. Are, not were. The sheer brilliance of the Ten Commandments is that they codify, in a handful of words, acceptable human behavior. Not just for then or now but for all time.[72]

Even Ted Koppel knows what God gave us was not the Ten Suggestions but the Ten Commandments, by which we are meant to live our lives.

And these commandments are not set up to make God happy, but to make *us* holy, which brings contentment.

For example, one of the places I recently was invited to speak was the Officers' Christian Fellowship, the largest club at the United States Military Academy at West Point. I can't even begin to describe what a blessing it was to be there. It was a humbling and emotional experience knowing how many great cadets had walked those halls, then gone on to influence the culture of America.

God allowed me to speak for an hour and a half to one-tenth of the Corps of Cadets. What a blessing it was to meet these young men and women! The army is in good hands with the future officers I met.

> *"The sheer brilliance of the Ten Commandments is that they codify, in a handful of words, acceptable human behavior. Not just for then or now but for all time."*
> — Ted Koppel

When I finished speaking, one of the cadets gave me a book entitled *Absolutely American*, by David Lipsky — a phenomenal book that follows a group of cadets through their four years at West Point. The author specializes in writing about college-age students for *Rolling Stone* magazine.

One of the things that he wrote in his book amazed me. He said that after visiting students at thirty different colleges around America, he found that the students at West Point were the happiest students that he had met anywhere.

He was shocked at what he found. He thought that all of the rules and regulations there would make the cadets unhappy. Of course, there is a bit of moaning and groaning, but they were without a doubt the happiest of all the college students he had gotten to know.

I began to wonder why that is. But it is easy to figure out when you think about it. If we live in a world with no rules, we actually have no freedom. We can't really be happy. But when there are boundaries and rules, we have "all the freedom in the world." We can be happy people. Does that sound strange?

As I talked with a guy one day, I gave him this example: If you were staying on the thirtieth-floor of a hotel, would you go out on the balcony if it were just a slab of concrete, but no railings? Would you put your child out there?

Of course, you wouldn't. It would be too dangerous. But once you put some good strong railings on the balcony, would you go out there? Would you go out there with your child?

Sure! Not only would most of us go out there, we would even lean on the railings while we were out there! Why would we do this? Once there is a boundary, you have all the freedom you want inside that boundary. You can have lunch out there if you want. Boundaries provide freedom.

One time in Myrtle Beach, I was talking with two 18-year-olds. They told me that they would never become Christians. I asked them why. They said that it would take all the fun out of life.

I looked them in the eye and said, "Today there is a zero-percent chance that I am going to get someone pregnant. There is a zero-percent chance I am going to get AIDS today. There is a zero-percent chance that I am going to get a DUI today. You know there are some pretty good benefits to becoming a Christian?"

Both young men's jaws dropped. They told me that they had never thought about that before. They had *thought* they had freedom, but they didn't. They thought they could do whatever they wanted to, but they didn't realize that they would be slaves to the consequences of their choices.

God gives us rules and laws to go by. When we stay within these boundaries, we are the freest people in the world.

When we step outside these boundaries, it's like stepping over the railings and trying to walk away from the edge of the thirtieth-floor balcony. What happens next isn't punishment; it's just the consequence of being rebellious and short-sighted.

An interesting study by John Hagee says that 97 percent of Americans "believe in" the Ten Commandments, but only 5 percent can actually name three or more.

We read before that the Law can tell us everything we need to know to guide our lives toward heaven. And we've found that the Law is the Ten Commandments.

So let's take a look at these commandments that so many people believe in, but so few know much about. Let's use the list of commandments in Exodus 20:1–17 to see how we are going to stack up next to God's standard for human behavior when we stand before Him.

. . .97 percent of Americans "believe in" the Ten Commandments, but only 5 percent can actually name three or more.

First Commandment

And God spake all these words, saying,

I *am* the Lord thy God, which have brought thee out of the land of Egypt, out of the house of bondage.

Thou shalt have no other gods before me. (*Exodus 20:1–3*)

The first commandment means that God should be the focal point of all of your affections. Your relationship with Him should be the most important part of your life.

A perfect example is the rich young ruler Matthew tells us about in the New Testament:

> And, behold, one came and said unto him, Good Master, what good thing shall I do, that I may have eternal life?
>
> And he said unto him, Why callest thou me good? *there is* none good but one, *that is*, God: but if thou wilt enter into life, keep the commandments.

> He saith unto him, Which? Jesus said, Thou shalt do no murder, Thou shalt not commit adultery, Thou shalt not steal, Thou shalt not bear false witness,
>
> Honour thy father and *thy* mother: and, Thou shalt love thy neighbour as thyself.
>
> The young man saith unto him, All these things have I kept from my youth up: what lack I yet?
>
> Jesus said unto him, If thou wilt be perfect, go *and* sell that thou hast, and give to the poor, and thou shalt have treasure in heaven: and come *and* follow me.
>
> But when the young man heard that saying, he went away sorrowful: for he had great possessions.
>
> Then said Jesus unto his disciples, Verily I say unto you, That a rich man shall hardly enter into the kingdom of heaven.
>
> And again I say unto you, It is easier for a camel to go through the eye of a needle, than for a rich man to enter into the kingdom of God. (*Matthew 19:16–24*)

We will all worship something. Whether we are atheists, agnostics, or believers in some religion, we are all worshipers.

It is interesting to see how Jesus talked with the rich young ruler using the Ten Commandments as the starting point in a discussion of "what shall I do to inherit eternal life?" And with those commandments He was able to show the man his self-righteousness. This is an amazing story. The rich young ruler could not even get past the first commandment: He *did* have another god before the God of the universe, and it was his money.

We will all worship something. Whether we are atheists, agnostics, or believers in some religion, we are all worshipers.

Where do you turn your mind and heart to gain meaning, fulfillment, control, protection, and significance in your life? What has your affection? What do you meditate upon? When you lay your head on your pillow at night, what do you think about? Who or what is your God?

Now ask yourself this question: Have I broken the first of the Ten Commandments?

Second Commandment

Thou shalt not make unto thee any graven image, or any likeness *of any thing* that *is* in heaven above, or that *is* in the earth beneath, or that *is* in the water under the earth:

Thou shalt not bow down thyself to them, nor serve them: for I the Lord thy God *am* a jealous God, visiting the iniquity of the fathers upon the children unto the third and fourth *generation* of them that hate me;

And shewing mercy unto thousands of them that love me, and keep my commandments. (*Exodus 20:4–6*)

The second commandment has to do with the worship of idols. We break this commandment when we create a god to suit our own sins. That is, when we say, "My god doesn't get mad at lying. My god would never punish people by sending them to hell. My god will let good people go to heaven," we are creating an idol in our own image.

The problem is that we cannot create our own god. We can *imagine* doing it, but God Almighty remains who He is. We don't have the power to make God what we want Him to be. We can only create or believe in idols, and pretend they are God.

Whether we made them up, or whether they've been presented to us by our culture, idols hold a certain power over us. Possessions, money, sports, following sports teams, food, drugs, boyfriends, girlfriends, TV, movies, jobs, etc., can all become idols in our lives.

Think about the "American Idol" television show. All these people want to be the idol that everyone will look up to! We can even make *ourselves* out to be idols.

I was speaking one time at a Christian high school on the west coast. After talking with some students in a first-period class, I walked outside after the bell rang.

I watched a student as he wiped down his beautiful Mustang — I believe it was a 1966 model — white with a blue racing stripe down the middle. It was a beautiful car. I walked over and asked him what he was doing. "I want to make sure no tree sap or anything got on my car." I said, "We've only been inside the school for fifty minutes! What do you think is going to happen to your car in fifty minutes?" It was obvious that he loved his car.

I was wondering *how much* he loved it, though, so I asked him, "Can I drive your car?" He answered, "No way. Only my Dad and I drive this car." I told him that when I go to visit Charles Barkley, a friend of mine from college, he will throw me the keys to his $100,000 Mercedes and let me drive it. He still wouldn't let me drive his Mustang, though. We stood there talking for another minute or so before he finally said, "I'll think about it."

Later that day, he came up to me and said, "OK. You can drive my car as long as I am in it with you." I responded, "I don't really want to drive your car. I just wanted to see if you would let me drive it. I was trying to find out if your car was your idol, and it is." The look on his face showed that he knew what I was saying was true. Isn't it amazing that we can love a car more than the God of the universe?

We can probably look at the posters on our walls to find out what we really worship.

But God doesn't want you loving and adoring something else, when He knows it cannot satisfy you. Only His love can satisfy you. Is that what you are yearning for? Or something less?

I heard a guy say one time about the Ten Commandments, "What part of 'thou shall not' don't you understand?" It's not that we don't *understand* what God is saying. It's that we don't want to *do* what God is saying.

It seems pretty straightforward that God says "No" to some things, but somewhere deep within us is a rebellious spirit that wants to do otherwise.

However you cannot serve two gods at the same time. One will always have preeminence over the other one. For instance, in the book of Matthew, Jesus warns about the love of money:

> No man can serve two masters: for either he will hate the one, and love the other; or else he will hold to the one, and despise the other. Ye cannot serve God and mammon. (*Matthew 6:24*)

Man's instinct is to worship something. And what you worship will control you.

> Know ye not, that to whom ye yield yourselves servants to obey, his servants ye are to whom ye obey; whether of sin unto death, or of obedience unto righteousness? (*Romans 6:16*)

What do you worship in your life?

Now ask yourself this question: Have I broken the second commandment by having idols in my life?

Third Commandment

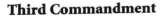

> Thou shalt not take the name of the Lord thy God in vain; for the Lord will not hold him guiltless that taketh his name in vain. (*Exodus 20:7*)

What does "in vain" mean? It means "uselessly," or "to no avail." For instance, we might say, "My efforts to achieve the goal were in vain."

What does "in vain" mean? It means "uselessly" or "to no avail." For instance, we might say, "My efforts to achieve the goal were in vain."

Taking the name of God in vain means to speak it irreverently, uselessly, because we're not really addressing Him.

To do this shows Him that we have contempt for Him. Perhaps without knowing it, we are taking something weighty and powerful and trying to diminish it, cheapen it, by the way we use it.

In the Old Testament, people were given the death penalty for speaking God's name irreverently. Some Jews consider the name of God so holy that they won't *speak* it or *write* it at all, lest they inadvertently break this commandment.

How can someone fear God *and* use His name in vain? Some people speak evil of God or accuse Him of evil. Some make promises to God that they do not keep. Some say, "I swear to God" and haven't a clue as to what they just said.

If we complain against God, or denigrate His name and character, we are taking His name in vain.

Here's a sad example: On a flight to Newark recently, no one was sitting next to me. That was kind of odd since I had prayed for someone to sit next to me so that I could talk to them about the Lord. But there was a guy next to me across the aisle.

I usually don't talk across the aisle because there are people walking back and forth, and that cuts the flow of conversation. After a while, though, and after praying, I decided to see if that guy wanted to engage in a conversation. He did.

In the Old Testament, people were given the death penalty for speaking God's name irreverently. Some Jews consider the name of God so holy that they won't use it at all.

His name was Michael. He told me that his birthday was on September 11th. He said that on his birthday in 2001, his sister-in-law who worked in the World Trade Center wanted him to come there to get his gift.

So he went there. She came down at 8:45. Three minutes later, the first plane hit that building. He told her to run. She worked on one of the floors where everyone was killed except her. He told me that he was right there as the second plane hit.

He said it was terrifying. He told me that he was standing there as a lady came hurtling down, hit a street sign, and was split in two.

Because he is a professional masseur, he stayed there to work on the firemen. As we talked, he told me that he was homosexual and wanted to know if he was going to hell because of that. Twice he motioned toward his bag and said, "If I am going there, I have my suntan lotion right here."

During our conversation, he would continually mock God and the things of God. It made me want to never ever mock God or use His name wrongly again. It makes me thankful for God's life-changing presence with His people. I continue to pray for the salvation of Michael. He lives in a world that has contempt for God and has no fear of using His dear name as a curse word.

How many times, watching a sporting event have you read the lips of players and coaches as they took the holy name of God in vain? Even using His name in a flippant or joking manner is not right with God. JC or GD are *not* respectful ways to talk about the Creator of the universe.

Philippians 2:9–11 says:

> Wherefore God also hath highly exalted him, and given him a name which is above every name:
>
> That at the name of Jesus every knee should bow, of *things* in heaven, and *things* in earth, and *things* under the earth;
>
> And *that* every tongue should confess that Jesus Christ *is* Lord, to the glory of God the Father.

The most righteous, holy name in the universe has been brought down to common use as a vile curse word. Ask yourself: Have I broken the third commandment by taking the name of God in vain?

Fourth Commandment

> Remember the sabbath day, to keep it holy.
>
> Six days shalt thou labour, and do all thy work:
>
> But the seventh day *is* the sabbath of the LORD thy God: *in it* thou shalt not do any work, thou, nor thy son, nor thy daughter, thy manservant, nor thy maidservant, nor thy cattle, nor thy stranger that *is* within thy gates:
>
> For *in* six days the LORD made heaven and earth, the sea, and all that in them *is*, and rested the seventh day: wherefore the LORD blessed the sabbath day, and hallowed it. (*Exodus 20:8–11*)

God has set aside one day a week for us to rest. It is a gift that God has given us. We are not supposed to do our jobs, or any other work on the Sabbath. God cares about our entire being.

During the time of Moses, those who worked on the Sabbath would be stoned to death. People today say the death penalty is not a deterrent to crime, but studies show that when it's enforced, the crime rate is low. I believe that's why the Bible records only one account of stoning someone for breaking the Sabbath. (*Numbers 15:32–36*).

Most Christians consider the first day of the week (Sunday) to be the Sabbath. Do we set aside the day to spend extra time with God? Or is it the day we catch up on our sleep from the week?

Why do we see so many soccer tournaments on Sunday mornings now? Is it a day we catch up on our exercise that we missed during the week? No matter how we define keeping the Sabbath, none of us has kept it the way that God designed it to be kept.

No matter how we define keeping the Sabbath, none of us has kept it the way that God designed it to be kept.

Fifth Commandment

> Honour thy father and thy mother: that thy days may be long upon the land which the Lord thy God giveth thee. (*Exodus 20:12*)

This is a completely unconditional statement. We are supposed to honor our parents just because they are our parents. We don't get to choose who our parents are. We are to obey them just because God put them over us. We are to acknowledge the significance and great value of our parents.

In return, we get a great blessing: long life. This is emphasized in the New Testament:

> CHILDREN, obey your parents in the Lord: for this is right.
>
> Honour thy father and mother; which is the first commandment with promise;
>
> That it may be well with thee, and thou mayest live long on the earth. (*Ephesians 6:1–3*)

We dishonor our parents when we treat them lightly or with disrespect. Our attitude toward our parents will precondition our attitude toward the authority figures that we encounter in life.

This commandment has nothing to do with our opinion of our parents' worthiness, but deals with the obedience and respect children should show toward their parents, no matter how worthy or unworthy the parents may seem.

"Foolishness," says the Bible (*Proverbs 22:15*) "is bound in the heart of a child; but the rod of correction shall drive it far from him." That is, we learn to be wise by the correction of our parents, which deters us from obeying foolish childish impulses. We don't like being deterred from foolishness, but it serves to help us grow in wisdom. If we rebel against our parents' care for us, we are being worse than foolish:

> For rebellion *is as* the sin of witchcraft, and stubbornness *is as* iniquity and idolatry. (*1 Samuel 15:23a*)

God considers rebellion the same as witchcraft. Why would that be? Because witchcraft is turning to a source other than God to get results. And rebellion is refusing guidance and determining, instead, to impose your own will on a person or situation.

Stubbornness is as iniquity and idolatry. If we do not submit to our parents we do not, and cannot, submit to God either.

Basketball was my sport when I was a young man. When I was in high school, we were playing Columbia High School for the sub-region championship. The first time we played them, we beat them 69–66. That night, I scored 36 points. If you ever score more than half of your team's points, you've had a good game.

The next time we played them for the championship, I scored nine points, and we lost. I was terrible. Late in the game, I felt that the referee had made a bad call: I'd been knocked to the ground, but he didn't call the foul.

I slapped the floor and said, "Get in the game, Ref!" He gave me a technical foul. I flipped him off and actually cursed at him. He gave me another technical foul. I definitely earned *that* one.

As this was happening, my parents had a perfect view of their lovely, disobedient son making a fool out of himself. When I went home that night after the game, my parents didn't say a word.

They didn't have to. I knew I had stepped way over the line of bad behavior. I actually did the Carl Lewis long jump over the line of bad behavior. I was not a believer in God at that point in my life, but even then I knew I should not have dishonored my parents like that.

Once, during the night after I had spoken at an event, an 18-year-old young man came up to talk to me. But he couldn't talk at first. He just sat there and wept. Eventually he told me that when I mentioned this commandment of God to honor our parents, God brought to mind all the things he had done to disobey his parents since he was five years old.

Have you honored your parents from the moment of birth until now? Just like the rest of us, you have broken this commandment.

Sixth Commandment

Thou shalt not kill. (*Exodus 20:13*)

Traditionally, this commandment is presented as "Thou shalt not kill," but the Hebrew words for "kill" and "murder" are different. In this commandment, the word used is "murder."

Why is that difference important? Because the Bible says we have the right to defend our lives, our families, our homes, and our nations — even if we have to kill the people attacking us.

It is not murder to kill someone who is trying to kill you. You are actually *preventing* a murder by stopping the murderer.

The first murder recorded in history occurred when one of Adam's sons, Cain, killed his brother Abel.

That was the first murder, but it certainly wasn't the last. There are an average of forty-four murders a day in America. Up to 4,000 unborn babies are murdered by being torn apart (aborted) in America each day. Columbine High School. Hitler. Saddam Hussein. It is amazing the murder that we see around us.

We see tens of thousands of unjust killings during our lifetime portrayed on TV, in movies, and on video games. We see so many "acted out" murders in the media that it doesn't seem to have much effect on us. We've become desensitized to it all.

The bar section of any town always draws interesting people. I was hanging out one night in the bar area of Denver, talking to people about God, and I walked up to three folks to get into a conversation. One of the guys wanted me to go into a liquor store to buy some alcohol for the group. That wasn't going to happen, so he and the girl went looking for someone else to help them.

But one guy stayed behind because he wanted to talk with me. During the conversation, I asked him if he had ever sinned. He told me "Yes," but then he asked, "What do you mean by 'sin'?"

I said, "Well, like the Ten Commandments."

"Oh, I've broken all of those."

"Have you ever killed anyone?" I asked.

Very nonchalantly he responded, "Yah."

"Ten people?"

He replied, "I don't know how many."

He told me that he had grown up in a gang in Long Beach, California, and he truly did not know how many people he had killed.

When he was fourteen years old, he was shooting baskets in his driveway when some gang members drove by and shot his girlfriend. She bled to death in his arms. "She was the one that I knew I was going to marry," he said. "She was the one I was going to have kids with, and she died in my arms."

Can you imagine having to go through that at fourteen years of age? Can you imagine not knowing how many people you have killed? But that's something you won't have to worry about, right? Well, let's see.

Jesus said:

> Ye have heard that it was said by them of old time, Thou shalt not kill; and "whosoever shall kill shall be in danger of the judgment:
>
> But I say unto you, That whosoever is angry with his brother without a cause shall be in danger of the judgment: and whosoever shall say to his brother, Raca, shall be in danger of the council: but whosoever shall say, Thou fool, shall be in danger of hell fire. (*Matthew 5:21–22*)

And John writes of this:

> Whosoever hateth his brother is a murderer: and ye know that no murderer hath eternal life abiding in him. (*1 John 3:15*)

Therefore, if you have been angry or hateful toward someone, it is the same as murder in the eyes of Almighty God. Why is that? God checks our insides as well as our outsides. He sees our thoughts as well as our actions. That is why all of us are in trouble by this standard.

Ask yourself this question: Have I broken this commandment, according to God's standard, by being angry or hateful toward someone even once in my lifetime?

Seventh Commandment

Thou shalt not commit adultery. (*Exodus 20:14*)

Most of us probably think we have not done this. But, again, the words of Jesus make this commandment a bit more interesting:

> Ye have heard that it was said by them of old time, Thou shalt not commit adultery:
>
> But I say unto you, That whosoever looketh on a woman to lust after her hath committed adultery with her already in his heart. (*Matthew 5:27–28*)

If you have looked at anyone with lust, even once, you have broken this commandment, not by the letter but by the spirit. And Jesus says we're going to be judged by the spirit, not the letter. So it is not OK with God for you to dwell on adulterous thoughts. Who will know? People can't read minds, but God can and God does.

It's been said that the first look isn't lust, but the second one is. It is not the glance that gets you, it's the gazing that does.

In addition, if you've looked at pornography at all, you have broken this commandment. Many different types of media, including music, can cause you to lust. And we can be so numbed and desensitized to evil thoughts that they can eventually lead to action. It's been said that the first look isn't lust, but the second one is. It is not the glance that gets you, it's the gazing that does. How many times have you taken a second look at someone? That would make you guilty by the standard God has set.

Every forty-eight seconds a rape is committed in America. Sexually transmitted diseases run rampant because of unbridled lust in our culture. Lust separates you from God, and takes you places that you really do not want to go. Ask yourself this question: Am I putting myself in danger with God by the things I think about or look at?

Eighth Commandment

Thou shalt not steal. (Exodus 20:15)

Sometimes we don't consider that we're really "stealing" when the value of the item is small, but theft is theft, irrespective of value. Whether you stole $1 or $20 from Mom's purse back in your childhood, it was still stealing. If you cheated on a test in school, you stole an answer from someone else's test. You're stealing from the government if you cheat on your income tax. Stealing time from an employer is also theft. The Bible describes Satan as a thief, but all of us have done the same. Criminals steal. If I have stolen, it would make me a criminal — a thief.

On the way to Florida for a vacation during my college days, some buddies and I stopped to put gas in my car. I pumped the gas and went in to pay for it. When I got back in the car, one of the football players shouted at me to drive away quickly.

I did, but as I drove, I asked him why. He said that while I was inside, he had gone into the storage area next to the convenience store and stolen a case of beer and put it in the car.

My heart started to beat very fast as I sped away. Why didn't I turn around? Why was my heart beating fast? Everything in my system told me what we just did was wrong, but still I drove on.

The Bible says:

> For when the Gentiles, which have not the Law, do by nature the things contained in the Law, these, having not the Law, are a Law unto themselves,
>
> Which shew the work of the Law written in their hearts, their conscience also bearing witness, and *their* thoughts the meanwhile accusing, or else excusing, one another… *(Romans 2:14–15)*

Here God clearly states He has written His Law onto the hearts of mankind, and our conscience (con-science = with-knowledge) will bear witness with the knowledge of right and wrong.

Sometimes we don't consider that we're really "stealing" when the value of the item is small, but theft is theft, irrespective of value.

Even though we don't like to admit it, we do have knowledge of our sin. We *know* when we do something wrong.

I once saw a video of a missionary who was working in Papua New Guinea. The missionary stated that the people in that area had no written language; everything was passed down by word of mouth. Interestingly, though, they had an oral code of conduct to live by. One of their rules was to not touch their neighbor's wife. This sounds like the seventh commandment to not commit adultery.

Another rule was to not take other people's things. That is what the eighth commandment says when it tells us not to steal. Other rules were to not murder people or tell falsehoods about them. Even though the villagers didn't have written communication, the Law of God was written on their *hearts*, and they knew right from wrong.

As I was talking with one young man in a mall, I asked him if he had ever stolen anything. He told me about an incident one day when he went to pick up his sister who worked at a gift store. When he walked into the mall, he saw that the security guard was at the other end of the mall, and he knew that there were no security cameras in that store.

While he was waiting for his sister, he noticed a Camaro key chain hanging on a display rack. His mother had a Camaro and he wanted to get her that key chain. What was this item worth — around $1.99? Yet he put the key chain in his pocket and began to walk away from the key-chain rack. He admitted that all of a sudden his heart began to race and small beads of sweat appeared on his forehead.

I asked, "What did you do?" He said that he quickly turned around and walked over to the rack, took the key chain out of his pocket, and hung it back on the hook. At that point his heartbeat began to slow down and his perspiration stopped. No one had to tell this young man that stealing was wrong. His whole system was sounding the alarm — which is just the way God said He designed us: He has written the Law on our hearts!

Ask yourself this question: Have I ever stolen one thing in my life, small or large? That would make me a thief in the eyes of a holy, righteous God.

Ninth Commandment

Thou shalt not bear false witness against thy neighbour. (*Exodus 20:16*)

A headline in the *Chicago Sun-Times* read "The Truth Is — Everybody Lies!" Is that true?

Some people claim that they have told only "white lies." But I really don't think God is impressed with the color of our lies.

Our entire justice system is based on the premise that witnesses will "tell the truth — the whole truth, and nothing but the truth." Perjury, which is lying in court, is a felony for good reason: How can there be justice when the truth isn't known?

One survey found that 91 percent of all Americans admit to lying on a regular basis. Some may insist that they haven't lied — just stretched the truth a little. But how far do we have to stretch the truth before it becomes a lie? Leaving out part of the truth to benefit ourselves is also lying. We also lie when we know untruth is being told and we just let it stand. And telling even one makes us liars. In a teen survey conducted in 2000, seven out of ten students admitted to cheating on a test within the last month. In essence, they lied by making it appear that they knew the information they wrote on the test.

Sometimes we lie because we think it is easier than telling the truth. *We* think. But what does *God* think of lying?

> But the fearful, and unbelieving, and the abominable, and murderers, and whoremongers, and sorcerers, and idolaters, **and all liars**, shall have their part in the lake which burneth with fire and brimstone: which is the second death. (*Revelation 21:8*) *[emphasis added]*

One of the things I realized as I went through the Ten Commandments is that God takes sin much more seriously than I do.

Jesus said:

> But I say unto you, every idle word that men shall speak, they shall give account thereof in the day of judgment.
>
> For by thy words thou shalt be justified, and by thy words thou shalt be condemned. (*Matthew 12:36–37*)

Every idle word we speak will be held against us on Judgment Day. If *idle* words are judged, what about *cruel* words? *Profane* words? *Blasphemous* words?

The Bible tells us to keep our speech simple and clear and honest:

> But let your communication be, Yea, yea; Nay, nay: for whatsoever is more than these cometh of evil. (*Matthew 5:37*)

In the Bible, one eyewitness could not convict someone of a crime. The witness might be lying or mistaken. So two or three witnesses were needed in order to convict a person.

And here is something even more interesting: If someone was given the death penalty — usually death by stoning — do you know who had to throw the first stones? The eyewitnesses!

Why? To discourage witnesses from lying. God knew when He gave this law that people who might be willing to lie about someone — out of envy or revenge or for money — would *not* be willing to stand face to face with them, and throw a stone at their head in an effort to kill them. And if they threw the stone half-heartedly or seemed ashamed when they confronted the accused, then their testimony against the condemned person would be brought into question, and the false accuser might find himself facing execution for attempted murder.

God wanted true judgment, not false. How are your words going to stack up on Judgment Day?

God's Word warns us:

> ... behold, ye have sinned against the LORD: and be sure your sin will find you out. (*Numbers 32:23*)

We often think we can hide our sins, but our sins will certainly find us out. Everything is laid bare before the eyes of Almighty God:

> Neither is there any creature that is not manifest in his sight: but all things *are* naked and opened unto the eyes of him with whom we have to do. (*Hebrews 4:13*)

George O'Leary, former football coach at Georgia Tech, was offered his "dream job": head coach at the University of Notre Dame. You could see how excited he was by the look on his face at his press conference. Someone from his hometown wanted to write a positive piece on him for the local paper. So the reporter got his résumé, started looking things up, and found a couple of discrepancies about his education.

Everything is laid bare before the eyes of Almighty God.

It turned out that O'Leary had fudged a résumé early in his career to get a coaching job, and had never changed it. By the time the storm reached its peak just six days later, he resigned — due to something on a résumé from thirty years earlier.

Time does not forgive sin. We like to think it does, but it doesn't. If George had corrected the lies, he would have been fine.

Is there a way for us to correct our sins before God? Since we just read Revelation 21:8, which says that "all liars shall have their part in the lake which burneth with fire and brimstone," we need to know if there is a way to correct our lies before then.

Charles Spurgeon, the great nineteenth-century preacher who, by the age of twenty-one, was the most popular preacher in London, and preached to thousands every Sunday for more than forty years[73], said:

> The very least offense against God is so intolerable that, if hell fire were put out, one sin could kindle it again.[74]

God takes lying very seriously. Do you? Ask yourself this question: Have I ever told one lie in my entire life? If I have, that makes me a liar in the eyes of Almighty God.

Tenth Commandment

Thou shalt not covet thy neighbour's house, thou shalt not covet thy neighbour's wife, nor his manservant, nor his maidservant, nor his ox, nor his ass, nor any thing that *is* thy neighbour's. (*Exodus 20:17*)

> *"A lot of people are rooting for me to get to heaven. Why? Because if I go, then everybody goes!"*
> — Jerry Springer

Coveting — desiring something that isn't rightfully ours — opens up the floodgates for so many sins in our lifetime. We covet before we steal. We covet someone before we commit adultery. We covet something and are tempted to disobey our parents or the law of the land to get it.

Coveting involves craving to get life's possessions or life's circumstances — success, marriage, fame — in a wrong way.

Advertisers work on people's hopes and desires to make them want to buy a particular product. If that hope or desire is awakened in people they may begin coveting — being envious or jealous of what others have. The wrong next step is taking what you want, rather than earning it or doing without. We slap God in the face and display dissatisfaction over what He has chosen to give us. God is looking at your heart.

Have you ever in your life broken this commandment?

God tells us:

> But we are all as an *unclean* thing, and all our righteousnesses *are* as filthy rags; and we all do fade as a leaf; and our iniquities, like the wind, have taken us away. (*Isaiah 64:6*)

Our sin has become a stench to God. We are all unclean. We could do millions of good deeds, but they do not have the power to wipe away one sin from our life.

Jerry Springer once said, "A lot of people are rooting for me to get to heaven. Why? Because if I go, then everybody goes!" Springer may want to joke about it, but it is not a joke. By saying this, he reveals that he at least knows that most people think God's standard for going to heaven is that you have to be good — but he isn't taking that standard seriously.

And now *you* know that standard, and the question to ask yourself is: How do I measure up?

Mark Twain said it wasn't the part of the Bible that he didn't understand, but the part he did understand, that troubled him the most!

What a statement! None of us knows everything about God's Word. But when each of us looks at the Ten Commandments, God's Law, we find it most troubling that even if we have broken one of them, it is just like we have broken all of them.

What? Is that true?

Here's what God has said about it:

> ... whosoever shall keep the whole Law, and yet offend in one *point*, he is guilty of all. (*James 2:10*)

Another point that may surprise you is that being religious, or doing good works, or being an active member of a congregation or denomination, or contributing to good causes has zero impact on whether or not we get into heaven.

Here's what Jesus said about that:

> Not every one that saith unto me, Lord, Lord, shall enter into the kingdom of heaven, but he that doeth the will of my Father which is in heaven.
>
> Many will say to me in that day, Lord, Lord, have we not prophesied in thy name? And in thy name have cast out devils? And in thy name done many wonderful works?
>
> And then I will profess unto them, I never knew you: Depart from me, ye that work iniquity. (*Matthew 7:21–23*)

If being religious won't help us, what will? That passage from the Bible lets us know that hell is going to catch many people by surprise. Will you be one of those people?

Our search for eternal truth is getting closer and closer to finding that right answer.

"When you die, what do you think
is on the other side?"

Chapter 6
The Bad News

The high-minded man must care more for the truth
than for what people think.
— Aristotle, philosopher, 384 – 322 B.C.

Imagine a man in a courtroom who is a liar, a thief, a murderer, and a rapist. But some people stand up and testify that he was a good next-door neighbor: He kept his yard clean, he looked out for other people in the neighborhood, and he always went to work on time.

Would the judge let him off because of these good deeds? You and I both know that there is no way a good judge would let him off.

A good judge must make a just ruling. The man has broken the law, and there are consequences that he must face. He knew about the law when he broke it, so it's not a surprise to him. He just hoped he wouldn't get caught.

We know that judges should make just decisions. And we know deep down that we *want* that judge to make a just decision — especially if the accused has done something against us.

So doesn't that mean that the just God of this universe will also have to make just decisions when *we* stand in front of *Him*?

We all want justice in this world. However, each of us is going to face a just Judge at the end of this life — will justice be what we want *then*?

After reviewing the Ten Commandments, we may think we're not too bad if we have broken only a few of them. We may have missed the mark, we think, but we can try a little harder from now on.

However, as I quoted a little earlier:

> Whosoever shall keep the whole law, and yet offend in one point, he is guilty of all. (*James 2:10*)

So if we have broken even one of the Ten Commandments, it is as if we have broken all of them. That is a pretty tough standard to live up to.

By that standard, Adolph Hitler, Mother Teresa, Joseph Stalin, Billy Graham, Timothy McVeigh, Osama bin Laden, you, and I — we'd all be found guilty. I was amazed when I learned that all six billion of us on earth are guilty. That's because none of us meets the standard that God has set for us in the Law.

All of us are guilty. I have offended God with my sins. You have offended God with your sins. We are all in the same boat. And the seriousness of our sin is measured not only by the deed, but also by who it was committed against: God Almighty.

Is that true? Have we sinned against God, not just other humans? Yes, the Bible makes that clear.

For example, King David stole a man's wife while her husband was off fighting the enemy. Then she got pregnant. So David called her husband back from the front, thinking that he would be with his wife, and then the expected child would seem to be his.

But the man was a good and honorable man, so when he came to see David, he slept in a corner and wouldn't go home.

> And Uriah said unto David, The ark, and Israel, and Judah abide in tents; and my lord Joab, and the servants of my lord, are encamped in the open fields; shall I then go into mine house, to eat and to drink, and to lie with my wife? *as* thou livest, and *as* thy soul liveth, I will not do this thing." (*2 Samuel 11:11*)

Eventually David had Uriah murdered to cover up his sin. God sent a prophet to face David and declare to him the wrong he had done. Until then, he'd felt he was the king and could do as he pleased. But when the thing was shown to him from God's point of view, it woke him up to the reality of what he'd done. His reaction is quoted in 2 Samuel 11, and in the prayer-song in which David spoke to God about it:

> Against thee, thee only, have I sinned, and done *this* evil in thy sight: that thou mightest be justified when thou speakest, *and* be clear when thou judgest. (*Psalm 51:4*)

The problem is that most of us don't think like that.

I was speaking at a basketball banquet that included kids from second grade up through high school. Now I don't do much speaking to second-graders, so I wasn't quite sure what to do with them.

When I began my talk, all of the second-graders crowded around the stage to hear me speak. I walked through each of the Ten Commandments. Then I threw names out to the crowd and asked them, by the standard of the Ten Commandments, and knowing that breaking just one would make you guilty, how would each of these people do by that standard?

I mentioned the names Timothy McVeigh, Hitler, Osama bin Laden, and, of course, everyone yelled out, "Guilty." Then I mentioned Mother Teresa and asked the crowd whether, by that standard, she would be guilty or not guilty on Judgment Day?

It is always interesting when I do that because some people will shout out, "Guilty," and others shout out, "Not guilty." In our minds, we have impressions of certain people that are hard to break. At this event, people were saying both answers. Suddenly one of the second graders stood up and said, "Wait a minute, sir. Don't you think she lied at least one time in her life?" Wow! The second grader knew the truth, but many of the adults didn't.

> For all have sinned, and come short of the glory of God; (*Romans 3:23*)
>
> As it is written, There is none righteous, no, not one: (*Romans 3:10*)

By the standard of the Ten Commandments, none of us can say, "Not guilty."

On a flight one day, I was sitting next to a scientist in the Air Force. He was very intrigued and wanted information on the proofs for God and for the Bible's reliability.

Once he heard the evidence, he wanted to know what it took to go to heaven. So I went through the Ten Commandments with him. I asked, "Have you ever told a lie?" He replied, "Yes." I said, "So what does that make you if you told a lie?" He said, "Human." Pretty good answer. Also very true!

I said, "If someone murders, he is a murderer. If someone rapes, he is a rapist. If you tell a lie, what does that make you?" He said, "A liar." I asked, "Have you ever stolen something?" He said, "Yes." I asked, "What does that make you?" He said, "A thief."

I asked, "Have you ever lusted in your heart?" He said, "Yes." I told him that Jesus said if we lust in our hearts it is the same as committing adultery.

"Have you ever taken the Lord's name in vain?" He said that he had. I told him that is blasphemy in the eyes of God.

"Have you ever been angry with someone?" He said he had. I told him that anger is the same in God's eyes as murder. It's murdering someone in your heart.

I then looked at him and said, "You just told me that you are a liar, a thief, an adulterer, a blasphemer, and a murderer according to the standard of God's Law. By that standard, would you be guilty or not guilty on Judgment Day?" He answered, "Guilty."

I asked, "Would that mean heaven or hell?" He said, "Hell." I then asked him, "Does it bother you that you would be going to hell?" He said, "Yes."

Then he asked me what it would take to make sure he *didn't* go to hell for eternity. And I got happy.

You see, the Law of God leads us to discover that we will be guilty on Judgment Day so that we will begin to earnestly seek a way to go from "guilty" to "not guilty" when we finally stand before God as our Judge. The Bible tells us:

> Wherefore the law was our schoolmaster *to bring us* unto Christ, that we might be justified by faith. (*Galatians 3:24*)

When you face the Law of God, it speaks to your conscience, just like it did to the Air Force scientist's. Our conscience informs us that we have broken the commands of Almighty God, whose Law, as we have seen, is written on our hearts, and our conscience tells us about it continually:

> ... which shew the work of the law written in their hearts, their conscience also bearing witness, and *their* thoughts the mean while accusing or else excusing one another... (*Romans 2:15*)

By God's standard right now, how are you doing?

Tiger Woods and the Ten Commandments

If Tiger Woods were judged by God's standard right now, how do you think *he* would do? The following account reveals what his answer was.

While I was in Florida, I learned that my friend Charles Barkley would be about half an hour away, filming a new commercial for Nike with Tiger Woods. I didn't have Charles' phone number with me, so I decided to just swing by where they were doing the shoot.

The Law of God leads us to discover that we will be guilty on Judgment Day just so we will begin to earnestly seek a way to go from "guilty" to "not guilty" when we finally stand before God as our Judge.

But there was a small problem. I knew that there would be a lot of security at the shoot, and wasn't sure how I was going to get through that to hook up with Charles. So as I was driving over there, I began to pray. (If you don't already know it, praying really changes things!) I pulled up to the Grand Cypress Resort and began to talk with a security guard. He told me that the shoot wasn't at the hotel but at the country club.

Then a lady went to pick up the phone. I guessed she was calling to see who was on the list to get in. I knew that I wasn't, so I called her over to my car. I began to chat with her, and then asked her, "If you died tonight, are you 100 percent assured that you would go to heaven?"

Well then it got fun. She told me that she loves the Lord, teaches a Bible-study class, and so on. Well, I told her that I had written a book, my first one, and she said she wanted a copy.

So I pulled one out of a box in the back seat and signed it for her. Then the first security guard, who was *not* a believer, wanted a copy of the book! Pretty cool.

Then the woman guard told me that she would take me over to where the commercial was being shot! So she got in her car and I followed her over there. She took me right through all of the security!

When I got to the set, Charles Barkley was in his trailer waiting for the shoot. So I hung out with him and his agent and some others. All of a sudden, the door opened up, and an older man walked in. Charles introduced us to him. The man sat down, and it turned out that he was the director of the commercial. As I sat there listening, it hit me who he was: This man is probably the most famous commercial director in the world.

He had directed four or five commercials that appeared during one of the Super Bowls. I had actually seen a special on him on one of the news-magazine shows. But in spite of his success, he was not a happy man. He was one of the most arrogant, angry, unhappy men I've met in my life. He mentioned going through a divorce, which he said was really tough on him. But I felt that wasn't where his anger was coming from. I felt that his anger was really toward God. I would soon find out the accuracy of that intuition.

As we were sitting in the trailer, he asked what each of us did. When he got to me, I told him that I was in town doing some speaking for the Fellowship of Christian Athletes. He looked at me and said, "You're not one of *those,* are you?" For the next ten or fifteen minutes, this guy tried to dog Christians as much as he could. He would start talking about other subjects, but then come back and direct a hostile question at me.

Finally, he looked at me and said he wanted to play me in a game of one-on-one basketball! So he stood up and started walking out of the trailer. I told him, "One of my knees is messed up." He said, "I have no cartilage in my knees, so let's go!"

It had already been mentioned by Tiger's people that Tiger was getting a little "itchy" and wanted the shoot to get going. But the director wanted to play basketball!

So they had a goal set up and we went and played. I was wondering why this elderly man wanted to play me one-on-one in basketball. Maybe he wanted to beat up on a Christian. So we played. During the game, I decided to take that time to witness to him. I would just ask him questions to make him think. It seemed to work OK. I finally put him out of his misery and beat him so that he could start shooting the commercial!

When we got over to the tee box, Charles introduced us around. He introduced me to Tiger, who smiled and walked on. So they went about the business of shooting the commercial.

Well, if you know me, you know I had to find someone to talk with. So I walked over and got into a talk with a guy, Richard, who turned out to be Tiger Woods' body double.

I said, "What do you do? His stunts?" I couldn't figure out why he would need a body double.

He told me that when there is a hand shot or a shot from a long distance of Tiger in a commercial, that it is actually him! Richard grew up in Mississippi and — because he had been drifting away from what he'd been taught as a child — really needed a challenge to start standing up for his beliefs.

Then I got into a talk with Vince Coleman, who used to play major-league baseball. He was a tremendous player and played a lot of years with the New York Mets and the St. Louis Cardinals. I had actually met him before at Charles' house in Phoenix.

As we talked, he told me that he goes to church every Sunday in Phoenix. Then I showed him my first book. He looked at it and said twice, "I want your book right now." He told me that he was going to begin reading it at his hotel that night.

He had just gotten to Orlando to do some work with the Atlanta Braves' instructional-league players on their base running.

I told him that I had thought I was coming there that day to witness to Tiger, but maybe the whole reason I was there was to challenge him to boldly begin to stand up for Jesus with his friends.

Meanwhile, every ten or fifteen minutes during the shoot, the commercial's director would fire some hostile question at me from fifteen feet away, in front of everybody. He thought he would antagonize me with his questions. But it was Satan trying to mess with me while I was doing the Lord's work.

One time, the director fired off the statement, "Jesus could not be the Son of God because He would have been a vegetarian." I began to smile. He said that Jesus ate fish, so He couldn't be the Son of God. I started to laugh. He looked at me twice, and both times, said, "Don't laugh!" He told me that the Son of God would not have killed another creature. He'd mentioned some Indian beliefs earlier, so I was pretty sure that this guy worshiped the creation and not the Creator.

I looked at him and said, "Jesus made fish. He can eat one if He wants to!" Everyone but the director looked like they were trying to hide a smile. What was interesting was that this man obviously was trying to get under my skin in front of a lot of other people. But as I tried to hold my ground in a very loving way, you could tell it was backfiring on him.

I saw this guy run roughshod over many of the workers and verbally cut them down. He could not have been a real fun guy to work for. So the people on the set appreciated my taking a stand.

A few hours later, Charles finished his part of the commercial shoot, and was saying his good-byes. People were walking up to Tiger and Charles getting autographs. So I walked up to Tiger, who was there giving autographs. As I approached, it was like God parted the Red Sea; everyone walked away, and it was just Tiger and me standing there.

So I pulled my book out of my pocket and told him I'd just written my first book and wanted to sign a copy for him. I asked where his assistant was so that I could give it to that person. He pointed out who he wanted me to give the book to, and we began to walk off of the tee box.

Now I knew I was supposed to do more than just give him my book. But I got nervous and clammed up. I asked myself, "Will I let the fear of man win out in this situation? Or my love for God?"

I had been praying during the past two months for a chance to tell Tiger Woods about God, and now God had provided this opportunity, and I didn't want to wimp out.

As we began to walk off of the tee box, I felt the Lord saying, "This is what you've been praying for. Just go for it."

So as we were walking, I said, "Tiger, I have always wanted to ask you a question." He said, "Go for it." The same answer God had just given me!

I said, "When you die, what do you think is on the other side? What do you think is out there when you walk out of here?"

Tiger stopped dead in his tracks, looked up at me and said, "I don't know." I responded, "Whether it is Payne Stewart dying [Payne was a famous golfer who died a couple of years ago, and I knew that Tiger had gone to his funeral], or John Ritter, or Johnny Cash, we all think about these things." He was just nodding his head.

I looked at him and said, "Did you hear what happened to Charles' brother?" He said "No," and I could tell he was intrigued.

Charles' brother, Darryl, once had a heart attack, flat-lined, and died. The doctors zapped him with those paddles and he came back to his body. He told me that when he flat-lined and died, his soul rose out of his body. He said that he went to the waiting room and could tell you who was in the waiting room, what they were saying, and what they were wearing while he was clinically dead.

There is no way this could just be in his head since he has such clear external evidence (from the waiting room) to show that he was outside of his body while his body was dead.

He told me that he then took off on a journey and that he could see trees on fire, ground smoldering around the trees, and a lake of fire in front of him.

I asked, "What did you see, Darryl?"

He said, "I saw hell."

And what he saw, he said, was much more real than the book that you now hold in your hands.

He said his senses worked to an amazing degree, and that he could literally feel the heat coming off of that lake of fire.

Tiger naturally has large eyes, but his eyes were about twice the normal size at that moment. He was amazed that someone had seen such a thing. And that it was the brother of the man he'd just been making a Nike commercial with!

So I looked at him and told him, "This is how you can find out where you will be spending eternity. Have you ever heard of the Ten Commandments?"

He said, "Yes."

I said, "Have you ever told a lie before?"

He said, "Yes."

I responded, "What does that make you?"

He didn't even hesitate. "A liar."

I then said, "Have you ever stolen anything?"

He said, "Yes."

He was getting edgy as I continued with my questions. (*The Law of God is written on our hearts and consciences. Confronting our sins puts each one of us in an uncomfortable situation.*) I wasn't looking for details, so I quickly responded with, "We've all done that in some small or large way. That makes us all thieves. Have you ever lusted for someone before?"

He said, "Yes."

I replied, "Jesus said that is the same as committing adultery. He will check our insides as well as our outsides. Have you ever been angry with someone before?"

He said, "Yes."

I responded, "Jesus said if you have been angry with someone, it's the same as committing murder. He will check our thoughts as well as our actions."

I then said, "Tiger, you just told me you are a liar, a thief, an adulterer, and a murderer by the standard of God's Law. Would you be guilty or not guilty on Judgment Day?"

He looked at me and said, "Guilty."

I said, "Would that mean heaven or hell?"

He responded, "Probably hell."

Right at that point, some guy walked up to get Tiger's autograph and told him that they needed to move to the next place to finish the commercial. Tiger began to walk off the tee box, and that was about to be the end of my conversation.

So I told him that I would give my book to the lady he'd indicated, and said, "Have a great day." I felt odd after this cut-off conversation but decided to trust the whole thing to God. He could tell the rest of the story to Tiger Woods when the time was right. To his credit, Tiger had a heart very open to the truths of God and answered those tough questions with an openness and honesty I appreciated.

Confronting our sins puts each one of us in an uncomfortable situation.

Now, forget Tiger for a second. Will you be as honest? How about your heart? How open is it? Whether it's me or you, each one of us would have to say we are a liar, thief, adulterer, and murderer by God's standard. We would say, "guilty" on Judgment Day by that standard. It's a sobering thought. Thank God he has provided a solution to that problem for each one of us. Is your heart ready to get right with God?

As the film crew went to the next hole, I went to get a couple of books from my car for people who'd asked for them. When I came back and gave them to some folks, the director looked over and told the people, "Don't read that trash!"

So I told him that I'd enjoyed chatting with him. He wouldn't shake my hand — but ended up hugging me goodbye! Maybe that change happened because I'd been speaking the truth to him in a loving way, in response to his hostility.

"For all have sinned..."

Since we all are guilty by God's standard, hell is the destination where we all will be going — unless God has made a way out *and* we take the way out He has provided.

Charles Spurgeon said:

> You are hanging over the mouth of hell by a single thread, and that thread is breaking. Only a gasp for breath, only a stopping of the heart for a single moment, and you will be in an eternal world — without God, without hope, without forgiveness. Oh, can you face it?"[75]

Since we all are guilty by God's standard, hell is the destination where we all will be going — unless God has made a way out and *we take the way out He has provided.*

Jesus was talking to a sick man and asked him a very interesting question:

> When Jesus saw him lie, and knew that he had been now a long time *in that case*, he saith unto him, Wilt thou be made whole? (*John 5:6*)

Sin is very expensive. It costs us a lot in this lifetime … and in the next one. Question for you: "Wilt thou be made whole?" Do you wish to get well? What's your answer?

It's amazing to realize every one of us is guilty by the standard God has set. Even if I try to ignore my sin, it doesn't mean God will.

Six billion of us are guilty by that standard. That means six billion of us are going to hell when we die unless we embrace God's solution to this massive problem.

The path leading to eternal truth continues to narrow, and the remedy for our sin problem is just a page-turn away.

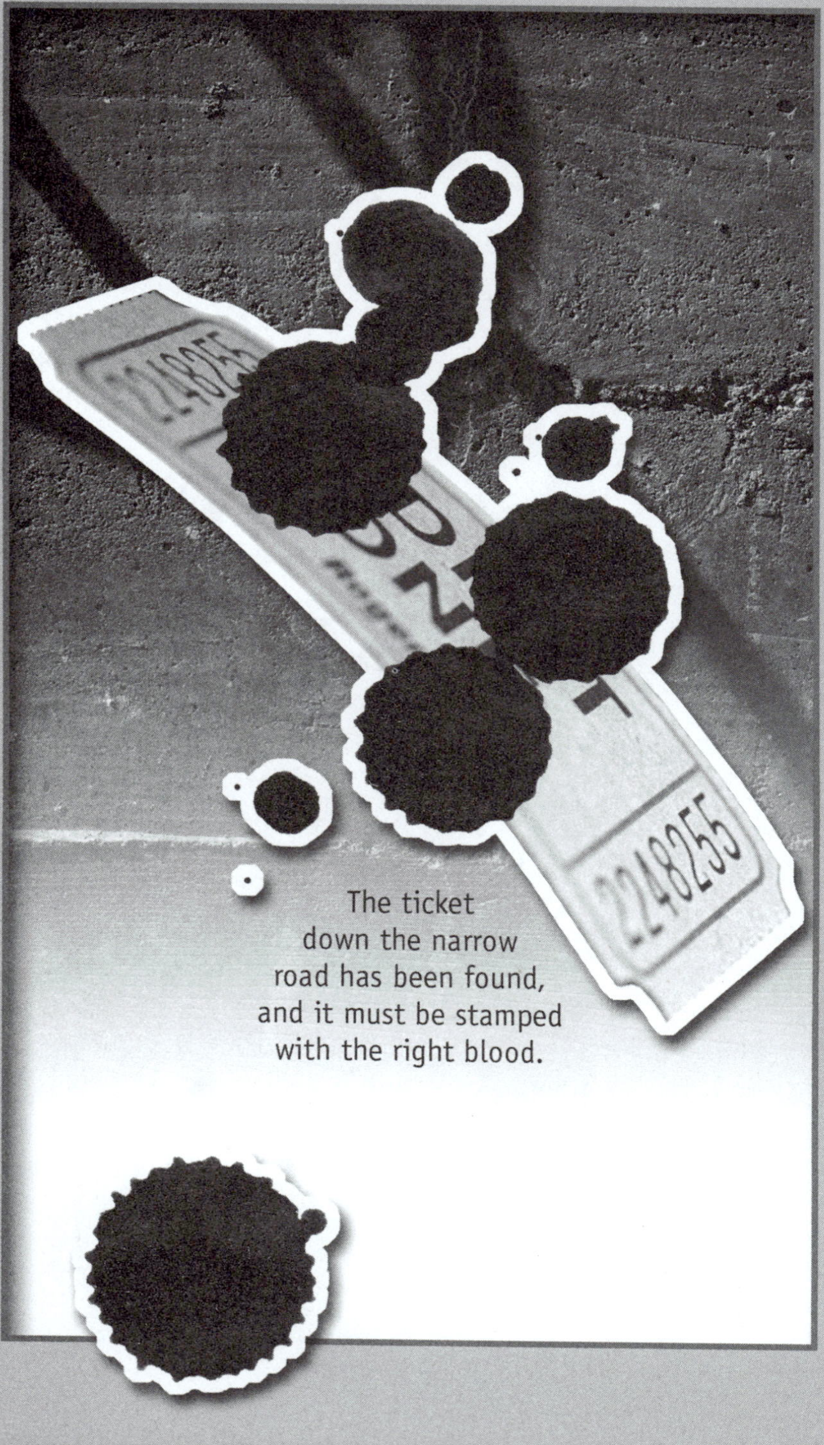

The ticket
down the narrow
road has been found,
and it must be stamped
with the right blood.

Chapter 7
The Good News

Eureka! [I have found it!]
— Archimedes, 287–212 B.C.

"Eureka!" is what Archimedes, the great Greek engineer, was said to have shouted when he solved a very difficult problem involving the density of the king's crown: The king wanted to know whether the crown was pure gold or mixed with silver.

Archimedes sat down in his bathtub to ponder the problem, noticed that the water overflowed onto the floor, and realized that the volume of water pushed out of the tub was the same as his body's volume.

That is, when an object is submerged in water, the level of the water rises because the object has moved some of the water out of the way to make room for itself. "Eureka!" He'd found a way to determine the volume of the crown: Since he knew the weight of gold, he could now answer the king's question by calculating the weight of that volume of gold.

Similarly, we all have a question of great importance that we find difficult to solve: How can we get on the good side of God and avoid hell? You might just shout "Eureka!" when you read the answer in this chapter.

Just before actor W. C. Fields died, a friend visited Fields' hospital room and was surprised to find him thumbing through a Bible. Asked what he was doing with a Bible, Fields replied, "I'm looking for loopholes."

Now that we know the Bible to be true — and that there aren't any loopholes — some interesting things begin to happen. God says:

> Look unto me, and be ye saved, all the ends of the earth: for I *am* God, and *there is* none else. (*Isaiah 45:22*)

God says that He is the only God out there. There is no other. But how can I be right with Him? What is that pathway? God says there is one Savior:

> Neither is there salvation in any other: for there is none other name under heaven given among men, whereby we must be saved. (*Acts 4:12*)

What is the one name of the one person who can save us all? God says…

> For *there is* one God, and there is one mediator between God and men, the man Christ Jesus; (*1 Timothy 2:5*)
>
> Whosoever denieth the Son, the same hath not the Father: *[But] he that acknowledgeth the Son hath the Father also.* (*1 John 2:23*)
>
> And this is the record, that God hath given to us eternal life, and this life is in his Son.
>
> He that hath the Son hath life; *and* he that hath not the Son of God hath not life. (*1 John 5:11–12*)
>
> He that believeth on him is not condemned: but he that believeth not is condemned already, because he hath not believed in the name of the only begotten Son of God. (*John 3:18*)
>
> … if ye believe not that I am *he*, ye shall die in your sins. (*John 8:24b*)
>
> Jesus saith unto him, I am the way, the truth, and the life: no man cometh unto the Father, but by me. (*John 14:6*)

… and there are many other verses that say that Jesus is the *only* way to make peace and find friendship with God.

Since Jesus is this "one mediator," what makes Him so special? Why is He the only right answer?

Well, there must be a right answer to comfort us when we walk out of here into eternity. There must be a right answer that will keep us from going to hell. And here it is: You need to bring the right sacrifice. Sacrifice? Read on.

What is so interesting as you read the Old Testament is that from the very beginning, God used animal sacrifices for the forgiveness of sin. Later, the Jewish people would bring animal offerings to the Temple in Jerusalem to atone for their sins.

When the innocent animal's blood was shed, it was understood to be a trade for their own blood. Because of their sin, they deserved to die. But because of the substitute animal's blood being shed on their behalf, their sin was taken away.

> For the life of the flesh *is* in the blood: and I have given it to you upon the altar to make an atonement for your souls: for it *is* the blood *that* maketh an atonement for the soul. (*Leviticus 17:11*)

Each family of the enslaved Children of Israel took the blood of a lamb without blemish and put it on the doorposts of their dwellings so that the death angel would "pass over" them.

A couple of years ago, I got a call from ESPN Classic. They were doing a special about Charles Barkley and were coming to Atlanta to interview people for it.

Somehow, they found my name in a search engine, and located me. A young guy just out of college asked me the questions on camera.

Each family of the enslaved Children of Israel took the blood of a lamb without blemish and put it on the doorposts of their dwellings so that the death angel would "pass over" them.

After the interview, he and I got into a conversation. He told me that he grew up half Lutheran and half Jewish as a kid. I asked him if he still went to synagogue. He said that he went on the High Holy Days.

The interview was two days before the Day of Atonement (Yom Kippur in Hebrew), so we talked about that holy day. It is the day on which all Israel is supposed to confess their sins, sacrifice animals as substitutes for themselves, and receive forgiveness.

As we talked about sin, I asked him what Jews did on that day to get rid of sin. He knew that they used to sacrifice animals for the sin offering, but that they didn't do that anymore because the sacrifice has to be made at the Temple in Jerusalem, which was destroyed in 70 A.D.

I mentioned that we can't just change the way God gets rid of sin. If He demands a blood sacrifice, that is what it must be.

The young man was curious as to what that blood sacrifice would be now, since the Temple in Jerusalem has been destroyed for almost 2000 years. So I told him what I'm about to tell you.

At the end of the conversation, he said, "How do you know so much about what you believe?" He loved hearing the truth that you have read so far in this book, but what he was most interested in was the *reason* for the blood sacrifice — and why it is no longer possible or necessary to do it.

Two of Jesus' disciples said of Him:

> The next day John seeth Jesus coming unto him, and saith, Behold the Lamb of God, which taketh away the sin of the world. (*John 1:29*)
>
> Forasmuch as ye know that ye were not redeemed with corruptible things, as silver and gold, from your vain conversation received by tradition from your fathers;
>
> But with the precious blood of Christ, as of a lamb without blemish and without spot: (*1 Peter 1:18, 19*)

And here is where it all begins to fit together. God, who demands a blood sacrifice for sin, says:

> And almost all things are by the law purged with blood; and without shedding of blood is no remission. (*Hebrews 9:22*)
>
> Who his own self bare our sins in His own body on the tree, that we, being dead to sins, should live unto righteousness: by whose stripes ye were healed.
>
> For ye were as sheep going astray; but are now returned unto the Shepherd and Bishop of your souls. (*1 Peter 2:24–25*)

We cannot, and will never be able to, change God's standard. Jesus is also called the perfect sacrifice who paid the penalty for all sin once and for all. We have to remember that God demands a perfect sacrifice. If Jesus was a sinner just like us, man and man alone, then that payment

We cannot, and will never be able to, change God's standard. Jesus is also called the perfect sacrifice who paid the penalty for all sin once and for all. We have to remember that God demands a perfect sacrifice.

won't cut it. Many people have died on a cross, but Jesus had to be different. And He was — and is:

> For we have not an high priest which cannot be touched with the feeling of our infirmities; but was in all points tempted like as *we are, yet* without sin. (*Hebrews 4:15*)
>
> Who did no sin, neither was guile found in his mouth:
>
> Who, when he was reviled, reviled not again; when he suffered, he threatened not; but committed *himself* to him that judgeth righteously. (*1 Peter 2:22–23*)

That is the difference. Jesus never sinned. Not once. Never. He was tempted as we are, but he never fell into sin. Because He always chose to do what He knew in His heart was the right thing, He and He alone can be that perfect once-and-for-all sacrifice for all sin of all sinners. That is how He could be the Lamb without blemish. He is the perfect atonement for all of our sins to the Almighty God of this universe.

I was in Kansas City, getting onto my plane. I put my bag in the seat I was going to sit in. The lady next to me was dressed all in black, with silver hair and gold jewelry. It was a real nice contrast; she appeared to be about 60 years old.

I said, "Hello," and she was friendly back. But I noticed that she was reading the *New York Times*, which is a very liberal (there-is-no-God) newspaper.

I remember thinking this was going to be a short conversation. (*By the way, be careful what you think; you might be totally wrong.*) After getting settled, we introduced ourselves; her name was Sheila. Then I asked her why she had been in Kansas City. She told me she'd been to a funeral. My hopes for a good conversation increased because I knew that she would be thinking about death.

I asked her who had died, and she told me it was her nephew. I asked her how he had passed away. She looked at me and said, "I just met you. I don't know if I should tell you."

I looked at her and told her that if she felt comfortable with telling me, that would be fine. Then she told me that her nephew had committed suicide. I told her that one of my students had done that a few years ago. So we began to really talk.

About twenty minutes into the conversation, something truly amazing happened. I had mentioned "God" kind of generically at one point. She had mentioned "spiritual" at another point. But nothing with any depth had happened so far, as far as talking about spiritual things.

I asked Sheila if she was Jewish, and she told me she was.

Suddenly she looked at me and asked, totally out of nowhere, "Why does someone like me need to receive Jesus for the forgiveness of my sins? Why can't I just be a good Jewish person who keeps the Ten Commandments to be right with God? Why do I need to receive Jesus for the forgiveness of my sins? It would be much easier for me to become a Christian and go from the minority to the majority. Why do I need to do that?"

My jaw about hit the floor. I couldn't believe this lady asked me that. It's amazing that I often think people won't talk with me when it comes to eternal matters. Then God puts someone next to me who is in "search mode," and I only have to be obedient in what I say to them. God has worked in their hearts and they are ready. All that is required is to plant the seed of truth or to water the seed that's already there.

After Sheila asked that enormous question, or series of questions, I stood up and got my Bible from my bag in the compartment above me, and we talked the whole flight about Yeshua being mentioned in the Old Testament. (Jesus' original Hebrew name is Yeshua, which means "Salvation.")

I once listened to a tape about a guy who was a completed Jew — that is, he had accepted Jesus as the Jewish Messiah. He said that he came to believe this after a Jewish person who believed in Jesus suggested that he read four things in the Old Testament, and then ask himself the question: "Who is this referring to?"

He thought that sounded fair, so he tried it.

1. Isaiah 53 talks about a suffering servant. His answer was that chapter was talking about Jesus.

2. Psalm 22 talks about the crucifixion of the Messiah. He knew that described Jesus' death.

3. Jeremiah 31:31–34 talks about how there is an old covenant and one day there will be a new one. He hadn't known about a new covenant. Now he did.

4. Daniel 9:24–27 talks about how the Messiah will be cut off and then the city will be destroyed. When the Old Testament talks about "the city," it is always in reference to Jerusalem. And we know from history that Jerusalem was destroyed in 70 A.D. So the Messiah had to have come before that!

This man said that at that point, he knew it was Jesus, and Jesus alone, who could have fulfilled that prophecy.

I also like a fifth verse:

5. Proverbs 30:4 tells us there is a God and then asks the question: "and what is his son's name?"

So the Jewish Scriptures proclaim, in these and many other passages, that the Son of God would come in a particular time and manner.

Sheila was really doing some thinking as we talked about all of this. We talked about her sin by reviewing the Ten Commandments, which she had mentioned as a way to be OK with God. It was an amazing conversation.

At the end of our talk, I took a copy of my first book, signed it, and gave it to her. She looked at me and said, "I have been wanting to have this conversation for a long, long time now."

I told her that, on the way to the airport, I had been praying that the person next to me on the flight would have an open heart for a conversation about Jesus. I looked at Sheila and told her, "You were the answer to that prayer."

The look on her face was priceless. Sheila looked at me and said, "I am going to remember this conversation for a long, long time." I pray for Sheila to accept Yeshua/Jesus as her Savior, if she hasn't done it already, so that she won't be judged by the Law.

One time in Winter Park, Colorado, I was doing a lot of skiing during the day. I like to talk about eternal matters with people on ski lifts. I mean, what are they going to do, jump? They always ride right up with you to the top!

One day on the ski lift, I was talking with a teacher from a Jewish synagogue and his son. We were talking about the forgiveness of sin. The Day of Atonement was a few days away, so he told me about the fasting and prayer that is done on that day.

As we talked, I found that he knew that the Jewish Scriptures talk about the sacrifice of animals and that their blood is understood to be a covering for sin. He also knew that, for almost 2000 years, Jews have not been able to offer animal sacrifices because the Temple where they must be offered was destroyed by the Romans almost 2000 years ago.

So I explained to him about Jesus being the perfect sacrifice for all sin, making the Temple sacrifice not needed anymore. That's why the Temple was gone.

We had a great talk on the lift. Then right when we got to the top — where you tilt your skis up so that they don't clip the landing area and pop off your feet — he looked at me and said, "I have never thought about the fact of a human sacrifice for sin before."

Two and two began to equal four in his mind. He knew the Jewish law that needed to be fulfilled for an effective sin offering, and now, for the first time, he was realizing why Jesus really came to this earth: To be that perfect once-and-for-all-time sin offering.

God says of Jesus:

> Who being the brightness of *his* glory, and the express image of *his* person, and upholding all things by the word of *his* power, when he had by himself purged our sins, sat down on the right hand of the Majesty on high; (*Hebrews 1:3*)

Remember that, from the outset, the search in this book has been for truth. Knowing truth and living by that truth will always set you free.

> Then said Jesus to those Jews which believed on him, If ye continue in my word, *then* are ye my disciples indeed;
>
> And ye shall know the truth, and the truth shall make you free." (*John 8:31–32*)

Buddha said at the end of his life, "I don't even know if there is a God. I am still searching for truth."

The Koran, written many years after Mohammed's death, quotes Mohammed as saying, "I am in need of forgiveness."

But listen to what Jesus says:

> ...I am the way, the truth, and the life: no man cometh unto the Father, but by me. (*John 14:6*)

At this point, when Jesus says that He is the only way to heaven, we have a dilemma. We have to decide who and what Jesus really is: a lunatic, a liar, or the Lord. Let's look at this.

When Jesus says that He is the only way to heaven, we have a dilemma. We have to decide who and what Jesus really is: a lunatic, a liar, or the Lord.

If He is lying and *doesn't know* he is lying, then He would be a lunatic. He would be out of His mind. It is not every day that someone claims to be God and the only way to heaven. If you make a statement like that, you had better be able to back it up.

Did this man who had such an impact on 2,000 years of history behave like someone who is crazy? Could the man whose birth split history into B. C. and A. D. actually have been crazy?

But if He is lying and He *knows* He is lying, He then would be the greatest deceiver that the world has ever seen — telling people that He was the way to heaven when He was not.

Jesus' sayings permeate society to this day and they have the ring of truth to most people. His enemies could not find any sin in him. He had spotless character.

Can someone whose words are the greatest moral teachings the world has ever known, and whose words and deeds have had the greatest impact on this world — could that man at the same time have been a liar about Himself, God, and where humanity would spend eternity?

We see that it makes no sense to think that Jesus was a lunatic, and it makes no sense to think that He was a liar. That leaves only one option: He was telling the truth, and He *knew* He was telling the truth. That makes Him God manifested in a human body, as prophesied in the Bible.

Scholar C. S. Lewis wrote:

> Either this man was, and is, the Son of God or else a madman or something worse. You can shut Him up for a fool, you can spit on Him and kill Him as a demon; or you can fall at His feet and call Him Lord and God. But let us not come with any patronizing nonsense about His being a great human teacher. He has not left that open to us. He did not intend to.[76]

The claims of Christ are unique compared with the claims of the founders of all other religions. Josh McDowell says:

> Mohammed never claimed to be God; Buddha remained silent on the question of God; Confucius refused to discuss the idea of God; Moses merely claimed to be a prophet of God. Only Jesus claimed to be God incarnate [in the flesh]. People have described Him as a "wise teacher," a "great master," but it wasn't just His words, but miracles which were seen as genuine and authentic. And together with the ancient writings (Old Testament), all speak of Him as Deity in the flesh.[77]

Jesus, whose very name means "salvation," was telling the truth: He is the only way to heaven. The pathway we have been looking for to get to heaven has been found. The mystery has been solved. He and He alone can forgive your sin. He is the only way to get to the Father and be right with God:

> Enter ye in at the strait gate: for wide *is* the gate, and broad *is* the way, that leadeth to destruction, and many there be which go in thereat:
>
> Because strait *is* the gate, and narrow *is* the way, which leadeth unto life, and few there be that find it. (*Matthew 7:13–14*)

The search for truth is always a narrow search, because truth is only just what it is, and excludes every other way or answer. The ticket to the narrow road to heaven has been found, and it must be stamped with the blood of Jesus. Just as there are many wrong answers, there is one right answer when you face God on Judgment Day: "Jesus paid it all!"

> … if we walk in the light, as He is in the light, we have fellowship one with another, and the blood of Jesus Christ His Son cleanseth us from all sin. (*1 John 1:7*)

His blood can cleanse us from all sin. And that means *all* sin. The only way a holy God can let us into heaven is if we are clean of all of the sin we have committed in our lifetime. That's why our "good works" will never be enough to allow us into the presence of an all-holy God.

Come now, and let us reason together, saith the Lord: though your sins be as scarlet, they shall be as white as snow; though they be red like crimson, they shall be as wool.
— Isaiah 1:18

Consider this: If you take a burnt cake and put white icing on it, how does it look? Sure, it looks good on the outside, but when you take a bite of it, how does it taste? Probably most of us have taken a bite out of a burnt cookie or piece of cake, and were happy until we hit the burnt part. It tastes horrible.

It's the same way with good works: If we are trusting our good deeds to gain us entrance into heaven, we try to look good on the outside. On the inside, however, we are still nasty and horrible because we're still breaking the Ten Commandments day by day.

To get into heaven, where no unclean thing is allowed, we can't merely cover our sin with good deeds; we must get rid of it altogether. The blood of Jesus, and the blood of Jesus alone, can make your sins as pure and white as a beautiful, fresh snowfall, getting rid of them once and for all:

> Come now, and let us reason together, saith the Lord: though your sins be as scarlet, they shall be as white as snow; though they be red like crimson, they shall be as wool. (*Isaiah 1:18*)

There is only one thing that will get rid of all of our sins, once and for all: the pure cleansing blood of Jesus the Messiah (or Christ, as it is in Greek).

> But now in Christ Jesus, ye who sometimes were far off are made nigh by the blood of Christ. (*Ephesians 2:13*)

Then we can stand before God dressed in the righteousness of Jesus, and our plea will be neither "Guilty" nor "Not guilty," but, "the blood of Jesus his Son cleanseth us from all sin." (*1 John 1:7*)

Charles Spurgeon said:

> The heart of Christ became like a reservoir in the midst of the mountains. All the tributary streams of iniquity, and every drop of the sins of his people, ran down and gathered into one vast lake, deep as hell and shoreless as eternity. All these met, as it were, in Christ's heart, and he endured them all.[78]

He was the only one who could wipe out the sin of all of mankind, and He did just that for us.

Spurgeon said this about this selfless act of God's Son:

> The marvel of heaven and earth, of time and eternity, is the atoning death of Jesus Christ. This is the mystery that brings more glory to God than all creation.[79]

There was nothing we could do to save ourselves. Any current good deed would be the right thing only for that moment, and it wouldn't pay for anything past. We were spiritually bankrupt; only a sinless person could pay our debt:

> For when we were yet without strength, in due time Christ died for the ungodly.
>
> For scarcely for a righteous man will one die: yet peradventure for a good man some would even dare to die.
>
> But God commendeth his love toward us, in that, while we were yet sinners, Christ died for us.
>
> Much more then, being now justified by his blood, we shall be saved from wrath through Him.
>
> For if, when we were enemies, we were reconciled to God by the death of his Son, much more, being reconciled, we shall be saved by his life. (*Romans 5:6–10*)

I was talking with a guy in the mall one day, trying to help him understand what the blood of Jesus had done for him. As we were talking, someone walked out of a store and the alarm buzzer went off because the salesperson had forgotten to remove the security tag from an item.

I asked the guy, "If someone left the security tag on your jeans and you walked out of a department store, what would happen?" He replied that the alarm would go off. I said, "Here is a word picture for you. Imagine that the gates of heaven have sensors, one on each side, and as you walk through, only one thing will set the alarm off. What would that be?"

His answer was, "My sin."

I said, "Exactly. But if all of your sins have been forgiven and washed away, can you enter through those gates once you walk off planet earth forever?"

His eyes suddenly lit up and he said, "Yes!" Just like none of us wants that alarm to go off when we walk out of a store, we most definitely don't want that alarm to go off when we try to enter heaven.

Just like none of us wants that alarm to go off when we walk out of a store, we most definitely don't want that alarm to go off when we try to enter heaven.

The blood of Jesus, when you trust in it, will wipe away all of your sins. Period. No alarm will be going off as you approach the throne of God.

Charles Spurgeon said:

> My heart was fallow and covered with weeds, but on a certain day the great Farmer came and began to plow my soul. Ten black horses were his team, and it was a sharp plowshare that he used, and the plowers made deep furrows.
>
> The Ten Commandments were those black horses, and the justice of God, like a plowshare, tore my spirit. I was condemned, undone, destroyed, lost, helpless, hopeless. I thought hell was before me.
>
> But after the plowing came the sowing. God who plowed the heart in mercy made it conscious that it needed the Gospel, and then the Gospel seed was joyfully received.[80]

The purpose of the Law is to show men they need a Savior. No one can keep the Law, so if that is what we are trying to do, we are without hope. When we realize our hopeless condition, we should be very happy to hear about what Jesus has done for us.

Are you ready to joyfully receive what Jesus has done for you, as was the man in the account below?

> And when they were come to the place, which is called Calvary, there they crucified him, and the malefactors, one on the right hand, and the other on the left.
>
> Then said Jesus, Father, forgive them; for they know not what they do. And they parted his raiment, and cast lots.
>
> And the people stood beholding. And the rulers also with them derided *him*, saying, He saved others; let him save himself, if he be Christ, the chosen of God.
>
> And the soldiers also mocked him, coming to him, and offering him vinegar,
>
> And saying, If thou be the king of the Jews, save thyself.
>
> And a superscription also was written over him in letters of Greek, and Latin, and Hebrew, THIS IS THE KING OF THE JEWS.
>
> And one of the malefactors which were hanged railed on him, saying, "If thou be Christ, save thyself and us.
>
> But the other answering rebuked him, saying, Dost not thou fear God, seeing thou art in the same condemnation?
>
> And we indeed justly; for we receive the due reward of our deeds: but this man hath done nothing amiss."
>
> And he said unto Jesus, Lord, remember me when thou comest into thy kingdom.
>
> And Jesus said unto him, "Verily I say unto thee, To day shalt thou be with me in paradise.
>
> And it was about the sixth hour, and there was a darkness over all the earth until the ninth hour.
>
> And the sun was darkened, and the veil of the Temple was rent in the midst.
>
> And when Jesus had cried with a loud voice, he said, Father, into thy hands I commend my spirit: and having said thus, he gave up the ghost.
>
> Now when the centurion saw what was done, he glorified God, saying, Certainly this was a righteous man."
>
> And all the people that came together to that sight, beholding the things which were done, smote their breasts, and returned.
>
> And all his acquaintance, and the women that followed him from Galilee, stood afar off, beholding these things. (*Luke 23:33–49*)

The truth is that all of us are like one or the other of the two thieves who were crucified next to Jesus: One mocked Him, and the other recognized that He was God and looked to Him for the forgiveness of his sins.

The passage above also makes the point that we get to heaven not by being good but by repenting of our sins, and placing our faith and trust in what Jesus has done *for* us.

Now, if everything depends on faith, just what is faith anyway? One thing faith is NOT is a feeling. You can be exercising great faith without any emotion or physical sensation. You believe that what you're sitting on now will hold you up. You believe it with perfect faith, yet you feel nothing about it.

Doubt is a feeling, not a spiritual element at all. But faith is not a feeling. It is a settled choice arrived at by a decision of your will.

On the other hand, doubt *is* a feeling. You can certainly feel emotionally and physically disturbed if you believe that what you're now sitting on may collapse at any moment. So doubt is a feeling, not a spiritual element at all. But faith is not a feeling. It is a settled choice arrived at by a decision of your will. "That chair looks OK to me." And you sit without thinking further. You're just trusting in your choice of views.

It's the same with faith in Jesus' love for you and His arrangements for you to be saved. Once you decide, there is not necessarily any feeling or emotion involved. You just know that Jesus is your savior, and you rest in His promises without entertaining doubts.

Each thief had a choice of how to treat Jesus. As a result, one went to hell and one went to heaven. You too have a choice. Whatever you decide to do with Jesus will determine where you will spend eternity. Think about why He came and what it means to you personally:

> This *is* a faithful saying, and worthy of all acceptation, that Christ Jesus came into the world to save sinners; of whom I am chief. (*1 Timothy 1:15*)

> Howbeit for this cause I obtained mercy, that in me first Jesus Christ might shew forth all longsuffering, for a pattern to them which should hereafter believe on him to life everlasting. (*1 Timothy 1:16*)
>
> Blotting out the handwriting of ordinances that was against us, which was contrary to us, and took it out of the way, nailing it to his cross; (*Colossians 2:14*)

"Blotting out" means "canceling, writing 'paid in full' on the list of our debts to God." When Jesus said, "It is finished," He meant that all prophecy had been fulfilled regarding Messiah's work on earth of paying humanity's sin debt "in full."

And think about this: Your debt was paid 2,000 years ago! Justice has been served, your debt has been paid, and God no longer looks at you as a sinner headed for hell, but as a beloved child getting ready to return Home to Him.

The only "if" in the situation is this: All this is yours IF — and only IF — you decide to accept it.

God will not force you to love Him. That's the real purpose of life in this world: We're here for an attitude adjustment. God has created us with free will, and we're here to exercise it. The big question we must answer is: Will I run my own life, or will I ask God to run it?

If I set myself up as my own god, He will sorrowfully allow me to do it. But He will also continue drawing me to Himself.

However, if I tell Him I'm sorry for the wrong I've done, especially against Him, and ask to live in fellowship with Him here, and to go to Him when I die, His answer is sure to be "Yes!"

That's because Jesus paid it all, so I am free to come to God and look Him in the face without fear. That's what the Gospel, the Good News, is all about: God desires to show mercy toward me, and offers me the most loving gift of all time — total and complete forgiveness through Jesus Christ. If I receive God's gift of forgiveness, I will be with Him after I die, not in hell.

This offer is yours, too, if you turn from your sinful ways, with His help, and determine to live a godly life in Christ Jesus.

Yes, you are free from the debt of your transgressions if you decide to accept what He has done for you and live in appreciation of it.

Not only did Jesus die on the cross for our sins, He did something amazing so that we could know for sure who He was:

He rose from the dead:

Now upon the first *day* of the week, very early in the morning, they came unto the sepulcher, bringing the spices which they had prepared, and certain *others* with them.

And they found the stone rolled away from the sepulcher.

And they entered in, and found not the body of the Lord Jesus.

And it came to pass, as they were much perplexed thereabout, behold, two men stood by them in shining garments:

And as they were afraid, and bowed down *their* faces to the earth, they said unto them, Why seek ye the living among the dead?

He is not here, but is risen: remember how he spake unto you when he was yet in Galilee,

Saying, The Son of man must be delivered into the hands of sinful men, and be crucified, and the third day rise again.

And they remembered His words,

And returned from the sepulcher, and told all these things unto the eleven, and to all the rest.

It was Mary Magdalene, and Joanna, and Mary *the mother* of James, and other *women that were* with them, which told these things unto the apostles.

And their words seemed to them as idle tales, and they believed them not.

Then arose Peter, and ran unto the sepulcher; and stooping down, he beheld the linen clothes laid by themselves, and departed, wondering in himself at that which was come to pass. (*Luke 24:1–12*)

... and left his tomb empty:

Whom God hath raised up, having loosed the pains of death: because it was not possible that he should be holden of it. (*Acts 2:24*)

MOREOVER, brethren, I declare unto you the Gospel which I preached unto you, which also ye have received, and wherein ye stand;

> By which also ye are saved, if ye keep in memory what I preached unto you, unless ye have believed in vain.
>
> For I delivered unto you, first of all, that which I also received, how that Christ died for our sins according to the scriptures;
>
> And that he was buried, and that he rose again the third day according to the scriptures:
>
> And that he was seen of Cephas, then of the twelve:
>
> After that, he was seen of above five hundred brethren at once; of whom the greater part remain unto this present, but some are fallen asleep.
>
> After that, he was seen of James; then of all the apostles.
>
> And last of all he was seen of me also, as of one born out of due time.
>
> For I am the least of the apostles, that am not meet to be called an apostle, because I persecuted the church of God.
>
> But by the grace of God I am what I am: and his grace which *was bestowed* upon me was not in vain; but I laboured more abundantly than they all: yet not I, but the grace of God which was with me.
>
> Therefore whether *it were* I or they, so we preach, and so ye believed.
>
> Now if Christ be preached that He rose from the dead, how say some among you that there is no resurrection of the dead?
>
> But if there be no resurrection of the dead, then is Christ not risen:
>
> And if Christ be not risen, then *is* our preaching vain, and your faith *is* also vain.
>
> Yea, and we are found false witnesses of God; because we have testified of God that he raised up Christ: whom he raised not up — if so be that the dead rise not.
>
> For if the dead rise not, then is not Christ raised:
>
> And if Christ be not raised, your faith *is* vain; ye are yet in your sins.
>
> Then they also which are fallen asleep in Christ are perished.
>
> If in this life only we have hope in Christ, we are of all men most miserable. (*1 Corinthians 15:1–19*)

At least two eyewitnesses were needed to establish the truth of anything.

Remember what we said about eyewitnesses earlier? We showed that one eyewitness was not considered enough to prove anything in a Jewish court of law. At least two eyewitnesses were needed to establish the truth of anything.

When Jesus rose from the dead, He was seen by at least 552 people in thirteen different places over a period of forty days. The resurrection of Jesus and His active presence in the world for forty days *after* the resurrection, were not behind closed doors; rather, they were out in the wide open spaces so that everyone could see the marvelous work of God in the resurrection of His Son.

This proved to those who saw Him, beyond a shadow of a doubt, that He was God incarnate: The Messiah. Think about that. He had to make sure that people throughout time, including us today, had enough evidence to make the correct eternal decision.

And Paul went even further. He said that if Jesus did not rise from the dead, our faith is in vain. It is nothing but a big hoax. And yet all of Jesus' followers were willing to die for their faith because *they had each seen the resurrected Savior!*

> The former treatise [the book of *Luke*] have I made, O Theophilus, of all that Jesus began both to do and teach,
>
> Until the day in which He was taken up, after that He through the Holy Ghost had given commandments unto the apostles whom He had chosen:
>
> To whom also He shewed himself alive after his passion by many infallible proofs, being seen of them forty days, and speaking of the things pertaining to the kingdom of God: (*Acts 1:1–3*)

I was at an arts festival one day talking with two ladies. They told me how they just could not believe that Jesus was the only way to heaven. I spent some time talking with them about the life of Jesus, the death of Jesus, and then the resurrection of Jesus.

When I got done talking about the resurrection, one lady looked at me and said, "If that man rose from the dead, He can make the statement that He is the only way to get to heaven."

Even she, who did not believe in Jesus, knew that if someone predicts his own death, predicts that he will get out of the grave, and then actually does it, then you can believe what else he says.

A lot of things can be said about Jesus, but one thing is for certain: His resurrection from the dead puts Him in a different category from everyone else who has ever walked on planet earth.

He predicted His death and predicted He would rise from the dead, and He did just that. Mohammed couldn't do it. Buddha couldn't do it. Confucius couldn't do it. Not only *could* Jesus do it, He *did* it.

Pascal's Wager

Blaise Pascal, the great mathematician and philosopher, suggested living as if there is a God is a better wager than living as if there is no God. This has come to be known as "Pascal's Wager."

Here is the wager, written out: If you live as if God doesn't exist and you're *right*, you just die and go to your grave. But if you live as if God doesn't exist, and you're *wrong*, you go into eternal misery in hell. Conversely, if you live as if God does exist and you're *wrong*, then you would just die and go to the grave. But if you live as if God does exist and you're *right*, you have just hit the jackpot for an eternity in heaven.

Pascal's point was: Why not take a gamble that there is a God? If you're wrong, you've lost nothing, and you've had a good life here. But if you're right, and God is real, you'll have eternity to be thankful that you chose wisely. We gamble every time we get into a car or an airplane, use an appliance, or eat in a restaurant. So why wouldn't we take a gamble on this, where there is everything to gain and nothing to lose?

As I was looking at this argument one day, I thought Pascal had missed something because he didn't mention Jesus. You can believe that a God exists, but if you don't choose the right God, Jesus Christ the Savior, you have made an eternal mistake.

Something can't be true and not true at the same time. Either Jesus is the Son of God who is the Way, the Truth, and the Life, who rose from the dead — or He is not, and did not.

On further investigation, I learned that Pascal was not only saying that one should believe in a God, but in God as represented in Christianity. He was also saying that if you believe something, you will act on it. So he was really recommending Jesus, but because he was speaking to atheists, he did it indirectly by starting with God.

Where do you stand on this question?

There is a 100 percent chance that you are going to die. Do you have the right ticket to get into heaven one day? That ticket must — and I do mean *must* — be stamped with the blood of Jesus. Either you will arrive in heaven as God's child, or you won't arrive there at all. No middle ground here. A choice must be made.

Here's how Josh McDowell spoke of faith in Jesus:

> Christianity is the largest religion in the world, but there is something very distinct about it. It is a religion in one sense, but it is all about one person. If there was no Joseph Smith, Mormonism would still be here. If there was no Buddha, Buddhism would still be here because so many have claimed to be Buddha. But if there is no Jesus, there would be no Christianity. The religion would be extinct. With no Jesus who walked and talked and was crucified and rose from the dead, there would be no Christianity. It all comes down to the Son of God, Jesus. The question now is, what are you going to do with Him?[81]

I once heard a guy say:

> Imagine that we are in a deep pit of sin. There is no way to climb out of this pit. Someone throws you down a ladder. There are ten steps on the ladder. You try to climb up, but each of the steps is one of the Ten Commandments and the rule is you can't place your foot on a step of one of the commandments that you have broken. There is no way out of the pit. You are stuck. All of a sudden, Jesus jumps in, and if you want, He'll put you on His back. And He climbs out of the pit, stepping on each step, as the perfect, sinless Savior who carries you out of the pit.

Do you want Jesus to carry you out of the pit of sin and death?

The mystery of eternal truth has been solved. Now you must decide what you want to do about it.

You're sitting astride your camel, baking in the sweltering heat, surrounded by the hot desert sand. The rest of the caravan is stretched out behind you, wondering why you've stopped...

Chapter 8
The Next Step

Sin and hell are married unless
repentance proclaims the divorce.
— Charles Spurgeon

Let's see where we stand: The evidence is overwhelming. We have each broken the commands of Almighty God. I will be guilty on Judgment Day. You will be guilty on Judgment Day.

So what is the next step for you and me to get right with God?

There is a word that we don't use much in everyday English anymore, and that's the word "repent." It represents an essential concept in human life, and the Bible mentions it more than one hundred times.

What does "repent" mean? In English, and the Latin from which much of it comes, "re" means "again," and "pent" means "think." So "re-pent" means to "think again," or to "rethink" something. In the Hebrew of the Old Testament, the word translated "repent" means to "return," with the implication that it means "return to God." In the Greek of the New Testament, the words translated "repent" mean "regret" and "reconsider."

So when we repent, we turn away from our sins and toward God, rethinking or reconsidering what we've been thinking and doing in the light of what He wants us to think and do. We are sorry for having offended Him, and we have an intention to change our ways, with His help. At the same time that we repent, we have an urge to cast away everything in our lives that invites us to do the things we're repenting of, and we determine, with God's help, not to return to that mess. God likens a return to sin after repentance and receiving God's cleansing forgiveness to returning to vomit or to a pig sty:

> But it is happened unto them according to the true proverb, The dog *is* turned to his own vomit again; and the sow that was washed to her wallowing in the mire. (*2 Peter 2:22*)

Simultaneously, we are placing our faith and trust in Jesus as our Savior. In other words, repentance and faith go hand in hand.

And this is how we are saved from being declared "guilty": As we repent and believe, we become new creatures born into God's family, and we are no longer under the condemnation of the Law.

Let's see what else the Bible says about this:

> I tell you, Nay: but, except ye repent, ye shall all likewise perish. (*Luke 13:3*)
>
> I say unto you, that likewise joy shall be in heaven over one sinner that repenteth, more than over ninety and nine just persons, which need no repentance. (*Luke 15:7*)
>
> I came not to call the righteous, but sinners to repentance. (*Luke 5:32*)
>
> And I gave her space to repent of her fornication; and she repented not.
>
> Behold, I will cast her into a bed, and them that commit adultery with her into great tribulation, except they repent of their deeds. (*Revelation 2:21–22*)
>
> And the rest of the men which were not killed by these plagues yet repented not of the works of their hands, that they should not worship devils, and idols of gold, and silver, and brass, and stone, and of wood: which neither can see, nor hear, nor walk:
>
> Neither repented they of their murders, nor of their sorceries, nor of their fornication, nor of their thefts. (*Revelation 9:20–21*)
>
> From that time Jesus began to preach, and to say, Repent: for the kingdom of heaven is at hand. (*Matthew 4:17*)

Jesus had all of eternity to think about what His first words would be when His ministry began. You know how important it is to say the right thing right at the start. That's why Jesus' first words in His public ministry were, "…repent ye, and believe the Gospel" (*Mark 1:15*).

So why did He choose "repent"?

> The Lord is not slack concerning his promise, as some men count slackness; but is longsuffering to us-ward, not willing that any should perish, but that all should come to repentance. (*2 Peter 3:9*)
>
> Repent ye therefore, and be converted, that your sins may be blotted out, when the times of refreshing shall come from the presence of the Lord; (*Acts 3:19*)

> But shewed first unto them of Damascus, and at Jerusalem, and throughout all the coasts of Judaea, and *then* to the Gentiles, that they should repent and turn to God, and do works meet for repentance. (*Acts 26:20*)
>
> And the times of this ignorance God winked at; but now commandeth all men every where to repent: (*Acts 17:30*)
>
> In meekness instructing those that oppose themselves; if God peradventure will give them repentance to the acknowledging of the truth. (*2 Timothy 2:25*)
>
> Now I rejoice, not that ye were made sorry, but that ye sorrowed to repentance: for ye were made sorry after a godly manner, that ye might receive damage by us in nothing.
>
> For godly sorrow worketh repentance to salvation not to be repented of: but the sorrow of the world worketh death. (*2 Corinthians 7:9–10*)

Being sorry that you got caught at something is not repentance.

Being sorry that you got caught at something is not repentance. "Repentance" in Greek, which is what the New Testament was written in, carries a strong indication of change. A change of heart and mind. A change in what you want to do.

Salvation is not: Drink beer, use drugs, have illicit sex, cheat on tests, disobey your parents, commit your life to Jesus Christ. Then drink beer, use drugs, have illicit sex, cheat on tests, disobey your parents. When you repent, there is visible change in your life. Your rethinking and regretting and reconsidering result in a change in the way you think and behave because when Jesus moves into a life, that life changes.

Once you are saved, you may still struggle with temptations, but with Jesus there to help you, you will overcome the temptations. So there will be changes in your life. You will avoid the things that used to separate you from God. You will want a different life.

My high-school buddies look at my life now and tell me that I am so different they hardly know me. They can see changes on the *outside* because of what has changed on the *inside* of me — my heart and mind! I changed my thoughts toward God, and He has been changing me to be what He wants me to be.

There are two distinct stages to repentance. Let me illustrate it this way: You're sitting astride your camel, baking in the sweltering heat, surrounded by the hot desert sand. The rest of the caravan is stretched out behind you, wondering why you've stopped. As you scan the horizon, you come to the inescapable conclusion that this is not the direction you need to go. That's the first stage. Next, in stage two, you turn your mount around and make your way back through the muttering crowd.... Repentance is not complete or valid until you turn your camel around.

Charles Spurgeon said:

> A man may hate sin just as a murderer hates the gallows, but this does not prove repentance. If I hate sin because of the punishment, I have not repented of sin. I merely regret that God is just. But if I can see sin as an offense against Jesus Christ, and loathe myself because I have wounded Him, then I have a true brokenness of heart. [82]

Consequences alone should not cause repentance. Offending God should make me want to make drastic changes in my life. We should want to leave that sinful life behind us. Do you? Do you want a changed life that will glorify God? Do you want all your sins to be forgiven? Do you want God to start preparing you for a life in heaven for eternity?

Charles Spurgeon said:

> To hate sin because it caused the brow of Christ to be girt with the thorn crown, and the face of Christ to be dishonored with the spittle, and the hands of Christ to be pierced with the nail — this is repentance — not because I am afraid of hell, not because sin brings pains and penalties with it, but because it made Jesus Christ to suffer for me such pangs unutterable.[83]

Traveling and speaking is always an adventure. I have spoken at the University of Florida several times. There are usually 600–700 college students at the talks, which always makes for a good time.

One time, I was leaving Florida for Los Angeles the morning after my talk. I had to get there in time for a live TV show. As I got to the airport in Florida, everything seemed fine. However, I soon learned that the fog had something to say about the situation! The plane I needed to get on wouldn't land because it was just too foggy. Due to the delay, I arrived late in Atlanta, where I needed to change planes for LA, and you guessed it: I arrived at the gate just as my plane was pulling away!

I was not happy!

After talking with the agents, I learned I could still get to LA on time, but I would have to land at a different airport. Now unless you know LA airport locations and traffic, that may not mean much to you. But after landing, I would have to get all the way across LA *during rush hour*, to make it in time for the show.

> *A man may hate sin just as a murderer hates the gallows, but this does not prove repentance. If I hate sin because of the punishment, I have not repented of sin. I merely regret that God is just. But if I can see sin as an offense against Jesus Christ, and loathe myself because I have wounded Him, then I have a true brokenness of heart.*
>
> — Charles Spurgeon

So I called the show's producers and asked them if they wanted me to cancel. They said to give it a shot and they would get me on at the end of the show. As we landed in LA, a driver from the studio picked me up and began to drive me toward the shoot location. His name was Anakhanda. He was from the Bahamas. I began to chat with him. As he drove, I asked him, "Who was the rudest person you have ever driven around before?" He told me that he couldn't say. But he eventually did, and it was a very famous celebrity.

One of the things he told me was that in his business, he is not allowed to talk to the client first. The client must make the first statement. He stated that many people never even say a word to him. To me, that is a sad commentary on the way we live our lives with those around us because it indicates that we do not realize the value of each person we see.

Think about it: What is a soul worth? God's answer to Jeremiah was:

> Before I formed thee in the belly I knew thee; and before thou camest forth out of the womb I sanctified thee, *and* I ordained thee a prophet unto the nations. (*Jeremiah 1:5*)

That was God's answer to Jeremiah, and His answer to you about the worth of *your* soul as well. It is just as loving and just as important.

Before God formed you in your mother's womb, He knew you! That's how He knew to make your body a proper reflection of your soul and a proper vehicle for His plan for your life.

You are so incredibly valuable to Him.

God said He made mankind in His own image and likeness:

> And God said, Let us make man in our image, after our likeness: and let them have dominion over the fish of the sea, and over the fowl of the air, and over the cattle, and over all the earth, and over every creeping thing that creepeth upon the earth. (*Genesis 1:26*)

Being made in the image of God is something that you should not take lightly. Every soul is of infinite value to God:

> For thou hast possessed my reins: thou hast covered me in my mother's womb.
>
> I will praise thee; for I am fearfully *and* wonderfully made: marvellous *are* thy works; and *that* my soul knoweth right well.
>
> My substance was not hid from thee, when I was made in secret, *and* curiously wrought in the lowest parts of the earth.
>
> Thine eyes did see my substance, yet being unperfect; and in thy book *all my* members were written, *which* in continuance were fashioned, when *as yet there was* none of them. (*Psalm 139:13–16*)

You are fearfully and wonderfully made in the eyes of Almighty God, no matter what anyone else might think or say.

During my conversation with Anakhanda, my driver, I asked him the question, "When you die, what do you think is out there when you walk out of here?"

That opened up an amazing conversation. He grew up half-Christian and half-Muslim. So we had this great talk as we traveled across the highways of LA. When I got to the point of mentioning repentance, he told me that he was sick of his life and wanted a change, and he knew it was time for it.

Later, as we talked, he called out to God and repented of his sins, confessing his faith in Jesus as his Savior. You could literally see the transformation on his face after we prayed. "Likewise, I say unto you, there is joy in the presence of the angels of God over one sinner that repenteth." (*Luke 15:10*)

He told me that he knew that God had sent me to talk with him that day. Now think about that. To meet this guy, I had to miss a plane flight, go to a different airport, and get the right driver out of them all. That is called a divine appointment. It wasn't by chance; we were supposed to meet because the God of this universe had set up this meeting.

Yes, God does that many times. Is it a divine appointment that you are reading this book right now? Truth has been laid before your eyes. Are you ready to repent and commit your life to Jesus?

Your appointment with God will come along one day. Do you want to make sure that you are right with Him *before* you meet Him? Before you finish this book, you will have that opportunity. Are you ready to put your life in God's hands and trust Him to do better for you than you could ever do for yourself? Are you ready to turn away from sin and get ready to go to Him? If so, some amazing news awaits you.

The mystery of eternal truth is coming into focus, and will be completely solved in the next chapter.

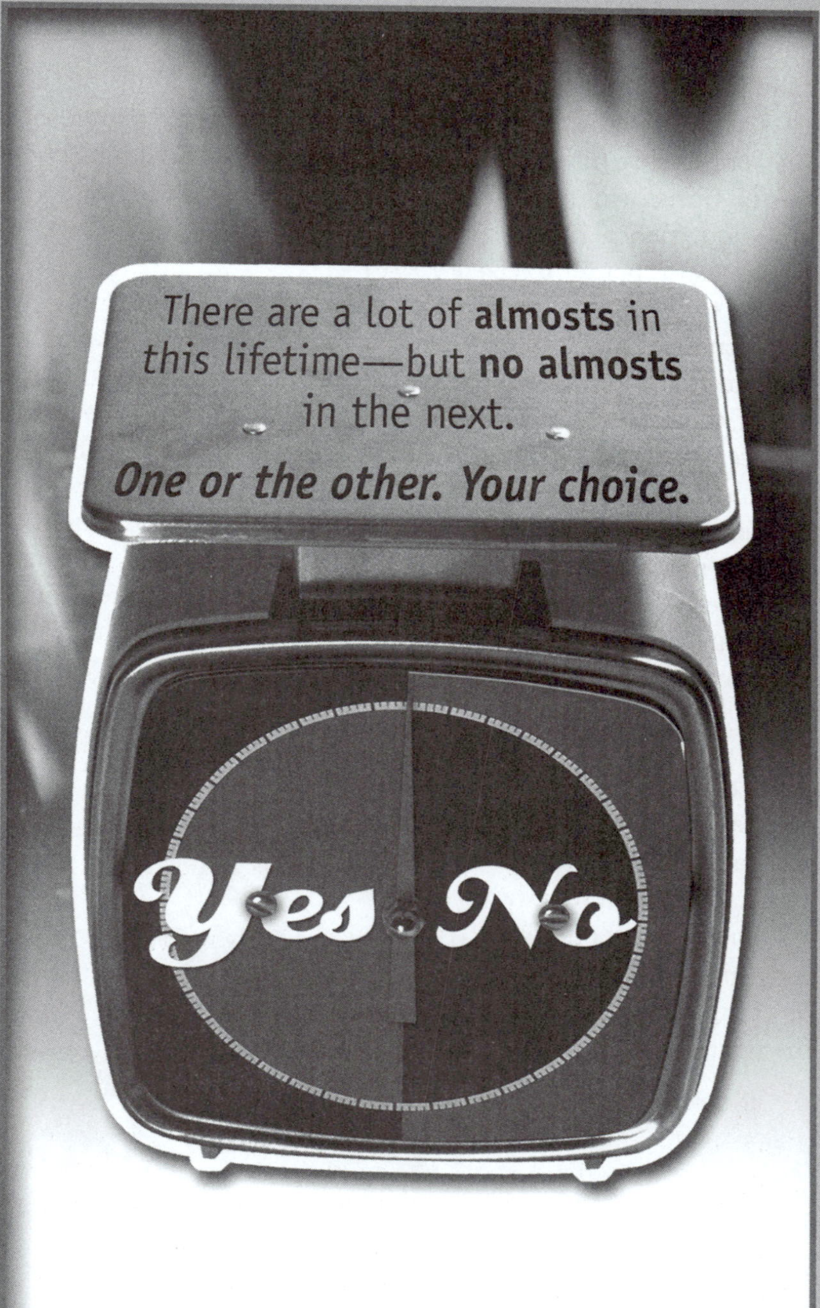
There are a lot of **almosts** in this lifetime—but **no almosts** in the next.
One or the other. Your choice.
Yes
No

Chapter 9
Decisions, Decisions

Christianity has not been tried and found wanting.
It has been found difficult and left untried.
— G. K. Chesterton

Timothy McVeigh said something very interesting before he died. His last words were, "I am the master of my fate. I am the captain of my soul." He was quoting from the poem *Invictus*. He was right in the sense that he got to make the decision where he would be spending eternity. But he was completely wrong if he thought he was in control for all of eternity. The God of the Bible is. However, He does allow you to decide who or what you will worship. By the way, what is your decision going to be?

One of Frank Sinatra's most famous songs was called, *I Did It My Way*. But my way, your way — nobody's way but God's way is going to cut it on Judgment Day. Are you ready to do it God's way? We all walk to the edge of the canyon of death. We all step off the edge. The only question is: Do you have the right parachute? Do you have the parachute that will softly land you in heaven? Or will your parachute not open, landing you in hell with a thud?

Some people think they will live this life the way they choose and then, when they are old, they will get right with God. But here's something to think about: Whether you are old or young isn't determined by your age, but by when you die. If you are 18, and you are going to die at age 80, you have a lot of life left. So, relatively speaking, you are still a very young person. But if you are 18 and you are going to die a week from now, then relative to your lifespan, you are very old. We think "old" people have walkers or wheelchairs, but that's not necessarily the case. It depends on when you die. That means you don't know if you are old or young, no matter what age you are. I have a simple question for you: Can you guarantee that you are going to wake up tomorrow morning? Of course, you know you can't guarantee that. The Bible says:

The choice is yours. Everyone has to make a choice, one way or the other. "Sitting on the fence" isn't really an option because Satan owns the fence.

> For yourselves know perfectly that the day of the Lord so cometh as a thief in the night. (*1 Thessalonians 5:2*)

Since you may not have tomorrow, make today your day of salvation.

> ... behold, now is the accepted time; behold, now is the day of salvation. (*2 Corinthians 6:2*)

You shouldn't put your head on your pillow tonight unless you know for certain that heaven is your eternal destination after you take your last breath.

As I was talking with a nineteen-year-old construction worker, I asked him what he liked to do for fun. He said he was a building jumper, so I asked what that was. "You know, like you see on TV, when people jump from the top of one building to another one," he replied. "It's a real rush."

I'll bet it is! Since I like to ask people questions, I asked him, "Have you ever missed?"

"Once," he said. He explained that one time when he jumped, he got only his fingers over the ledge of the building, and his body slammed against the wall. He hung there for a moment, and had barely enough energy to pull himself over the top of the building to safety.

Each one of us will get to the edge of death at some point in our lives. We are all hanging by our fingertips, one breath away from eternity. The problem is that we will *not* have enough strength on our own to pull ourselves "over the top." Only the nail-pierced hand of God can reach down and pull us to eternal safety. Are you ready to grab that hand now in order to make sure you are safe for all eternity?

To go to hell for eternity, all you have to do is nothing. You are born with a nature bent on rejecting God's commandments, so unless you do something to deal with that fact, hell is your default destination. But Jesus has arranged for you to go to heaven. He has paid for your sins, and paved the way. So to go to hell, do nothing. To go to heaven, turn to Jesus and "repent, confess, and get rid of your mess," as the old preacher used to say. The choice is yours. Everyone has to make a choice, one way or the other. "Sitting on the fence" isn't really an option because Satan owns the fence. Not choosing is, by default, choosing hell.

> For God sent not his Son into the world to condemn the world; but that the world through him might be saved.
>
> He that believeth on him is not condemned: but he that believeth not is condemned already, because he hath not believed in the name of the only begotten Son of God. (*John 3:17–18*)

Jesus says that non-belief is a decision to reject Him. Such a decision makes no sense after all the evidence that has been presented to you in this book. In fact, it is really difficult to go to hell once you look at the evidence and recognize your sin and realize that you've been invited to heaven. On the other hand, you don't have an invitation to go to hell, so why don't you go ahead and cash in the invitation to go to heaven?

But there is something else you need to know before you make that decision. God doesn't promise that everything will become smooth in your life and that there will not be any problems once you surrender your life to Jesus. Yes, the Bible promises over and over that God will forgive your sins and "provide all your needs according to His riches in glory" (*Philippians 4:19*). Still, following Jesus is not about life-enhancement. But then why does He make such promises as the following?

> And Jesus answered and said, Verily I say unto you, There is no man that hath left house, or brethren, or sisters, or father, or mother, or wife, or children, or lands, for my sake, and the gospel's,
>
> But he shall receive an hundredfold now in this time, houses, and brethren, and sisters, and mothers, and children, and lands, with persecutions; and in the world to come, eternal life. (*Mark 10:29–30*)

This seems to promise material abundance, but what is it really saying? It is giving us an important cluster of information that should help us cope with this world while we're here:

First, we are told that we can't lose by walking away from our worldly possessions for Jesus' sake. That is, if it's a choice between keeping close to Jesus or keeping close to our family, friends, and possessions, and we choose Jesus, He will restore everything we lost to us — and more. Many have seen and experienced this. And he will do it "now in this time." We don't hate our family and friends or want to lose our stuff, but if it's a choice between them and Jesus — and it's odd how the world often confronts believers with these choices — we can know that Jesus will see to it that we are blessed with much more than what we lost: "houses, and brethren, and sisters, and mothers, and children, and lands."

One way this is fulfilled is that when you are born into the Body of Christ, everyone already in it becomes your brother, sister, mother, father, and so on. And their homes, in a sense, become your homes. Read the Bible and see how often it says godly people were dining or visiting with people not of their family. Life in Jesus is a life of abundant provision. Not money in the bank so that we can say, "Hey, look what I've got!" but a sure supply of all we need.

So where does the difficulty come from? Reread that passage, and notice that little phrase "with persecutions." What does that mean? It means that people who are on the broad path that leads to destruction, spoken of by Jesus, will be raised up against us.

> Persecutions, afflictions, which came unto me at Antioch, at Iconium, at Lystra; what persecutions I endured: but out of *them* all the Lord delivered me.
>
> Yea, and all that will live godly in Christ Jesus shall suffer persecution. (*2 Timothy 3:11–12*)

Not everyone all the time. But from time to time, it happens. And the more we live life as unto the Lord, the more our lives are a testimony to the goodness of God, and the wickedness of people who hate God. Though we can expect people to reject us because of our faith in Jesus, we can also expect God to protect us and rescue us. Jesus said:

> ... when they persecute you in this city, flee ye into another: for verily I say unto you, Ye shall not have gone over the cities of Israel, till the Son of man be come.
>
> The disciple is not above his master, nor the servant above his lord. It is enough for the disciple that he be as his master, and the servant as his lord. If they have called the master of the house Beelzebub, how much more shall they call them of his household?
>
> Fear them not therefore: for there is nothing covered, that shall not be revealed; and hid, that shall not be known. (*Matthew 10:23–26*)

Persecution and tribulation follow those who truly live out their lives for Jesus. It is a promise. Why? This world is not in the business of glorifying God, and it does not want to change. Satan will also try to do anything to pull you away from your faith. I think he figures you will give Jesus Christ up and not follow the Son of God if he puts your faith to the test. But actually, it does just the opposite. The testing strengthens your faith.

Remember, never accept Jesus just in order to improve your life in this world. It is not about getting things in this life but about being right with the God we will stand in front of on Judgment Day. And during our time on earth, God gives us everything we need.

In fact, some of the persecution will come from ungodly religious people who are jealous of how happy you are and of how blessed you are in things of the Spirit, as well as in things of the world — those houses, lands, friends and family God gives you to replace the ones that fell away when you came to Jesus.

In other words, your life in Jesus may stir up envy in some who profess to believe in Jesus but don't. The temptation to hurt you, with gossip or any way they can think of, will be too much for them to resist.

There are only two possible relationships between a believer and any other person: ministry and fellowship.

Fellowship is a relationship a believer can only have with another believer. It may include ministry from one to the other, but it also may include sharing deep thoughts and questions, and requests for prayer or advice.

We can have ministry with anyone, believer or unbeliever. Ministry means that we are friendly and interested in the person's eternal destiny and that we are looking for opportunities to speak with them about Jesus. My experience with the LA driver was one of ministry.

Fellowship is a relationship a believer can have only with another believer. It may include ministry from one to the other, but it also may include sharing deep thoughts and questions, and requests for prayer or advice. A believer can't do these things with an unbeliever because an unbeliever's advice will be based on worldly considerations rather than on the Presence of God speaking through one believer to the other. That's why Jesus warns us not to get too close to those who are yet His enemies:

> Give not that which is holy unto the dogs, neither cast ye your pearls before swine, lest they trample them under their feet, and turn again and rend you. (*Matthew 7:6*)

It's not that casting pearls before the unappreciative is a waste of pearls. God has more pearls where those came from. It is that these swine have tusks to disembowel those who approach too closely. So when we're tempted to treat unbelievers as though they were believers, it's really a bad idea. It will provoke them to attack us — either to our face or behind our back.

Persecution that we didn't provoke, except by our existence as a friend of Jesus, brings us blessing!

> Blessed *are* they which are persecuted for righteousness' sake: for theirs is the kingdom of heaven.
>
> Blessed are ye, when *men* shall revile you, and persecute *you*, and shall say all manner of evil against you falsely, for my sake.
>
> Rejoice, and be exceeding glad: for great *is* your reward in heaven: for so persecuted they the prophets which were before you. (*Matthew 5:10–12*)

James Emery White wrote:

> Christian spirituality isn't about sitting at the feet of some guru for a seminar at a retreat. It isn't about having a nice, comfortable, safe dose of spirituality in your life to make you feel good whenever your thoughts run deep about ultimate questions and eternal destinies.
>
> Jesus called people to follow Him — and there was only one place He was going: a cross. The true nature of spiritual living involves sacrifice, duty, and commitment.[84]

Persecution comes with the territory when you follow Jesus Christ, but without a doubt, He is worth it. Yes, some people may call you a "Jesus freak" or a "holy roller," but that is a small price to pay compared to what He did for you on that cross.

Some people are literally disowned by their family when they trust Jesus for the forgiveness of their sins. Some Muslim or Jewish families will no longer have anything to do with their son or daughter if they make that decision. That is a big price to pay. But eternity with the Son of God is worth it. Jesus tells us what to do at those times: "But I say to you, love your enemies and pray for those who persecute you" (*Matthew 5:44*). When you begin to pray for the people who persecute you, it changes how you look at them. And often it changes how they look at you!

I had friends who once were very close to me who don't return my phone calls anymore. That's OK. I make sure that I pray for them to become friends with Jesus. Friendship with Jesus is worth more than anything the world holds. And it is God's greatest gift to us:

> But and if ye suffer for righteousness' sake, happy *are ye*: and be not afraid of their terror, neither be troubled;
>
> But sanctify the Lord God in your hearts: and *be* ready always to *give* an answer to every man that asketh you a reason of the hope that is in you with meekness and fear:
>
> Having a good conscience; that, whereas they speak evil of you, as of evildoers, they may be ashamed that falsely accuse your good conversation in Christ. (*1 Peter 3:14–16*)

Many people say they are Jesus' friends, but their behavior tells the truth of the matter:

> And it came to pass, that, as they went in the way, a certain *man* said unto him, Lord, I will follow thee whithersoever thou goest. And Jesus said unto him, Foxes have holes, and birds of the air *have* nests; but the Son of man hath not where to lay *his* head.
>
> And he said unto another, Follow me. But he said, Lord, suffer me first to go and bury my father.
>
> Jesus said unto him, "Let the dead bury their dead: but go thou and preach the kingdom of God.
>
> And another also said, Lord, I will follow thee; but let me first go bid them farewell, which are at home at my house.
>
> And Jesus said unto him, "No man, having put his hand to the plow, and looking back, is fit for the kingdom of God. (*Luke 9:57–62*)

Jesus also said we would be heading for trouble when ungodly people praised us:

> Woe unto you, when all men shall speak well of you! For so did their fathers to the false prophets. (*Luke 6:26*)

What does "woe" mean? According to the Merriam-Webster Online Dictionary (www.m-w.com), it means:

> 1: a condition of deep suffering from misfortune, affliction, or grief
>
> 2 : ruinous trouble : CALAMITY, AFFLICTION <economic woes>

So in the verse above, Jesus is saying that if the Devil's crowd likes you, you are headed for suffering and destruction. If *they* like you, it's a sure sign you're on the wrong track.

Of course, the opposite is true: The devil's crowd is never going to like us if we are faithful to Jesus. We have to accept that not everyone will like us. In fact, we have to realize that when the devil's crowd is hostile to us, it means we must be doing something right! Other people's opinions of us don't really matter. It is only God's opinion that matters. Following Him is all that matters. You don't want the following verse to be a description of you:

> For they loved the praise of men more than the praise of God. (*John 12:43*)

Always remember that no matter how people treat you, God's way is not just the best way, it is the *only* way that leads to eternal life in heaven. And while people are speaking ill of you, God is praising you and is very proud of you!

One of my friends is a stand-up comic. I went to one of his shows. Part of his routine was to mock Jesus Christ. It was about a twenty-minute part of his set. After the show, he asked what I had been up to lately. Well, I told him that I had become a Christian, then explained what I was doing. He asked me what I thought about that twenty-minute part of his routine. I just told him that I didn't think it was a good thing to mock the Son of God. We continued to talk and had a good night hanging out together.

A couple of years later, I was in another city and brought some friends to see him perform. When he got to that part of the routine, he made his first Jesus joke. As he did it, he looked right at me to see what my reaction would be. I just sat there. I didn't laugh. It was not funny. And he could tell by looking at my face that I didn't think it was funny — at all.

Many people will appreciate your decision and react positively when you decide to stand for what you believe. They are not far from the Kingdom.

All of a sudden, he skipped that part and went into a different part of his routine. He didn't believe in Jesus yet — though I'm trusting that God will get his attention — but he respected my faith.

Many people will appreciate your decision and react positively when you decide to stand for what you believe. They are not far from the Kingdom.

> Remember the word that I said unto you, The servant is not greater than his lord. If they have persecuted me, they will also persecute you; if they have kept my saying, they will keep your's also. (*John 15:20*)
>
> And when he had called the people *unto him* with his disciples also, he said unto them, Whosoever will come after me, let him deny himself, and take up his cross, and follow me.
>
> For whosoever will save his life shall lose it; but whosoever shall lose his life for my sake and the Gospel's, the same shall save it. (*Mark 8:34–35*)

Your life can only be found in Jesus. Are you ready to lose your life for His sake? Paul was. Here is what he wrote:

> For God, who commanded the light to shine out of darkness, hath shined in our hearts, to *give* the light of the knowledge of the glory of God in the face of Jesus Christ.
>
> But we have this treasure in earthen vessels, that the excellency of the power may be of God, and not of us.
>
> *We are* troubled on every side, yet not distressed; *we are* perplexed, but not in despair;
>
> Persecuted, but not forsaken; cast down, but not destroyed;
>
> Always bearing about in the body the dying of the Lord Jesus, that the life also of Jesus might be made manifest in our body.
>
> For we which live are always delivered unto death for Jesus' sake, that the life also of Jesus might be made manifest in our mortal flesh. (*2 Corinthians 4:6–11*)

Recently I spoke at a church in Florida. One of the church members worked for the Post Office. Every Christmas he would give each customer a Christmas card with a nice, generic, loving Christian message. After hearing me speak, he knew he needed to be more specific with the message he was giving his customers. He prayed about it, and the Lord led him to write the question: "If you died tonight, are you 100 percent assured that you would go to heaven?" on each card.

That is a great question, and he got some positive feedback from customers. But one man didn't like it and called the letter carrier's boss. The customer was not satisfied with that conversation, so he went one level higher in the management hierarchy.

They were going to fire him for what he did until they realized that the only thing they could find against him was that he had delivered his cards without postage on them. So they came back with a one-week suspension instead. With pay!

That mailman knew without a doubt that the hand of God was protecting him through this whole process. He was so glad he took a stand for the Lord. He stated that this situation had touched many lives well beyond his own. He got to talk to many people about what had happened, and he got to share his faith with many of his customers. The persecution was worth it, he said, because he knew he had stood up for the truth and that God had helped him and many others through it!

Paul writes of the sufferings and triumphs of the Old Testament saints. Here is Paul's summary:

> And what shall I more say? for the time would fail me to tell of Gideon, and *of* Barak, and *of* Samson, and *of* Jephthae; *of* David also, and Samuel, and *of* the prophets:
>
> Who through faith subdued kingdoms, wrought righteousness, obtained promises, stopped the mouths of lions,
>
> quenched the violence of fire, escaped the edge of the sword, out of weakness were made strong, waxed valiant in fight, turned to flight the armies of the aliens.
>
> Women received their dead raised to life again: and others were tortured, not accepting deliverance; that they might obtain a better resurrection:
>
> And others had trial of *cruel* mockings and scourgings, yea, moreover of bonds and imprisonment:
>
> They were stoned, they were sawn asunder, were tempted, were slain with the sword: they wandered about in sheepskins and goatskins; being destitute, afflicted, tormented;
>
> (Of whom the world was not worthy:) they wandered in deserts, and *in* mountains, and *in* dens and caves of the earth.
>
> And these all, having obtained a good report through faith, received not the promise:
>
> God having provided some better thing for us, that they without us should not be made perfect. (*Hebrews 11:32–40*)

These faithful saints eventually triumphed by entering the Kingdom of heaven, ushered in by Jesus Himself — what a great day that was for them!

Too many Christians live their lives trying to fit into this world. I want to live a life that is worthy in the eyes of God, not in the eyes of the world. I'm not seeking trouble, by any means. But when it comes to taking a stand, I want always to stand for Jesus. I want Him to be proud of me:

> Great *is* my boldness of speech toward you, great *is* my glorying of you: I am filled with comfort, I am exceeding joyful in all our tribulation. (*2 Corinthians 7:4*)

> Yea doubtless, and I count all things *but* loss for the excellency of the knowledge of Christ Jesus my Lord: for whom I have suffered the loss of all things, and do count them *but* dung, that I may win Christ, (*Philippians 3:8*)

Here is a letter I received from a friend, telling how she dared to tell a young woman about Jesus:

> My friend Brandon and I were walking home from a coffee shop at 10 am when we passed a girl and said "Hi" to her. Well, we had not even walked a few steps past her when I felt that I needed to turn around, so I did.
>
> I asked her if she was okay, and she said, "No, I just need to find Jesus Christ!" Well, needless to say we were a bit taken aback by that answer! So we asked her to walk to the park with us to talk. We sat down and listened to her story.
>
> Her name was Heidi and she had been in jail, was taking drugs, and was struggling with homosexuality. In all of this she has always believed in God, but that morning she felt like she was going to meet Jesus. So she had been walking up to random homes, churches, and people asking how to find Jesus!
>
> We shared from the Bible with her and … she gave her life over to Christ right there in the park! Can I just say that the angels were throwing a party along with Brandon and me.
>
> She then came to my home and flushed her drugs down the toilet, smashed her pipe, and spent the next 24 hours with us as we talked with her, and listened to her, and ministered to her. It was INCREDIBLE!!!!

Would you have been courageous enough to do what these young people did? You can never tell when there is someone right near you who is aching to learn about Jesus. But if you fear rejection and the opinions of men, you will shrug off that feeling that you should tell someone about Jesus, and pass them by. You will let them go on into hell because you were afraid or ashamed to tell them about Jesus. Please don't let that happen.

In a publication from Voice of the Martyrs — a ministry that informs people about the millions of Christians who have died for their faith, or who are being persecuted for their faith — we read the story of Soon Ok Lee:

"I never knew what these prisoners were singing until I became a Christian."

Soon Ok Lee was a prisoner in North Korea from 1987 to 1992. She did not become a Christian, however, until she escaped to South Korea. When she first received Christ, she was overwhelmed by her memories of what she had seen and heard in prison.

They were simple things, like the Christians who sang as they were being put to death. At that time, she did not understand and had thought they were crazy. She was not allowed to talk, so she never had the chance to speak with a Christian. She does remember hearing the word "Amen."

"While I was there, I never saw Christians deny their faith. Not one. When these Christians were silent, the officers would become furious and kick them. At the time, I could not understand why they risked their lives when they could have said, 'I do not believe,' and have done what the officers wanted."

"I even saw many who sang hymns as the kicking and hitting intensified. The officers would call them crazy and take them to the electric-treatment room. I didn't see one come out alive."

It was the singing that stuck with her. Perhaps it was the singing of these precious saints that planted a seed in her spirit and eventually led her to Christ.

Like spies, those who are curious about Christianity zero in on believers so that they can evaluate the truth for themselves. They observe. They watch. They take mental notes. Whenever Christians go through trials, these silent observers often hope to see the believers fall, so that they can assure themselves that Christians are like everyone else after all.

However, when Christians smile through trouble, they are stumped. When believers clap instead of cry, they are amazed. When Christ followers sing amidst sorrow, they are drawn in by what they cannot explain.[85]

God is with His people:

Remembering without ceasing your work of faith, and labour of love, and patience of hope in our Lord Jesus Christ, in the sight of God and our Father. (*1 Thessalonians 1:3*)

Here is another incredible testimony of faith. Few believers are so tested, but those who are, including children and women, generally live up to this standard. We have to know God is at work, showing their tormentors that Jesus is real:

"Break him morally or destroy him physically!"

The Turkmenistan bureaucrats had no more patience for this street preacher. Shageldy Atakov was offered his freedom under President Saparmurat Niyazov's December 23, 2000 amnesty, provided he would swear the oath of allegiance to the president and recite the Muslim creed. Shageldy refused the amnesty — again.

Shageldy had been threatened by state officials before to stop preaching. He was arrested in December 1998 and sentenced to two years in jail, but a prosecutor appealed the verdict as "too lenient." He was then sentenced to two additional years in prison. Shageldy was in such pain from the harsh beatings that he asked his children not to touch him.

In February 2000, his wife and five children had been forcibly taken from their home and exiled to remote Kaakhka where they remained under "village arrest."

When his family visited him in early February of 2001, Shageldy said his farewells. His wife noticed that "during the visit [that] he was bruised and battered, his kidneys and liver hurt, and he was suffering from jaundice. He could barely walk and frequently lost consciousness." He did not expect to survive much longer.

Despite this, Shageldy was still not broken. He would not give in, and though release was within his reach, he would not accept it if it meant forsaking his allegiance to Christ.

Humans can live for many weeks without food, yet we cannot survive many days without water. In the same way, our spirits need spiritual nourishment as well. We may go several days, months, and even years without companionship — our spirits can survive despite loneliness. We may do without peace, enduring illness upon lingering illness — our spirits, though discouraged, will survive.

If we try to endure long without the hope of Jesus Christ, however, our souls diminish. We cannot live without hope, God's precious gift to His children. If you are feeling as though you cannot go on, ask God to encourage and motivate you. You will endure all things with a strong hope in Jesus Christ.[86]

As odd as this may sound, the death of His children is precious to God:

Precious in the sight of the Lord is the death of his saints. (*Psalm 116:15*)

And I heard a loud voice saying in heaven, Now is come salvation, and strength, and the kingdom of our God, and the power of His Christ: for

> the accuser of our brethren is cast down, which accused them before our God day and night.
>
> And they overcame him by the blood of the Lamb, and by the word of their testimony; and they loved not their lives unto the death. (*Revelation 12:10–11*)

Humans can live for many weeks without food, yet we cannot survive many days without water. In the same way, our spirits need spiritual nourishment.

Most of us will not have to suffer to that extent, even though many are suffering just like that for God around the world today in many places. It only makes sense to let you know some of the consequences that may arise before you make that decision to follow Jesus. But making that decision for Jesus is definitely worth the temporary, earthly persecution, especially when you compare it to what He has waiting for those who believe, once we walk out of here.

But all the rewards aren't just on the other side. When you see someone who has persecuted you come to a saving knowledge of Jesus Christ, it makes all the persecution well worth it in this lifetime! In Acts, chapter 17, the apostle Paul is preaching at Mars Hill in Athens. As he preaches about the resurrection of Jesus, there is an interesting response from the crowd. Some in the crowd mock him, some hesitate, and some believe.

That is exactly what happens today. If we make the choice to stand up for Jesus, some will mock us, some will hesitate, and some will believe. We must make that choice.

And remember, *not* to choose *is* to choose. People may think they are just sitting on the fence, not making a decision for God or for Satan, but as I said before, *Satan owns the fence.* You either choose to love Jesus Christ, or you choose to reject Him — one or the other.

Many people have watched one of the Crime Scene Investigation TV shows. The CSI shows have been highly rated since they came on the air. They do something very interesting on that show. They don't tell you who they think the culprit is in the first five minutes. They take a look at the evidence for about fifty-five minutes and see where it leads, and then at the end of the show they show you the person to whom the evidence led them.

Now that you have seen the evidence that has been laid out in this book, are you ready to make a commitment to the one the evidence has led you to: Jesus?

The Bible records (*Acts 25 and 26*) that Paul was trying to persuade King Agrippa of the truth of Jesus Christ. King Agrippa told Paul that he almost persuaded him to become a Christian. King Agrippa almost became a Christian that night.

You *almost* got a 4.0. You *almost* scored the last-second shot in that basketball game. You *almost* got that job. You *almost* won the lottery. There are a lot of "almosts" in this lifetime — but no "almosts" in the next. You won't *almost* make it to heaven. You won't *almost* commit your life to Jesus Christ. You either make that decision or you don't. One or the other. Your choice.

On the subject of "almosts," Charles Spurgeon said:

> There was a man who was almost saved in a fire, but he was burned. There was another who was almost healed of a disease, but he died. There was one who was almost reprieved, but he was hanged. And there are many in hell who were almost saved.[87]

In 1 Kings 18:21, we read:

> And Elijah came unto all the people, and said, "How long halt ye between two opinions? If the Lord be God, follow him; but if Baal, then follow him." And the people answered him not a word.

Who are *you* going to follow — Jesus or Satan? Jesus wants you to forsake all and follow Him. Don't do what the people did when Elijah challenged them to come down on one side or the other: "They answered him not a word"; they said nothing.

However, *indecision is an answer.* It means that you will not follow the Lord. Please be a follower of Jesus — for your eternal sake.

Spurgeon also said:

> We are lost willfully and willingly; lost perversely and utterly; but still lost of our own accord, which is the worst kind of being lost.

> We are lost to God, who has lost our heart's love, confidence, and obedience; lost to the church, which we cannot serve; lost to truth, which we will not see; lost to right, whose cause we do not uphold; lost to heaven, into whose sacred precincts we can never come; lost, so lost that unless almighty mercy shall intervene, we shall be cast into the pit that is bottomless to sink forever.
>
> Lost! Lost! Lost! Better a whole world on fire than a soul lost! Better every star quenched and the skies a wreck than a single soul to be lost.[88]

Read the following two prayers, and decide which one best describes you. Even if you don't consciously pray either one of them, you really are praying the first one by default — because when you put this book down, you will be serving someone. The only question is, whom will you be serving?

> **Dear Satan,**
>
> The Bible tells me that you are the god of this world and the father of lies. You deceive the nations and blind the minds of those who do not believe.
>
> God warns that I cannot enter His kingdom because I have sinned. I have lied and stolen; looked with lust, thereby committing adultery in my heart. I have harbored hatred, which the Bible says is the same as murder. I have blasphemed, refused to put God first, violated the Sabbath, coveted other people's goods, dishonored my parents, and I am guilty of the sin of idolatry — I have made a god to suit myself.
>
> I did all this despite the presence of my conscience. I know that it was God who gave me life. I have seen a sunrise. I have heard the sounds of nature. I have enjoyed an incredible array of pleasures, all of which came from His generous hand. I realize that if I die in my sins, I will never know pleasure again.
>
> I know that Jesus Christ shed His life's blood for my sins and rose again to destroy the power of death, but today I refuse to confess and forsake my sins.
>
> On the Day of Judgment, when I am cast into the lake of fire, I will have no one to blame but myself. It is not God's will that I perish. He showed His love for me in the death of His Son, who came to give me life. It was you, Satan, who came to steal, kill, and destroy. You are my spiritual father. I choose to continue to serve you and do your will. This is because I love the darkness and hate the light.
>
> If I do not come to my senses, I will be eternally yours. Amen.

* * *

Dear God,

I have sinned against You by breaking Your commandments. Despite the conscience You gave me, I have looked with lust and therefore committed adultery in my heart. I have lied, stolen, failed to love You, failed to love my neighbor as myself, and failed to keep the Sabbath holy.

I have been covetous, and I have harbored hatred in my heart, making me guilty of murder in Your sight. I have used Your holy name in vain, have made a god to suit myself, and because of the nature of my sin, I have dishonored my parents.

If I stood before You in Your burning holiness on Judgment Day, if every secret sin I have committed and every idle word I have spoken came out as evidence of my crimes against You, I would be utterly guilty, and justly deserve hell.

I am unspeakably thankful that Jesus took my place by suffering and dying on the cross. He was bruised for my iniquities. He paid my fine so that I could leave the courtroom. He revealed how much You love me. I believe that He then rose from the dead, according to the Scriptures.

I now confess and forsake my sin and yield myself to Jesus to be my Lord and Savior. I will no longer live for myself. I present my body, soul, and spirit to You as a living sacrifice, to serve You in the furtherance of Your kingdom. I will read Your Word daily and obey what I read. It is solely because of Calvary's cross that I will live forever.

I am eternally Yours.
In Jesus' name I pray. Amen.

Jesus tells us:

> No man can serve two masters: for either he will hate the one, and love the other; or else he will hold to the one, and despise the other. Ye cannot serve God and Mammon. (*Matthew 6:24*)

None of us can serve two masters. Whom will you choose to serve for the rest of this life and for all eternity? If you answer "Myself," you have given the same answer to that question as Satan did, so you will really be aligned with him, in this life and the next.

> And if it seem evil unto you to serve the Lord, choose you this day whom ye will serve; whether the gods which your fathers served that *were* on the other side of the flood, or the gods of the Amorites, in whose land ye dwell: But as for me and my house, we will serve the Lord. (*Joshua 24:15*)

Whom will you serve? In reality, you are serving someone right now. The ice is very thick, and now you must make a decision. You are sitting on that snowmobile with the ramp ahead. Are you ready to turn on the ignition, take that ride, and make that jump into eternal salvation? If so, then from the deepest part of your soul, pray one of those two preceding prayers right now, depending on which of the two commitments you want to make.

Charles Spurgeon said:

> Will you do me a favor?... Will you take a little time alone this evening, and after you have weighed your own condition before the Lord, write down one of two words? If you feel that you are not a believer, write down Condemned. And if you are a believer in Jesus and put your trust in Him alone, write down Forgiven.
>
> Do it, even if you have to write down the word Condemned. We received into a church fellowship a young man who said, "Sir, I wrote down the word Condemned, and I looked at it. There it was. I had written it myself: Condemned." As he looked, the tears began to flow and the heart began to break. And before long he fled to Christ, put the paper in the fire, and wrote down Forgiven.
>
> This young man was about the sixth who had been brought to the Lord in the same way. So I ask you to try it. Remember, you are either one or the other — condemned or forgiven. Do not stand between the two. Let it be decided. And remember, if you are condemned today, yet you are not in hell. There is still hope.[89]

Please let me know what decision you made.

You can email me at: Mydecision@markcahill.org
My hope and prayer is that you will choose to serve
the God of this universe with every fiber of your being.
I earnestly hope to see you in heaven one day!

...Christ in you, the hope of glory.
-Colossians 1:27

Chapter 10
Who Am I?

> Therefore, if any man be in Christ, he is a new creature: old things are passed away; behold, all things are become new.
> — Apostle Paul, 2 Corinthians 5:17

An amazing thing happens when you become a Christian. The things you once loved, you now hate, and the things you once hated, you now love. Think about it, as the journey to serve the King continues.

If you have *not* made that decision to follow Jesus, read on to see what you will experience when you finally surrender your life to Him.

If you *have* made your decision for Jesus Christ, you are going to be amazed at what you read now. You are now officially a totally different person in God's eyes — a new creature in the eyes of God! You have been justified. The ransom has been paid in full. No debt remains to be paid for your sin. It is forgiven! You are a different person!

One guy put it this way:

> If you played football, you are as good as your talent and work level. But if one day Michael Vick came to live inside of you, look at the changes: You could run a 4.2 40-yard dash, you'd have lightning-quick moves, and an arm that could throw a football down the field with a flick of the wrist. You are now a totally different player. Why? Something changed on the inside.

This leaves out one thing: Having Michael Vick inside you wouldn't give you Michael Vick's body. So the *desire* to be great might be there, but would you have the *ability* to be great?

But when the Son of God is living inside of you, and has changed your life by what He did for you, life is truly worth living! Although Michael Vick living inside of you *might* change your life, you better believe that the Son of God WILL change your life in unimaginable ways, now that you believe in Him!

God tells us that:

> *Even* the mystery which hath been hid from ages and from generations, but now is made manifest to his saints:
>
> To whom God would make known what *is* the riches of the glory of this mystery among the Gentiles; which is Christ in you, the hope of glory: (*Colossians 1:26–27*)

You now have the Son of God living inside of you. You are going to be humbled by the changes that will be occurring in your life! Look at who you become as a follower of Jesus Christ:

> I am crucified with Christ: nevertheless I live; yet not I, but Christ liveth in me: and the life which I now live in the flesh I live by the faith of the Son of God, who loved me, and gave himself for me. (*Galatians 2:20*)

Jesus now lives in you and through you. As Spurgeon said:

> The more you reaffirm who you are in Christ, the more your behavior will begin to reflect your true identity![90]

Now take a look at who you have become! (from *Victory Over the Darkness*, by Dr. Neil Anderson.)

WHO AM I?

I am accepted...

- I am God's child: *John 1:12*
- I am Christ's friend: *John 15:15*
- I have been justified: *Romans 5:1*
- I am united with the Lord, and I am one spirit with Him: *1 Corinthians 6:17*
- I have been bought with a price. I belong to God: *1 Corinthians 6:19–20*
- I am a member of Christ's body: *1 Corinthians 12:27*
- I am a saint: *Ephesians 1:1*
- I have been adopted as God's child: *Ephesians 1:5*
- I have direct access to God through the Holy Spirit: *Ephesians 2:18*
- I have been redeemed and forgiven of all my sins: *Colossians 1:14*
- I am complete in Christ: *Colossians 2:10*

I am secure…

- I am free forever from condemnation: *Romans 8:1–2*
- I am assured that all things work together for good: *Romans 8:28*
- I am free from any condemning charges against me: *Romans 8:31–34*
- I cannot be separated from the love of God: *Romans 8:35–39*
- I have been established, anointed, and sealed by God: *2 Corinthians 1:21–22*
- I am hidden with Christ in God: *Colossians 3:3*
- I am confident that the good work God has begun in me will be perfected: *Philippians 1:6*
- I am a citizen of Heaven: *Philippians 3:20*
- I have not been given a spirit of fear, but of power, love, and a sound mind: *2 Timothy 1:7*
- I can find grace and mercy in time of need: *Hebrews 4:16*
- I am born of God, and the Evil One cannot touch me: *1 John 5:18*

I am significant…

- I am the salt and light of the earth: *Matthew 5:13–14*
- I am a branch of the true vine, a channel of His life: *John 15:1,5*
- I have been chosen and appointed to bear fruit: *John 15:16*
- I am a personal witness of Christ's: *Acts 1:8*
- I am God's temple: *1 Corinthians 3:16*
- I am a minister of reconciliation to God: *2 Corinthians 5:17–21*
- I am God's co-worker: *2 Corinthians 6:1*
- I am seated with Christ in the Heavenly realm: *Ephesians 2:6*
- I am God's workmanship: *Ephesians 2:10*
- I may approach God with freedom and confidence: *Ephesians 3:12*
- I can do all things through Christ who strengthens me: *Philippians 4:13*[91]

All this is the literal result of the transformation that takes place within a believer in Jesus. The power of God to change us is startling.

Once you know who you are in the eyes of God as one of His followers, the next question is: What does He want to do through me? You are going to feel humbled by the glorious plans that God has for you in this life. ***Read on!***

The Potter wants
to mold our lives
for us because
He has great
things to do
in and through
us...

Chapter 11
Reflect the Light of the Son

Though no one can go back and make a brand new start,
anyone can start from now and make a brand new ending.
— Anonymous

Now that you have been justified, it is time to become sanctified. What that means is that God is in the business of molding and shaping you into the man or woman of God that He wants you to be. The analogy in the Bible is of a potter and clay:

> But now, O Lord, thou *art* our father; we *are* the clay, and thou our potter; and we all *are* the work of thy hand. (*Isaiah 64:8*)

Just as a potter sits at a potter's wheel and molds the clay into what he wants it to be, God wants to mold our lives and do great things in us and through us while we are still here on earth.

If the potter doesn't like what the clay is becoming, he doesn't throw the clay away; he just pushes it down and starts forming it into what he *does* want it to be. It's the same way with God. He doesn't throw His children away when we do something wrong. Instead, He puts a desire into our hearts to humble ourselves — to push ourselves down and repent to Him. Then He starts to reshape us.

This is where the fun is in following God. As He continues that shaping process, we become more and more fulfilled in our individuality. And at the same time, we become more like Him. Then we're on a journey to become so obedient to Him that He can use us in ways that we cannot even imagine at this moment in our lives!

Charles Spurgeon said:

> It is remarkable that the Holy Spirit has given us very few deathbed scenes in the book of God. We have very few in the Old Testament, fewer still in the New. And I take it that the reason may be, because the Holy Ghost would have us take more account of how we live than how we die, for life is the main business. He who learns to die daily while he lives will find it

> no difficulty to breathe out his soul for the last time into the hands of his faithful Creator.[92]

Paul, speaking of his experience of meeting the glorified Jesus on the road to Damascus, said he couldn't stop telling people about Jesus:

> But shewed first unto them of Damascus, and at Jerusalem, and throughout all the coasts of Judaea, and *then* to the Gentiles, that they should repent and turn to God, and do works meet for repentance. (*Acts 26:20*)

As with Paul, now that you are saved, God wants to work through you, to make your life a true reflection of repentance and faith. Once you repent and receive Jesus, the Spirit of God is in you, and your gratitude for what He has done and will do for you will fill you with a desire to do great deeds for Him.

What you truly believe is what drives you to action. Now it is time for action:

> They profess that they know God; but in works they deny *him*, being abominable, and disobedient, and unto every good work reprobate. (*Titus 1:16*)
>
> For the love of Christ constraineth us; because we thus judge, that if one died for all, then were all dead:
>
> And *that* he died for all, that they which live should not henceforth live unto themselves, but unto him which died for them, and rose again.
>
> Wherefore henceforth know we no man after the flesh: yea, though we have known Christ after the flesh, yet now henceforth know we *him* no more.
>
> Therefore if any man *be* in Christ, *he is* a new creature: old things are passed away; behold, all things are become new. (*2 Corinthians 5:14–17*)
>
> For we are his workmanship, created in Christ Jesus unto good works, which God hath before ordained that we should walk in them. (*Ephesians 2:10*)

God has created His people to live a life filled with good works. He wants you to live your life to glorify Him. For better or for worse, your works will attest to what and whom you love. One of my friends says, "You may not do what you say, but you *will* do what you believe." Our actions are determined by our beliefs. If I believe stealing is wrong, I won't do it. If I believe murder is wrong, I won't do it. If I believe helping the poor is right, I will do it. And now that you are a child of God, your works will show the love that you have for Him.

Charles Spurgeon said:

> I have now concentrated all my prayers into one, and that one prayer is this, that I may die to self, and live wholly to him.[93]

Our actions are determined by our beliefs. If I believe stealing is wrong, I won't do it. If I believe murder is wrong, I won't do it. If I believe helping the poor is right, I will do it.

You don't have to do the doing. You only have to be willing for Him to do the doing through you. Are you ready to give all that you've got for Him? It is the only way to live this life.

During the scandal about the moral character of President Clinton, Alan Keyes commented on the situation on a TV show, and he made a very interesting observation. He said that the president claimed that these things were part of his personal life and did not affect his job as president.

Mr. Keyes said that the president of the United States is the leader of the free world. Once you accept a job of that magnitude, you are president twenty-four hours a day, seven days a week. In fact, you are never not the president of the United States.

Similarly, now that you have chosen to be a believer in Jesus Christ, you are a believer in Jesus Christ twenty-four hours a day, seven days a week. You are always a believer, and people will always be watching you — either hoping for you to fail or hoping for you to succeed.

> But, beloved, we are persuaded better things of you, and things that accompany salvation, though we thus speak.
>
> For God *is* not unrighteous to forget your work and labour of love, which ye have shewed toward his name, in that ye have ministered to the saints and do minister.
>
> And we desire that every one of you do shew the same diligence to the full assurance of hope unto the end:

That ye be not slothful, but followers of them who through faith and patience inherit the promises. (*Hebrews 6:9–13*)

If Jesus is living IN you, you don't have to wonder what His will is at any time. You can *just ask Him*. Read your Bible and ask Him to teach you His truth. If He is telling you to behave a certain way, ask Him to help you behave that way. And talk to Him all the time about everything. That's called "praying." Go to a Bible-believing fellowship or assembly of believers. Worship God when you're alone and when you're with other believers.

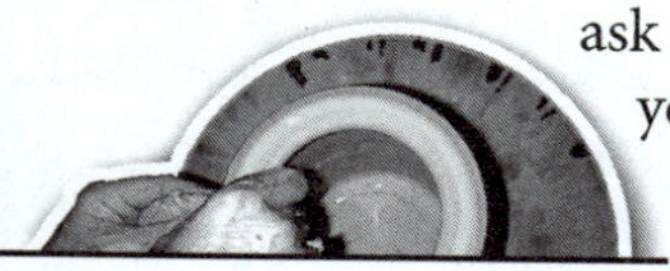

If Jesus is living IN you, you don't have to wonder what His will is at any time. You can just ask Him.

Help others without expecting help in return. You can volunteer at the hundreds of organizations that help the poor, the homeless, the ill, the abused, or the abandoned. There is plenty of Jesus work at crisis pregnancy centers, homeless shelters, and other institutions. Volunteer to read to the blind, or visit hospitalized babies who have no one coming to see them. Teach reading to adults. When you love Jesus, you will love people because it is Him in you loving them. And you will seek the interests of others before seeking your own interests because it is Jesus in you seeking their interests.

The Bible refers to us as co-*laborers* with Jesus Christ, not as co-*watchers* with Him. We need to be about the business of working to further His kingdom by showing Him to the people around us — whether we know them or not. Remember, God knows them and wants them to come to Him.

In the Bible, Satan is recorded as saying, "I will…" over and over and over. But Jesus is recorded as saying, "not my will, but thine, be done." We need to live a life where it is not "my will" being done but "His will." If we live close enough to Jesus, we will want to glorify God with every fiber of our being. We will want to do what He wants us to do. Jesus said in the Bible, "Follow Me." All I know is that when we say "OK" and start following Him, everything in this world makes so much more sense. Old and intractable problems start to be worked out.

We need to obey and follow Him to have the highest quality of life we can experience, and a life that brings glory to God. Obedience is a choice, and what a great choice it is!

> And to her was granted that she should be arrayed in fine linen, clean and white: for the fine linen is the righteousness of saints. (*Revelation 19:8*)

Once saved, you are a saint of God. You were created to glorify God with your righteous acts. God wants you to forsake all and glorify Him. Go for it!

> For we must all appear before the judgment seat of Christ; that every one may receive the things *done* in *his* body, according to that he hath done, whether *it* be good or bad. (*2 Corinthians 5:10*)

This is a judgment that all believers go through once they have physically died. It is not a judgment of whether you will go to heaven or hell. After all, you're already in heaven. It is a judgment of how well you let Jesus run your life here on earth.

> Now if any man build upon this foundation gold, silver, precious stones, wood, hay, stubble;
>
> Every man's work shall be made manifest: for the day shall declare it, because it shall be revealed by fire; and the fire shall try every man's work of what sort it is.
>
> If any man's work abide which he hath built thereupon, he shall receive a reward. If any man's work shall be burned, he shall suffer loss: but he himself shall be saved; yet so as by fire. (*1 Corinthians 3:12–15*)

Your whole life after you commit to Jesus will be judged. Every action. And what you did for God will be rewarded in heaven.

> For the Son of man shall come in the glory of his Father with his angels; and then he shall reward every man according to his works. (*Matthew 16:27*)

No two people get the same rewards in heaven because no two people were created to be the same; therefore, no two lives are the same. Jesus will reward you for what you did with your life *after* you committed your life to Him. And His judgment will not entail comparison with someone He created to be different but with the way He created you to be. The things you let Him do through you will be rewarded, and the things you do yourself — things that have only temporary value and no eternal value — will be burned up like a brush fire.

This desire to tell people about Jesus, or to behave like Jesus toward them, is nothing new. We read that the same thing happened to people in the Bible when they had an encounter with Jesus. They wanted to tell other people about what Jesus had done for them. Andrew, Peter, the woman at the well, Paul, John — all had an encounter with the Son of God, and they just had to tell someone.

When a woman has a baby, she tells everybody. Why? Because she has good news! She has to tell somebody.

It brings glory to Jesus to tell others about Him. God can use you in a way that may cause them to repent and place their faith in Jesus. That is one major reason God leaves us here on earth after we get saved: to reach the lost before they die and go to hell.

When a woman has a baby, she tells everybody. Why? Because she has good news! She has been carrying this baby for nine months, the baby is born, and Mom is excited. She has to tell somebody.

The word "gospel" means "good news." The truth is that it is *great* news: God isn't mad at me. I know how to be forgiven of my transgressions against Almighty God. Jesus died for my sins, then rose from the dead! If people want to share the good news of a new baby with others, why wouldn't they want to share this great news with everybody they meet?

Now that you are a follower of Jesus Christ, it is time to fish for men:

> And He saith unto them, Follow me, and I will make you fishers of men. (*Matthew 4:19*)

Someone once told me that if you are not fishing, you are not following. Let me repeat that: If you are not fishing for the souls of men, you are not following Jesus the way He commands you to follow Him. It is time for us to reach the lost. It is time to make sure that no one dies and goes to hell for all eternity. It is time to take your light to a very dark world and let it shine very brightly.

Jesus said that we are the salt of the earth. Salt makes people thirsty. People should see our lives and hear our voices and be thirsty for Jesus, and Jesus alone.

> For the Son of man is come to seek and to save that which was lost. (*Luke 19:10*)

Jesus said that we are to seek and save that which is lost. If it is important to Jesus to reach the lost, it ought to be important to us to do the same. There can't be a simpler command than that. We are here to preach the gospel to every person God leads us to. We are here to make disciples. We are here to plant seeds in hearts that God has prepared, and then He can make the seed grow. We are here to plunder hell and populate heaven.

Charles Spurgeon said:

> The saving of souls, if a man has once gained love to perishing sinners and his blessed Master, will be an all-absorbing passion to him. It will so carry him away, that he will almost forget himself in the saving of others. He will be like the brave fireman, who cares not for the scorch or the heat, so that he may rescue the poor creature on whom true humanity has set his heart.[94]

While driving to my parents' house one day, I stopped at a red light, and a woman walked in front of my car. There was a bus coming on the cross street, and another woman was yelling to her to hurry up so she wouldn't miss the bus. She began to run across the street in front of me and darted across the other street to catch the bus. All of a sudden, an SUV hit the running woman. She flew up in the air, hit the windshield, and rolled off to the side.

As soon as I could, I pulled over and went to where she was lying on the ground. There were already people there taking care of her. They called 911, and I prayed.

From what I could hear her friend saying to her, the woman was apparently Eastern European. Then something struck me: When that lady got hit, *everybody* ran over to her. Males, females, whites, blacks, Hispanics — everybody ran to her.

There were no racial barriers. No economic barriers. They saw someone in need, and they went to help. Nothing stopped them.

I don't know what happened to that woman, but I know I was there to pray for her. Now, just think about all the people who are in spiritual need and falling into hell as you read this. There are so many people who are not right with God and not ready for eternity. They are eternally condemned.

How can I run to those people who are temporarily hurt *physically* but not run to those who are eternally hurt *spiritually*? If I walk past a swimming pool while someone is drowning, I can't just keep walking. I *must* do something.

One guy told me that all he would do is "react" and go save that drowning person. Well, if you are believing in Jesus for the forgiveness of your sins, you should just "react", and do anything you can to make sure that no one around you goes anywhere near hell for all eternity.

Spurgeon said:

> You cannot stop their dying, but, oh, that God might help you stop their being damned! You cannot stop the breath from going out of their bodies, but, oh, if the Gospel could but stop their souls from going down to destruction![95]

There is one thing you cannot do once you get to heaven, and that is share your faith with lost people. They won't be there, so your time to reach them is *now!* There is only one place you can reach them and that is *here* on earth.

My first book is called *One Thing You Can't Do in Heaven*. Many people have told me this book awakened in them a passion to boldly reach the lost. You can go to a bookstore or to www.markcahill.org and pick up a copy.

Living on in this world is a good thing, so we can reach the lost. That's why Paul was so determined to live as long as he could, even though he was yearning to go to heaven:

> But I would ye should understand, brethren, that the things *which happened* unto me have fallen out rather unto the furtherance of the Gospel;

> So that my bonds in Christ are manifest in all the palace, and in all other *places*;
>
> And many of the brethren in the Lord, waxing confident by my bonds, are much more bold to speak the word without fear.
>
> Some indeed preach Christ even of envy and strife; and some also of good will:
>
> The one preach Christ of contention, not sincerely, supposing to add affliction to my bonds:
>
> But the other of love, knowing that I am set for the defense of the gospel.
>
> What then? notwithstanding, every way, whether in pretence, or in truth, Christ is preached; and I therein do rejoice, yea, and will rejoice.
>
> For I know that this shall turn to my salvation through your prayer, and the supply of the Spirit of Jesus Christ,
>
> According to my earnest expectation and *my* hope, that in nothing I shall be ashamed, but *that* with all boldness, as always, *so* now also Christ shall be magnified in my body, whether *it be* by life, or by death.
>
> For to me to live *is* Christ, and to die *is* gain.
>
> But if I live in the flesh, this *is* the fruit of my labour: yet what I shall choose I wot not.
>
> For I am in a strait betwixt two, having a desire to depart, and to be with Christ; which is far better:
>
> Nevertheless to abide in the flesh *is* more needful for you.
>
> And having this confidence, I know that I shall abide and continue with you all for your furtherance and joy of faith;
>
> That your rejoicing may be more abundant in Jesus Christ for me by my coming to you again. (*Philippians 1:12–26*)

Remember, Jesus has not *asked* us to reach the lost. He has not made it an option. He has *commanded* us to reach the lost. Think about that while you read His words on the subject:

> And He said unto them, Go ye into all the world, and preach the gospel to every creature.
>
> He that believeth and is baptized shall be saved; but he that believeth not shall be damned. (*Mark 16:15–16*)

There are two things we need to notice here. One is that believers are commanded to go and to preach the gospel "to every creature." Another is that anyone who believes what they're told about the good news will go to heaven, while those who reject what they're told will go to hell.

In the military, if you disobey the order of a commander, it is called "insubordination." If you take authority away from the captain of a ship, it is called "mutiny." What is it called to disobey the Commander, Captain, and Savior of all creation? We shouldn't even begin to think about it. Just obey Him and reach the lost.

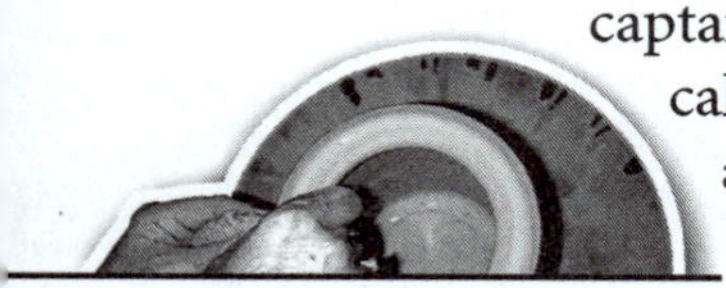

In the military, if you disobey the order of a commander, it is called "insubordination." If you take authority away from the captain of a ship, it is called "mutiny." What is it called to disobey the Commander, Captain, and Savior of all creation?

A friend of mine got a letter from an atheist. You will not believe what he wrote. Read on with an open heart:

> You are really convinced that you've got all the answers. You've really got yourself tricked into believing that you are 100 percent right. Well, let me tell you just one thing. Do you consider yourself to be compassionate [toward] other humans? If you're right about God, as you say you are, and you believe that, then how can you sleep at night?
>
> When you speak with me, you are speaking with someone who you believe is walking directly into eternal damnation, into an endless onslaught of horrendous pain which your loving God created, yet you stand by and do nothing.
>
> If you believed one bit that thousands every day were falling into an eternal and unchangeable fate, you should be running the streets mad with rage at their blindness. That's equivalent to standing on a street corner and watching every person that passes you walk blindly directly into the path of a bus and die, yet you stand idly by and do nothing. You're just twiddling your thumbs, happy in the knowledge that one day that Walk signal will shine your way across the road.
>
> Think about it. Imagine the horrors hell must have in store if the Bible is true. You're just going to allow that to happen and not care about saving anyone but yourself? If you're right, then you're an uncaring, unemotional, and purely selfish [expletive] that has no right to talk about subjects such as love and caring.

I find it amazing that an atheist knows Christians should be sharing their faith with everyone they meet, but some Christians haven't figured it out yet. His point is that Christians who don't share their faith are the most selfish of all people. Don't be that type of Christian. Please don't. Each soul is important to God. He died for them. Let them know what He has done for them.

I saw a t-shirt with a quote by General Douglas MacArthur:

> The enemy is in front of us, the enemy is behind us, the enemy is to the right, the enemy is to the left. They can't get away this time.

What a statement! I don't need to run from Satan and the lost. I need to run right *toward* them, knowing that God has my back! God has invitations for everyone to come to heaven. It is now our job to hand out these invitations to everyone we meet.

What I didn't tell you earlier, in the Vanilla Ice story, was something that really needs to be mentioned. I asked him during our conversation if he was into Christianity. He told me, "I used to be into that." I wondered how anyone could "used to be" into the Son of God. Then he showed me a cross tattooed on his forearm and told me that he had "the sacred heart of Jesus" (a Catholic symbol) tattooed on his chest.

I asked him what he was into now. He told me that he was into Scientology. I said, "How did you get into that?" I will never forget his answer to the day that I die. He said, "John Travolta had a talk with me."

I was amazed. What was John Travolta doing? He was standing up for what he believed. John Travolta will boldly stand up for untruth because he believes it, but here we are with the truth, and yet we hesitate to stand up and be heard? I don't think so! I cannot, I *will not* let John Travolta out-witness me. Don't ever let John Travolta out-witness you either!

One other thing to remember is that when you share your faith, God will water that seed you planted. And you may never know about it until you get to heaven and see who is there.

When I witnessed to Tiger Woods, and he walked away before I could tell him how to be declared "not guilty," I was disappointed because I had more to share. But later God showed me that I had planted the seed of truth and He had watered that seed. Here's the rest of the story.

Because I felt there was unfinished business with Tiger, I asked some people to pray for him, to pray that God would grow that seed I'd planted. Within a week, a friend of mine had the opportunity to talk to Tiger about eternal matters, *and* one of Tiger's friends got the chance to witness to him over dinner. God had all of this follow-up going on, and I didn't even know about it! I should have known that He'd take care of it because it's what HE wants to do:

> So then neither is he that planteth anything, neither he that watereth; but God that giveth the increase. (*1 Corinthians 3:7*)

If you have been talking to God, please ask Him now to save both Tiger Woods and the commercial director. Just stop and do it right now. And do it for your family and friends, too. God is *more* than faithful. The question is: Are you and I that faithful? Can He count on us to further His Kingdom?

My upstairs neighbor Jay has a little girl. They were going up to Minnesota for the holidays. He likes to drive instead of fly when he travels, so I thought he was going to drive there. I handed him an envelope with some money in it to help with expenses. He surprised me by saying he was flying, so I told him to get something for his daughter for the holidays.

About thirty minutes later, Jay knocked on my door and told me that he could not take the money — it was too much. I told him that I could not take it back because it was a gift — that God had a lot of people buy my first book, so I had a few extra dollars in my pocket, and I love to bless others with it. I also told him that I have finally learned that it is "more blessed to give than to receive." I said, "Why not take the basketball team you coach out to dinner after the season?" So off to Minnesota he went.

When he got back from his trip, Jay told me that during the entire trip he'd been thinking about me and the money I had given him. You could look in his eyes and see that the gift had really blessed him. Then he gave me a gift he had bought for me in Minnesota, and he stated that he'd intended to read my book on the trip but just got too busy.

The next day, Jay was going over to a lady's house. This woman had four kids and was struggling with lupus. He had decided to take half of the money that I had given him and bless her with it! So off he went.

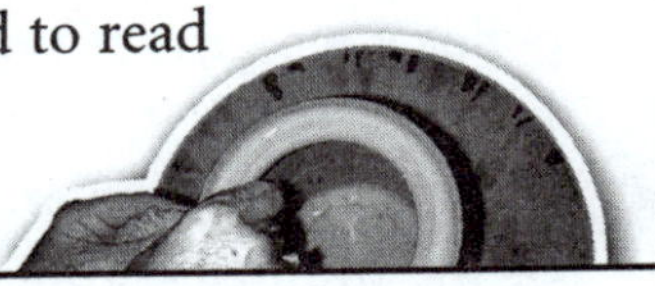

God is more *than faithful. The question is, are you and I that faithful? Can He count on us?*

The day after that, there was another knock on the door! Jay had this look in his eyes. He was so excited. When he had given the money to that lady, she had begun to cry. She was struggling financially, and the money was a huge blessing. You could see the impact it was having on Jay. A day later, I opened my door and found a note taped to it. Jay had written me a two-page letter thanking me for the money. He stated in the letter that he had $29 and some change left over and that he was going to get his three-year-old daughter, who lives with her mom, her first Bible.

Think about that. He doesn't go to church, but he now wanted to get a Bible for his daughter. There was a children's Bible at my parents' house, so I brought it over for Jay to give to his daughter. He was so thankful. I asked if he had a Bible; he didn't. "Would you like one?" He would. I gave him a Bible, and he asked for some help on how to start reading it.

Reach out to others as God has reached out to you. It happens in a thousand different ways. But you have to be listening to the "still, small voice" of Jesus in your heart, and have to obey.

Spurgeon said:

> If we had to preach to thousands year after year, and never rescued but one soul, that one soul would be full reward for all our labor, for a soul is of countless price.[96]

I was speaking to a bunch of Korean adults and teens from various youth groups from around the US. The conference was taking place at North Central College in a suburb of Chicago.

When I arrived at the college, I noticed that there were some college-age girls sitting at a table next to the dorm I was staying in. So I struck up a conversation with them. They worked with a group called Premier. The purpose of this group was to bring all of the minority students on campus for about six weeks prior to school starting so that they could "bond" before the other students showed up.

This sounded interesting, but I was looking to make an eternal difference in their lives. The power of God in the name of Jesus will break down all racial barriers. I began to witness to them, but they didn't want any part of this conversation. So I told them that I had written a book and wanted to sign a copy for each of them.

As I was signing a book for each of them, a young lady walked over to me and asked me what I was doing. Her name was Tamara, and she headed up the multicultural diversity department that was sponsoring the event. You could tell by the tone of voice and body language that she was not at all happy about my being there. So I told her what I was doing. She told me that it would be OK to talk to these staff ladies but that I should please not talk to the minority students when they arrived on campus! Nothing like a free, open society where we can exercise our first-amendment rights!

So I began to witness to her, and she didn't want anything to do with it. So I went and got her a book and signed it for her. I later checked a trash can nearby and didn't find any of the books in it! I thought I would find at least one.

The next day, I was talking with some of the people in my group when Tamara approached me. She said that I wasn't supposed to be talking with any of the college students here. I informed her that I had the right to do that. She stated that campus security had already been called. She looked up and said, "And here he is."

Around the corner came a security guard in his early twenties with sunglasses on. He looked at me and said, "You cannot be on this campus talking with people and handing out literature. If you do not leave campus right now, you will be arrested." Just another normal day in the life of Mark Cahill! So I looked at him and said, "I am with the Korean group that is here, and I do believe that I have the right to talk with people."

Now he was on the defensive. I guess he had thought I was just some stranger hanging out in the dorm. He then told me that I could talk to people in my group but not to people in other groups! I looked at him and asked, "Did I lose my first-amendment rights when I walked onto this campus?" I asked him this question three times, and he wouldn't answer me. He told me that we would have to talk to the person in charge of camps who had signed a contract allowing us to be there.

I then asked him, "What was the nature of the complaint against me?" He said that he could not tell me that. So I looked at him and said, "A question for you. If you died tonight, are you 100 percent assured that you would go to heaven?" What is interesting is that if what I was doing was illegal, he should have arrested me then and there! But, of course, he didn't.

He said, "I am going to decline to answer that question right now." What we all must remember is that people may decide to not answer that question now, but we will all *have* to answer it one day. So I went over to lunch. I ended up sitting with some football players from the college who were conducting a football camp for some young guys. We hit it off right away. Some were believers, some weren't. One Catholic guy told me that he had opened up his Bible for the first time two days earlier! He said that he had some questions, so I gave him some answers! Those guys all wanted my book, so I signed it for them. While I was signing, I looked to the side, and there was Tamara just staring at me! This was not going according to her plans.

I found out the next day that the Catholic guy read more than 80 pages of my book in one day! And later I found out that one of those football players started a Bible study on campus that, last I heard, has more than twenty people participating in it.

Pastor David, who was the leader of our group, went and talked with the head of the camps about what had happened to me. This was on a Monday.

On Sunday, the previous day, the Korean kids had split up and gone to different churches around town for Sunday service. The head of the camps told Pastor David that a group of the Korean kids were at his church on Sunday! He said it was a real blessing to have them there and told Pastor David what I was doing was just fine, that the security guard was out of line, and that he would deal with him accordingly.

Pastor David then told him that — after I talked to the teens that night — there would be about 90 Koreans doing the exact same thing! The head of the camps told Pastor David that would be fine, too. Wow!

> Then spake the Lord to Paul in the night by a vision, Be not afraid, but speak, and hold not thy peace:
>
> For I am with thee, and no man shall set on thee to hurt thee: for I have much people in this city. (*Acts 18:9–10*)

Do not be silent. The Lord wants us to radically take a bold stand for Him. He is with us. He has people in all the right places — like the head of camps — that we can't even imagine. Our job is to simply stand strong for the truth of Jesus Christ.

Some of the Korean kids had great talks with the college students that week. Please pray for the salvation of Tamara and the security guard.

Spurgeon said:

> If a man could tell me that he stopped Niagara at a word, I would not envy him his power if God will only allow me to stop a sinner in his mad career of sin. If a creature could put his finger on Vesuvius and quench its flame, I would not at all regret that I had no such power if I might but be the means of staying a blasphemer and teaching him to pray. This spiritual power is the greatest power imaginable, and the most to be desired.[97]

June is a great month. For many cities and states, it has become what many call "Pride Month." What that means is that it is the month to celebrate the gay and lesbian lifestyle. It is the time of year when that movement celebrates what is going on in their community, but their primary goal is to convince other folks that their lifestyle is really OK.

I have always found "Pride" to be an amazing title for their events. Pride has always had a bad name:

> Pride *goeth* before destruction, and an haughty spirit before a fall. (*Proverbs 16:18*)

All people need to realize that pride comes before eternal destruction; and to all who are prideful and haughty, that fall is certain to come one day.

June 2003 had special significance for the gay community because of the Supreme Court's decision that homosexual sex done in the privacy of the home is legal. Always remember that no matter what humans say, including humans on the Supreme Court, the Word of God stands supreme.

Do not be silent. The Lord wants us to radically take a bold stand for him. He is with us.

> In those days *there was* no king in Israel: every man did *that which was* right in his own eyes. (*Judges 21:25*)

If people don't follow King Jesus, they tend to follow the herd, or do whatever else they feel like doing. There will always be negative consequences in our lives if we insist on doing what is right in our own eyes rather than what is right in the eyes of God.

The last weekend in June is the time when major cities around the country host festivals that celebrate that hoped-for gay movement victory. In Atlanta, the event is called the "Pride Festival." This particular year, the festival took place just days after the Supreme Court ruling came out. So you can imagine that the gay people were very excited and ready to throw a party.

For the past six or seven years, I have gone to this festival. Atlanta has the second-largest gay-pride festival in the nation, with 200,000 to 300,000 people in attendance. And, of course, the reason that I go is to talk with some folks and share eternal truth with them. There were about ten of us doing some witnessing at the festival that weekend. We could sure use some help at these festivals. There are many lost people there, and there are few Christians who love them enough to try to reach them. Why do we run *away* from sinners instead of running right *to* them with the truth that they are really looking for?

On Saturday, I saw a group of about six people sitting. So I prayed, then walked over to them. One girl had moved away from the group in order to talk on her cell phone. I struck up a conversation with the rest of them, then asked them all this question: "When you die, what do you think is on the other side?"

All of a sudden, one of the guys looked at the girl with the cell phone and said, "Michelle, come over here right now." I couldn't figure out what was going on. When she came over, he asked me to repeat the question. I did, and all of a sudden her eyes got huge. "What is going on?" I asked. She said, "One week ago, we talked about that exact same question for four hours!" She then told me that they actually have a notebook in which they take notes about what they have been discussing! So we talked for well over an hour about what is out there after we die.

For example, during this conversation, I asked one guy how his relationship with his father was. He told me, "I hate my father!" He said his father hit him so hard one time that he actually knocked him out of a window. He told me how his father had put his cigarettes out on him when he was a kid. I then asked him if there had been any sexual abuse in his life. He told me that when he was fifteen years old, someone else's father had molested him at a Boy Scout camp. He stated that his homosexual thoughts began at that time. As he told me this, huge tears welled up in his eyes.

Later that day, I talked with a seventeen-year-old named Alex. He told me that he had a terrible relationship with his father. He also said that his uncle had sexually molested him for three years, between the ages of six and eight.

Often we think we see a problem, but really we only see a symptom. For example, most people think homosexuality is the problem. Actually, it is only the symptom. Researchers are learning that societal factors push people down the road of homosexuality. There are two big factors in this push. One is a break in the child's relationship with their same-sex parent. For example, there is a break in the relationship between a son and his father, or between a daughter and her mother. Often, there is a divorce or one parent is working all the time.

The second major factor that puts a child on the road to homosexuality is abuse, usually of a sexual nature. So here we deal with folks who have a tremendous amount of pain in their lives, and we actually have the answer to their pain. It is the power, healing, forgiveness, and deliverance of Jesus Christ. Yet how many times do we condemn gay people instead of bringing them the Truth that heals?

Help in getting delivered from the homosexual lifestyle can be found both at Exodus Global Alliance (www.exodusglobalalliance.org) and Stephen Bennett Ministries (www.sbministries.org). Both have lots of great information you can use to get delivered or to help you share your faith with gays.

Going back to the conversation with Michelle at the festival: Toward the end of our talk, she looked at me and said, "I have been dying to find anybody who passionately believes what they believe about eternity. I look at your eyes and the countenance on your face, and I know for a fact that you know this to be true."

Think about that for just a second. We always think it is our *words* that they need to hear. However, it is not only words but also the manner in which we deliver those words that can really affect these hurting people for Jesus. You can't fake passion. Either you love the Lord or you don't. When you truly love Him, it comes through loud and clear to those around you. Michelle and a friend of hers have since emailed me for a copy of my first book. Spiritually hungry people are looking for what can satisfy them for eternity. If you have Jesus, are you giving Him away to those hungry people?

Charles Spurgeon — have you noticed that I really like this guy? — said:

> If there existed only one man or woman who did not love the Savior, and if that person lived among the wilds of Siberia, and if it were necessary that all the millions of believers on the face of the earth should journey there, and every one of them plead with him to come to Jesus before he could be converted, it would be well worth all the zeal, labor, and expense… One soul would be full reward of the labor of myriads of zealous Christians, for a soul is of countless price.[98]

On a recent flight to Dallas, I sat next to a guy who lived in San Francisco, and he had this great French accent. He was born in France, but he had lived in the States for the past fifteen years.

We had a great time talking about life and the things of God. He wasn't a believer yet, but he was very open and had a lot of questions. After a while, he told me that he had to get some work done but wanted to tell me a story later.

A bit before we landed, he put his work away and told me that six months earlier his father had died. His father had lived in France, and due to the time difference, he hadn't learned of his father's death until about twelve hours later.

On the morning of his father's death, he woke up, then fell back to sleep. But it was a sort of in-between state — not really awake, not really sleeping — and he had this vision of a man talking to him. The man had white hair and was like a televangelist, he said, but so much more than that. He knew that the man was trying to tell him about God, but he couldn't hear him. I asked him why not, and he told me, "Because I didn't want to listen." Isn't that the truth! Some people just don't want to listen when God is trying to get their attention.

September 11th was a "wake-up call" for America. Many people began thinking about the things of God. But most of them soon moved away from God, back to the hustle and bustle of life.

Now listen to what happened next to this guy on the plane: The dream scene changed. Suddenly, he was in a big theatre or auditorium. The same mysterious man was standing on the stage with a lot of people in front of him. People would walk up to him one at a time.

The guy from San Francisco was watching all of this from the back of the stage. He said that the man speaking was the same man he'd seen before, but now he could see him only from behind. The man had long, white, flowing hair, and he had a long, white, flowing robe.

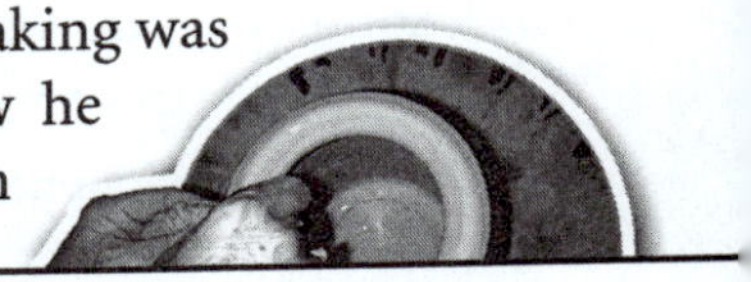

September 11th was a "wake-up call" for America. Many people began thinking about the things of God. But most of them soon moved away from God, back to the hustle and bustle of life.

My seat mate knew this scene was important, but he didn't know what to make of it. I pulled out my Bible and showed him Acts 2:17, which quotes the Old Testament prophet Joel, who said:

> And it shall come to pass afterward, *that* I will pour out my Spirit upon all flesh; and your sons and your daughters shall prophesy, your old men shall dream dreams, your young men shall see visions:
>
> And also upon the servants and upon the handmaids in those days will I pour out my Spirit. (*Joel 2:28–29*)

And God is doing this in these days! I have heard some amazing stories of dreams that people have had. I believed God was trying to reach this unbeliever through his dream. I showed him Revelation 1:14 which describes Jesus by saying, "His head and his hairs were white like wool, as white as snow...." Also, Mark 9:3 states that when Jesus was transfigured on the mount, His clothes were exceedingly white.

I let this man know that I believed he'd seen a vision of the Lord before whom he would stand one day. So I asked him, "Are you ready to stand there? Your dad stood there. And I will stand there, and you will stand there."

Judgment is coming for all. The question is: Are you ready for Judgment Day? If so, are you helping others get ready for that day? That is why we are here. My motto is: If they are breathing, they need Jesus.

> The fruit of the righteous *is* a tree of life, and he that winneth souls *is* wise. (*Proverbs 11:30*)

You always want to live your life as a wise person. In the eyes of God, someone who wins souls is a wise person. Be wise.

Charles Spurgeon said:

> Do you want arguments for soul winning? Look up to heaven, and ask yourself how sinners can ever reach those harps of gold and learn that everlasting song, unless they have someone to tell them of Jesus, who is "mighty to save." But the best argument of all is to be found in the wounds of Jesus. You want to honor Him, you desire to put crowns upon His head, and this you can best do by winning souls for Him. These are the spoils that He covets, these are the trophies for which He fights, these are the jewels that shall be His best adornment.[99]

One day, my apartment started flooding with water! There had to be a broken pipe somewhere, but the maintenance crew couldn't tell where it was coming from — though they were sure it wasn't from my apartment.

They finally found the problem in the apartment next door. They told me that if I hadn't been home to catch it, I would have had six inches of water covering my whole apartment by the time I got home. I would have needed an ark to get around!

Well, I began to pray. I asked God to let me handle this in a Christian manner, even though I was upset at having so much water on my carpet. I asked God to give me an opportunity to witness to the people He brought across my path because of all of this.

The maintenance guy's name was Ramadan. What a great Muslim name! As I began to witness to him, I discovered he was a strong Christian. He told me that he didn't want to change his name because it opened up many doors for him to share Jesus with others! I gave him my first book, and he was excited to get it.

A little bit later, a guy came by to cut up my carpet and throw it out. His name was Laurence. As I began to talk with him, he really opened up. He was not a believer, but we talked for more than twenty minutes about how to get saved from hell. He wanted a book about it, so I gave him one. Every other weekend he goes to visit his mom, who is dying of lupus. He's helping pay her medical bills. I had just received a monetary blessing from some folks in

Alabama, so I decided to bless him with it, to help with his mom's expenses.

I got a chance to pray for him before he left, and he was very moved. I could see it in his eyes, and he also told me how much it meant to him that I took the time to talk with him.

People are thirsty for truth. Give them the living water of God to satisfy the thirst in their soul. Get out of your old, dead comfort zone. Outside that zone, is the only place to really live. I spoke at a youth conference in Tennessee, and here is an abbreviated version of a letter from one of the youth pastors who was there:

> It was New Year's Eve coming on. On the way home [from the camp] we stopped at a Taco Bell to have lunch. When we got there a tire blew, so we contacted a mechanic. While waiting for him, Desi realized a part from the brake had broken off and hit the tire, causing it to go flat.
>
> Well, imagine Desi trying to find a part for an old school bus on New Year's Eve! AND me stuck at Taco Bell with 19 teenagers — for nearly four hours!
>
> This is when miracles started happening. One by one, the kids started coming on the bus and getting their *One Thing You Can't Do in Heaven* books they'd gotten from you. Most kids probably get those books and then never read them. But these kids were stuck, so they all were sitting there reading them. Then, one by one, they started witnessing — at Taco Bell, and at the gas station next to it.
>
> I was surprised when another bus came to pick us up. I asked the driver how this came about, because it had been nearly four hours since my husband left, and I still hadn't heard from him. She said in Knoxville, she happened to overhear my husband describing our problem, and since she owned a fleet of buses, she decided to come pick us up and take us back to our motel.
>
> The kids all started chipping in whatever money they had left, which paid for another night at the motel — after the manager kindly gave us a discount. Then those kids were so on fire for Jesus that the manager actually had to talk to us because he had some complaints about too many people talking about Jesus! (It turned out to be only one man, after we asked for specifics.)
>
> That night ended up being the most blessed of all. The kids said that book changed their lives! They were talking about how they were scared to death

to witness at first, and how it got easier the more they did it. They started getting really burdened for people back home, in Indiana.

They wanted to do that thing where they make lists of each grade and make it a goal to speak to each kid about Jesus.

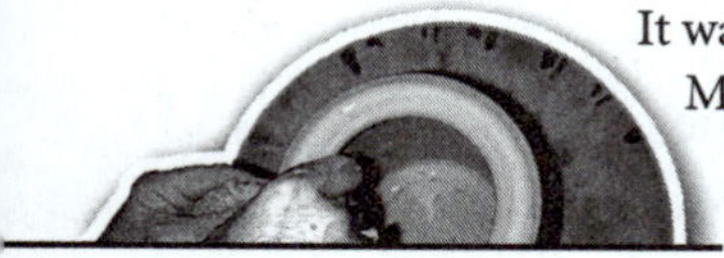

It was soooooooooo awesome how God worked it all out, Mark. What a blessing!

On a personal note, when I heard your message, I felt like scales dropped off MY eyes too! I'd been reading the Word more than ever, and "busy" in ministry … but the closeness I used to feel with God was missing, and I couldn't figure out why. (Interesting how Satan can even blind Christians.)

Then it hit me like a ton of bricks: I have nearly stopped personal one-on-one soul-winning. Yes, kids come to the Lord through the ministry. But personal one-on-one outside of the ministry is what I was missing! It's like I was "busy" in "God's work" but had forgotten how it is to REALLY be in God's work: the awesomeness of that oneness you feel with God when you soul-win; having the burden for souls that comes from personal soul-winning; watching Him arrange things and all — you know what I mean!

Your message really got through. God truly used you to reach our youth group AND its leaders!

The moon must be correctly angled toward the sun in relation to us in order for people to see the sun's light reflecting from the moon. Then it hit me: Isn't that the same for believers in Jesus Christ? Aren't we supposed to reflect the light of the Son?

Why do teens hear the truth about how to reach the lost and just go for it, while some of us adults think too much about it and then don't do anything?

For do I now persuade men, or God? or do I seek to please men? for if I yet pleased men, I should not be the servant of Christ. (*Galatians 1:10*)

For they loved the praise of men more than the praise of God. (*John 12:43*)

It doesn't matter what your boss or your friends say about you. All that matters is what Jesus says about you. So don't be a man-pleaser. Be a God-pleaser! It is the only way to live!

Charles Spurgeon said:

> If you never have sleepless hours, if you never have weeping eyes, if your hearts never swell as if they would burst, you need not anticipate that you will be called zealous. You do not know the beginning of true zeal, for the foundation of Christian zeal lies in the heart. The heart must be heavy with grief and yet must beat high with holy ardor. The heart must be vehement in desire, panting continually for God's glory, or else we shall never attain to anything like the zeal which God would have us to know.[100]

A great writer of prayer songs wrote:

> It shall be established forever as the moon, and *as* a faithful witness in heaven. Selah. (*Psalm 89:37*)

I was thinking about this verse one day. The moon is a faithful witness in the sky. Now we know from this book's first chapter (on creation) that the moon glorifies God by just being up in the sky.

We look at the moon, and we wonder how it just hangs there. We wonder how finely tuned this universe is, how scientists can tell you the exact day when a full moon or an eclipse will occur. We know that the moon plays a major role with the tides and even the earth's rotation. But to us regular folks, who are not so scientifically oriented, the moon does one major thing: It reflects the light of the sun. It can be a crescent moon, a half-moon, or a full moon. But here is the key: The moon must be correctly angled toward the sun in relation to us in order for people to see the sun's light reflecting from the moon.

Then it hit me: Isn't that the same for believers in Jesus Christ? Aren't we supposed to reflect the light of the Son? We should be reflecting the light of the Son of God. But what is the key? We must be angled correctly toward the Son.

When we read the Word of God, obey what we read, pray, worship, and live what we know, then we can reflect the light of Jesus Christ, the Son of God, into other people's lives. People are hungry for truth, and we want to "reflect" that for them to see.

Charles Spurgeon said:

> I am sure of this: It is impossible to know the value of salvation without desiring to see others brought in. Said that renowned preacher, Whitfield, "As soon as I was converted, I wanted to be the means of the conversion of

> all that I had ever known. There were a number of young men that I had played cards with, sinned with, and transgressed with. The first thing I did was, I went to their houses to see what I could do for their salvation. Nor could I rest until I had the pleasure of seeing many of them brought to the Savior."[101]

I recently spoke at a Bible study in Atlanta. One of the participants was Ernie Johnson, who hosts the "Inside the NBA" show on the TNT broadcasting network. He is a very humble man of God, and we had a nice talk afterward. He invited me to come to one of the tapings at the main TNT studios. So I went there on a Wednesday night. As I pulled into the parking area, I got into a talk with the security guard. He was a faithful churchgoer, but he was not 100 percent assured that he would go to heaven when he died. I signed a book for him and parked my car.

Ernie came and got me and took me up to his office. We had a good talk, but soon he had to go and get ready for the show. So he told one of the ladies who worked there that she should come and talk with me. She and I had an amazing talk. She was in "search mode" at that point in her life. She had grown up in a Catholic family, but she longed to find the truth for herself. I was signing a book for her as Ernie walked back into the room.

By the way, look for opportunities to reach the lost wherever you go in life. There are opportunities around every corner.

Ernie and I walked out to the set, and he showed me around. I was interested in how the whole show came together, and he basically took me through the ins and outs of the show.

Before the show gets started, Magic Johnson, Charles Barkley, and Kenny Smith, who co-host the show, hang out in a big control room and watch the game and talk. There is a ton of cutting up going on and not a lot of game watching!

After the halftime show, but before the after-game show, I got a chance to talk with Magic Johnson for about twenty minutes about the things of the Lord. It was an amazing conversation. Magic did not take his eyes off of me except once during that whole time.

Magic is a faithful churchgoer in LA, and he grew up in church. At one point, I looked across the room at Charles and said to Magic, "Do you want to see Charles in heaven one day?" He responded that he did. I looked at him and said, "What are you going to do about it?" It got a little tense at that moment, but people need to be challenged to stand up for Jesus with their lives. We may want to see someone in heaven, but the real question is: What are we going to do about it? I signed a copy of my book about witnessing and gave it to Magic. Ernie Johnson told me later that Magic had told him, "I really like that friend you brought tonight."

After the show, Charles and some of the staffers went out to a club in the bar section of Atlanta. I decided to go with them. In the first club, one guy told me at the end of my conversation with him, "Talking with you has been a very spiritually fulfilling evening."

One girl told me that she loved the Lord with all of her heart, but just likes to come out drinking and dancing. I asked her if she thought that anyone was dying and going to hell in this club. She responded "Yes."

I then asked her what she was going to do about it. She just began to weep. If we say that we believe but do nothing about the fact that people are dying and going to hell, then the question is: Do we really believe? Charles Spurgeon said: "Have you no desire to see others saved? Then you are not saved yourself, you can be sure of that." Most people who claim to be Christians *do* have the desire to see others saved. They just don't know how to share their faith.

I want to encourage you again to get a copy of my first book, *One Thing You Can't Do in Heaven*, so that you can learn how to effectively and biblically share your faith (www.markcahill.org).

A little bit later, we went to another club in the area. Terrell Owens, the wide receiver for the San Francisco 49ers and Philadelphia Eagles, was at the club. We got the chance to talk for awhile. I got to look him in the eye and ask the question, "If you died tonight, are you 100 percent assured that you are going to heaven?"

As I was walking out of the club, I handed some tracts to some of the bartenders, bouncers, and bystanders. One guy talked with me for a couple of minutes. I told him that I had written a book and gave him my card so that he could email me his address. I told him I would send him my book. I turned and walked out because it was 3:30 in the morning. But a few days later, that guy emailed me, and I sent him my book. People everywhere are waiting to hear the good news. Since you know this is true, go tell them!

Charles Spurgeon said:

> Etiquette nowadays often demands of a Christian that he should not intrude his religion on company. Out on such etiquette! It is the etiquette of hell. True courtesy to my fellow's soul makes me speak to him, if I believe that soul to be in danger.[102]

Spurgeon also said:

> Having joined the church of God, are any of you satisfied to be silent? Are you content to let those around you sink to hell? What! Never tell of Christ's love? What! Never speak of salvation to your own children? Can this be right? In God's name, wake up! What are you left on this earth for? If there is nothing for you to do, why are you in this sinful world?[103]

When you go to a funeral, don't buy into the lie that the person is dead. That simply is not a true statement. Yes, their *body* is dead, but the body is only the vehicle that the soul uses to navigate on earth. The soul is the true person, not the body. And the soul is immortal. It can never die — just relocate.

So the soul of every person whose body is in a casket is either alive and well in heaven, or alive in hell. One of two destinations: That is it. What are you doing to ensure that everyone you meet is going to be with you in heaven one day?

Now read the last will and testament of a man whose passion for souls grew from his love for Jesus:

FELLOWSHIP OF THE UNASHAMED

(An African martyr's last words)

I am part of the Fellowship of the Unashamed.
The die has been cast. I have stepped over the line.
The decision has been made. I am a disciple of Jesus Christ.

I won't look back, let up, slow down, back away, or be still. My past is redeemed, my present makes sense, and my future is secure.
I'm finished and done with low living, sight-walking, small planning, smooth knees, colorless dreams, tame visions, mundane talking, cheap giving, and dwarfed goals.
My pace is set, my gait is fast, my goal is heaven, my road is narrow, my way is rough, my companions few, my Guide reliable, my mission clear.
I won't give up, back up, let up, or shut up until I've preached up, prayed up, paid up, stored up, and stayed up for the cause of Christ.
I must go until He returns, give until I drop, preach until all know, and work until He comes.
And when He comes to get His own, He will have no problem recognizing me. My colors will be clear. "For I am not ashamed of the Gospel of Christ." [*Romans 1:16*][104]

This is the passion of a saved soul who understands the tragedy of people dying unsaved. He dedicated his life to bringing as many people as possible into the Kingdom of God with him.

I hope these stories encourage you as you now begin the journey of making sure everyone you meet will see you in heaven one of these days and say, "Hey, thanks for telling me about what Jesus did for me!"

There is a lost world to be reached, and now is the time to do it!

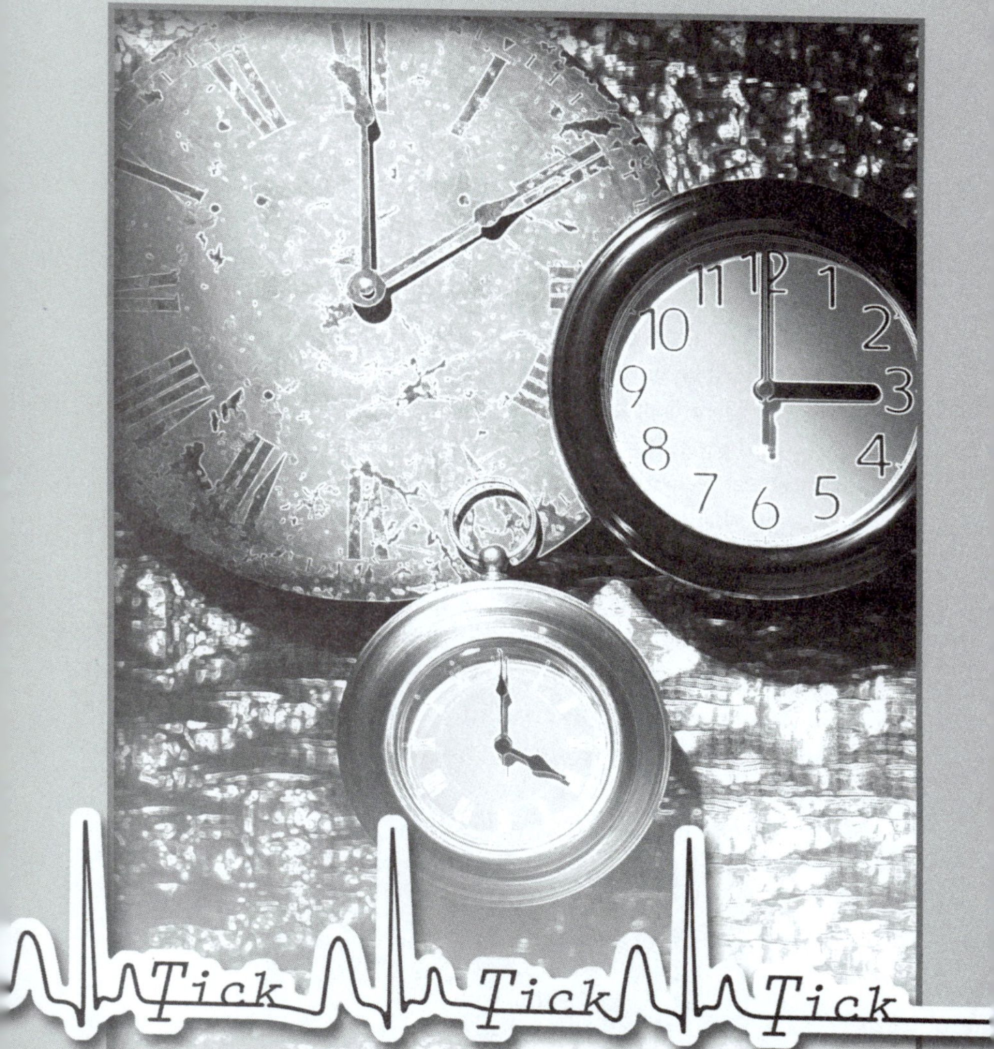

The one thing we don't know, though, is how much time we have left on the clock.

Chapter 12
Tick Tick Tick

Live every day as if it were your last
and someday you'll be right.
— Anonymous

When you walk into a basketball arena, there is always a scoreboard with a clock on it. I was looking at the clock one day as it was ticking down. Five, four, three, two, one, zero — the horn sounded, and the game was over.

Then it hit me: Our lives are just like that. Our clock is ticking down every day, and one day we will die. The clock is always ticking. The one thing we *don't* know is how much time is left on the clock.

But we do know one thing for sure: The clock continues to tick, tick, tick… What are you going to do with the time you have left?

Charles Spurgeon said:

> Listen for one moment to the ticking of that clock! It is the beating on the pulse of eternity. It is the footstep of death pursuing you! Each time the clock ticks, death's footsteps are falling on the ground close behind you![105]

Spurgeon also said:

> Listen to the ticking of the clock! As the pendulum swings back and forth, it says to some of you, "Now or never! Now or never! Now or never! Now or never!" Will you trust your soul with Jesus?[106]

God warns us that we should be making the most of every minute we have:

> Redeeming the time, because the days are evil. (*Ephesians 5:16*)

You must make the most of your time. We live in an evil time. We see things happening today that many of us thought we would never see in our lifetime; yet, they are happening.

If you give away your shirt, you can go to the store and get another one. If you give away $100, you can get a job and earn the money back. But time is one thing that, once it is given away, you can never get back.

God knows the day you were born and the day you will die. Your time on earth is finite and fleeting; it has a definite limit. But your time is infinite when you walk out of here.

What are you going to do with your time here to ensure that your eternity is a joy?

Charles Spurgeon said:

> Heaven and hell are not far away. You may be in heaven before the clock ticks again it is so near. Oh, that we, instead of trifling about such things because they seem so far away, would solemnly realize them, since they are so very near! This very day, before the sun goes down, some hearer now sitting in this place may see the realities of heaven or hell.[107]

Last Words

One of the most amazing things to do is to read what people said right before they died — the last statement they made with their very last breath. You can learn a great deal about what was important to these people by reading what they said. And it might give you some insight into what may have lain in store for them after they took that last breath.

These quotes are taken from *The Evidence Bible*, by Ray Comfort.

Cardinal Borgia: "I have provided in the course of my life for everything except death, and now alas, I am to die unprepared."

Elizabeth the First: "All my possessions for one moment of time."

Thomas Hobbs (atheist author of "Leviathan," written to justify the rule of absolute monarchs and the oppression of the people): "I am about to take my last voyage; a great leap in the dark."

Anne Boleyn (wife of Henry the Eighth, who had her executed): "O God, have pity on my soul. O God, have pity on my soul."

Henry, Prince of Wales: "Tie a rope round my body, pull me out of bed, and lay me in ashes, that I may die with repentant prayers to an offended God. O! I in vain wish for that time I lost with you and others in vain recreations."

Socrates: "All of the wisdom of this world is but a tiny raft upon which we must set sail when we leave this earth. If only there was a firmer foundation upon which to sail, perhaps some divine word."

Tony Hancock (British comedian): "Nobody will ever know I existed. Nothing to leave behind me. Nothing to pass on. Nobody to mourn me. That's the bitterest blow of all."

Phillip III, King of France: "What an account I shall have to give to God! How I should like to live otherwise than I have lived."

Voltaire (skeptic philosopher): "I am abandoned by God and man! I will give you half of what I am worth if you will give me six months' life. Then I shall go to hell; and you will go with me. O Christ! O Jesus Christ!"

This talented French writer once said of Jesus, "Curse the wretch!"

Aldous Huxley (humanist/atheist): "It is a bit embarrassing to have been concerned with the human problem all one's life and find at the end that one has no more to offer by way of advice than: Try and be a little kinder."

Karl Marx: "Go on, get out! Last words are for fools who haven't said enough!"

Napoleon: "I marvel that where the ambitious dreams of myself and of Alexander and of Caesar should have vanished into thin air, a Judean peasant, Jesus, should be able to stretch his hands across the centuries, and control the destinies of men and nations."

Diana, Princess of Wales (per police files): "My God. What's happened?"

James Dean: "My fun days are over."

Jonathan Edwards (evangelist): "Trust in God and you shall have nothing to fear."

Patrick Henry: "Doctor, I wish you to observe how real and beneficial the religion of Christ is to a man about to die…."

(In his will he wrote: "This is all the inheritance I give to my dear family: The religion of Christ which will give them one which will make them rich indeed.")

D. L. Moody (evangelist): "I see earth receding; heaven is opening. God is calling me."

William Shakespeare: "I commend my soul into the hands of God my Creator, hoping and assuredly believing, through the only merits of Jesus Christ my Savior, to be made partaker of life everlasting; and my body to the earth, whereof it was made."

Martin Luther: "Into Thy hands I commend my spirit! Thou hast redeemed me, O God of truth."

John Milton (British poet): "Death is the great key that opens the palace of Eternity."

Charles Dickens: "I commit my soul to the mercy of God, through our Lord and Savior Jesus Christ, and I exhort my dear children humbly to try and guide themselves by the teaching of the New Testament."

Daniel Webster: "I still live."

As he was dying, he said, "The great mystery is Jesus Christ, the Gospel. What would the condition of any of us be if we had not the hope of immortality? … Thank God, the Gospel of Jesus Christ brought life and immortality to light."

Andrew Jackson: "My dear children, do not grieve for me … I am my God's. I belong to Him. I go but a short time before you, and … I hope and trust to meet you all in heaven."

Henry Ward Beecher: "Now comes the mystery."

Beecher, a man with a great mind, did not know the answer to the mystery beyond death. Beecher may not have known, but, after reading this book, you do. The question is: What have you done with what you know?[108]

When John Owen, the great Puritan, lay on his deathbed, he had his secretary write to a friend, "I am still in the land of the living." Then, Owen cried, "Stop! Change that to say, 'I am yet in the land of the dying, but I hope soon to be in the land of the living.'"[109]

Time is progressing, but it eventually comes to a standstill for each one of us in this physical realm. Your last breath could be today. If so, what would your last words be?

You:____

____

____

____

____

What if you had more time in your life? What if you could live life differently than you have? What if you could write down what you hope your last words will be before you die? What if you then could live a life that would actually reflect those words? What would those words be?

You:____

____

____

____

____

… thou hast praised the gods of silver, and gold, of brass, iron, wood, and stone, which see not, nor hear, nor know: and the God in whose hand thy breath is, and whose are all thy ways, hast thou not glorified: (*Daniel 5:23*)

God holds your breath, indeed your very life, in the palm of His hand. He can snatch it away at any moment and take you off to eternity. He has chosen to let you have another breath at this moment. What are you going to do with that breath?

God holds your breath, indeed your very life, in the palm of His hand. He can snatch it away at any moment and take you off to eternity. He has chosen to let you have another breath at this moment. What are you going to do with that breath? Will you glorify Him or not? It's your choice.

This book was written by me, and now it has been read by you. When you put it down and go on with your life, remember this: You will be serving somebody.

Please remember, while you are still breathing, that God has given you that breath of life for this moment. The only question is: What are you going to do with it? If you are not saved, now is the time to surrender to God. If you are saved, live radically for Him. Once you die and go to heaven or hell, there is no crossing over from one side to the other.

Truth has been found. The journey of your life continues. Die with no unfinished business. Have no regrets on Judgment Day. Don't waste your life. There are still moments of your life to be lived. I wonder how those moments will be played out. Use your time wisely…

RESOURCES

The New Evidence That Demands a Verdict
Josh McDowell
101 Scientific Facts in the Bible
Ray Comfort
Creation: Remarkable Evidence of God's Design
Grant Jeffrey
God Doesn't Believe in Atheists
Ray Comfort
Reasons for Believing
Dr. Frank Harber
The Collapse of Evolution
Dr. Scott Huse
The Evolution of a Creationist
Dr. Jobe Martin
The Signature of God
Grant Jeffrey

Web Sites

www.answersingenesis.org
www.probe.org
www.roncarlson.com
www.str.org
www.livingwaters.com

ENDNOTES

[1] The Barna Group, *Americans Describe Their Views About Life After Death*, October 21, 2003.

[2] Ibid.

[3] Sir Winston Churchill, <http://en.wikiquote.org/wiki/Winston_Churchill>

[4] Robert Jastrow, *Until the Sun Dies*, (New York: W. W. Norton, 1977), 21.

[5] F. Darwin, ed., *The Life and Letters of Charles Darwin* (New York: D. Appleton & Co., 1905), 276.

[6] C. S. Lewis, *God in the Dock: Essays on Theology and Ethics*, (Grand Rapids, MI: Wm. B. Eerdmans Publishing Co., 2001), 211.

[7] Ray Comfort, *Way of the Master Evidence Bible* (Gainsville, FL: Bridge-Logos, 2003), 1454.

[8] Ibid.

[9] Dr. Scott Huse, *The Collapse of Evolution,* 2d ed. (Grand Rapids, MI: Baker Book House, 1993), 71–72.

[10] As quoted in *Austin American-Statesman*, October 19, 1997.

[11] Stephen Hawking, *A Brief History of Time* (New York:Bantam Books, 1988), 162

[12] Fred Hoyle, "The Universe: Past and Present Reflections," *Annual Review of Astronomy and Astrophysics*, 1982, 20:16.

[13] Paul Davies, *The Cosmic Blueprint* (New York: Simon and Schuster, 1988), 203.

[14] As quoted in Dr. Henry F. Schaefer, *Science and Christianity: Conflict or Coherence?* (University of Georgia, 2003), 71.

[15] As quoted in Fred Heeren, *Show Me God* (Wheeling, IL: Searchlight Publications, 1995), 200.

[16] As quoted in H. Margenau and R. A. Varghese, eds., *Cosmos, Bios, and Theos* (La Salle, IL: Open Court, 1992), 83.

[17] George Greenstein, *The Symbiotic Universe* (New York: William Morrow, 1988), 27.

[18] Ronald Clark, *The Life and Times of Einstein* (New York: World Publishing, 1971), 18–19.

[19] J. P. Moreland, *Scaling the Secular City: A Defense of Christianity* (Grand Rapids, MI: Baker Academic, 1987), 220.

[20] Ken Ham, *The Answers Book* (Green Forest, AR: New Leaf Press; Master Books, 2003), 125.

[21] Martin Moe, "Genes on Ice," *Science Digest*, December, 1981, 89 [11], 36, 95.

[22] G. G. Simpson, C. S. Pittendrigh, and L. H. Tiffany, *Life: An Introduction to Biology* (New York: Harcourt, Brace, and World, 1965), 241.

[23] Francis Crick, "In the Beginning," *Scientific American*, February 1991, 12.

[24] Charles Darwin, *The Origin of Species*, 6th ed. (London: John Murray, 1872), 49.

25 G. G. Simpson, *Tempo and Mode in Evolution* (New York: Columbia University Press, 1984), 106.

26 A. J. Marshall, *Biology and Comparative Physiology of Birds* (New York: Academic Press, 1960), 1.

27 H. W. Smith, *From Fish to Philosopher* (New York: Little Brown, 1953), 26.

28 As quoted in Arthur C. Custance, *Evolution or Creation?* (Ottawa: Doorway Papers, 1988), <http://www.custance.org/Library/Volume4/Part_I/chapter6.html.

29 David B. Kitts, "Paleontology and Evolutionary Theory," *Evolution*, Vol. 28, (September, 1974), 467.

30 Robert L. Carroll, "Towards a new evolutionary synthesis," *Trends in Ecology and Evolution*, 15, (2000), 27–32.

31 Adapted from "Questions for Evolutionists" <http://www.drdino.com/articles.php?spec=76>

32 Dr. Colin Patterson, letter to Luther D. Sunderland, April 10, 1979.

33 Niles Eldridge, *Reinventing Darwin: The Great Debate at the High Table of Evolutionary Theory* (New York: John Wiley & Sons, 1995), 95.

34 Fredrick Hoyle and Chandra Wickramasinghe, *Evolution from Space* (London: J.M. Dent and Sons, 1981), 24.

35 Carl Sagan, *Cosmos* (New York: Random House, 1980), 278.

36 Richard Dawkins, *The Blind Watchmaker* (New York: W. W. Norton & Co., 1987), 4.

37 Michael Behe, *Darwin's Black Box* (New York: Free Press, 1996), 39.

38 Charles Darwin, 146.

39 Dr. Scott Huse, *The Collapse of Evolution*, 2d ed. (Grand Rapids, MI: Baker Book House, 1993), 92.

40 Bruce Alberts, "The Cell as a Collection of Protein Machines: Preparing the Next Generation of Molecular Biologists," *Cell*, 92, February 8, 1998, 291.

41 Michael Behe, 252–253.

42 Richard Dawkins, *River Out of Eden* (New York: HarperCollins Publishers, 1995), 17.

43 Bill Gates, *The Road Ahead* (Penguin Books, 1996), 228.

44 James Shapiro, "In the Details... What?" *National Review*, September 19, 1996, 62–65.

45 "The Brainy Bug: What Makes Ticks Tick," *BreakPoint* with Charles Colson, Commentary #000912, September 12, 2000.

46 Ibid.

47 Ibid.

48 As quoted in Dr. Jobe Martin, *The Evolution of a Creationist* (Rockwall, TX: Biblical Discipleship Publishers, 2002), 106.

49 William McCall, *"Ocean Sponge May Be Best for Fiber Optics,"* August 22, 2003, <www.govtech.net/news/news.php?id=65317>.

50 Ibid.

51 Ibid.

52 Paul Davies, *Superforce: The Search for a Grand Unified Theory of Nature* (New York: Simon and Schuster, 1984), 235–236.

53 Dr. Jobe Martin, *The Evolution of a Creationist*, 131–133.

54 George Wald, *The Molecular Basis of Life* (San Francisco: W. H. Freeman and Co., 1968), 339.

55 As quoted in Dr. Scott Huse, *The Collapse of Evolution*, 2d ed. (Grand Rapids, MI: Baker Book House, 1993), 146.

56 Richard C. Lewontin, "Billions and Billions of Demons," *The New York Review of Books*, (January 9, 1997), 31.

57 Robert Jastrow, *Until the Sun Dies* (New York: W. W. Norton & Company, 1977), 51–52.

58 Ron Ayres, "The Truth about the Truth," 19, August 2002, <http://*www.ninetyandnine.com/Archives/200200 819/devotion.htm*>

59 Russell Ash, *The Top 10 of Everything* (New York: DK Publishing, 1998), 123.

60 Quote from Josh McDowell, *The New Evidence That Demands a Verdict* (Nashville: Thomas Nelson, 1999), 35.

61 Ibid., 49.

62 Ibid., 61.

63 Ibid., 100.

64 *Modern Century Illustrated Encyclopedia*, Vol. 12, as quoted in Ray Comfort, *Scientific Facts in the Bible* (Gainsville, FL: Bridge-Logos, 2001), 9.

65 From Columbus' diary, in reference to his discovery of the New World, quoted in Ray Comfort, *Scientific Facts in the Bible*, 10.

66 The Barna Group, *Americans Describe Their Views About Life After Death*, October 21, 2003.

67 Ibid.

68 Frank Harber, "10 Objections to Christianity and How to Respond," *Today's Christian Woman*, March/April 2000, *<http://www.christianitytoday.com/tcw/2000/002/7.62.html>*

69 *The Great Divorce*, 75; as quoted in W. Martindale and J. Root, *The Quotable Lewis* (Wheaton, IL: Tyndale, 1989), 293.

70 Maurice Rawlings, M.D., *Beyond Death's Door* (Nashville: Thomas Nelson, 1978), 19–20.

71 The Barna Group, *Americans Describe Their Views About Life After Death*, October 21, 2003.

72 Ted Koppel, 1987 commencement address at Duke University, MediaWatch, April 1989.

73 Excerpted from an introductory page to W. Y. Fullerton, *Charles Haddon Spurgeon: A Biography*, *<http://www.spurgeon.org/misc/biopref.htm>*

74 Tom Carter, ed., *Spurgeon At His Best* (Grand Rapids, MI: Baker Book House, 1988), 192.

75 Ibid., 69.

76 C. S. Lewis, *Mere Christianity* (New York: Macmillan Publishing, 1975), 56.

77 Josh McDowell and Don Stewart, *Answers to Tough Questions* (Wheaton, IL: Living Books, Tyndale House Publishers, 1980), 39.

78 *Spurgeon At His Best*, 16.

79 Ibid., 45.

80 Ibid., 45.

81 Josh McDowell and Don Stewart, *Answers*, 39.

82 *Spurgeon At His Best*, 174.

83 Ibid., 174.

84 James Emery White, *You Can Experience the Spiritual Life* (Nashville, TN: Word Publishing, 1999), 194.

85 Voice of the Martyrs, *Extreme Devotion* (Nashville, TN: W Publishing Group; Thomas Nelson, 2001), 150.

86 Ibid., 151

87 *Spurgeon At His Best*, 108.

88 Ibid., 122.

89 Ibid., 38.

90 Ibid., 46.

91 Dr. Neil T. Anderson, "*Who I Am In Christ*," <http://www.ficm.org/whoami.htm>

92 *Spurgeon At His Best, n.r.*

93 Ibid., 67.

94 Ibid., 68.

95 Ibid., 68.

96 Ibid., 69.

97 Ibid., 69.

98 Ibid., 70.

99 Ibid., 225.

100 Ibid., 219.

101 Ibid., 220.

102 Ibid., 220.

103 Ibid., 205.

104 Voice of the Martyrs, *Extreme Devotion*, 150.

105 *Spurgeon At His Best*, 205

106 Ibid., 67.

107 Ibid., 67.

108 Ray Comfort, *The Evidence Bible, 1504–1505*

109 John M. Drescher, *Pulpit Digest*, Summer, 1985, N. pag.

Mark Cahill has a business degree from Auburn University, where he was an honorable mention Academic All-American in basketball. He has worked in the business world at IBM and in various management positions, and he taught high school for four years. Mark now speaks to thousands of people a year at conferences, camps, retreats, etc. He has also appeared on numerous radio and television shows.

Mark's favorite thing to do is to go out and meet people and find out what they believe and why they believe it. You can find Mark at malls, concerts, art and music festivals, airports, beaches, sporting events, bar sections of towns, college campuses, etc., doing just that.

To arrange a speaking engagement,
contact the **Ambassador Agency** toll-free
at 877-425-4700 or
www.ambassadoragency.com

•

To order additional books or resources,
or to receive a free e-newsletter
http://www.markcahill.org

•

Contact Mark Cahill at:
P.O. Box 81, Stone Mountain, GA 30086
800-NETS-158 / 800-638-7158
Email: mark@markcahill.org